Possible Worlds

Also by Rod Girle and published by McGill-Queen's University Press

Modal Logics and Philosophy

Possible Worlds

Rod Girle

McGill-Queen's University Press
Montreal & Kingston • Ithaca

ISBN 0-7735-2667-6   (bound)
ISBN 0-7735-2669-2   (paper)

Published simultaneously outside North America
by Acumen Publishing Limited

McGill-Queen's University Press acknowledges the financial support of the
Government of Canada through the Book Publishing Development
Program (BPIDP) for its activities.

National Library of Canada Cataloguing in Publication Data

Girle, Roderic A.
    Possible worlds / Rod Girle.

Includes bibliographical references and index.
ISBN 0-7735-2667-6 (bound).—ISBN 0-7735-2669-2 (pbk.)

    1. Possibility. 2. Necessity (Philosophy). 3. Modality (Logic).
I. Title.

BC71.G57 2003   110   C2003-901759-1

Designed and typeset by Kate Williams, Abergavenny.
Printed and bound by Biddles Ltd., Guildford and King's Lynn.

Contents

Preface

This volume is an exploration of the ways in which the notion of possible worlds has been used in recent philosophy and logic. There is a bias towards looking at the topics from a philosophical logic perspective. Although this book is intended for the wider audience, it is written with an eye to making the topics readily available to senior undergraduates and postgraduates. I begin with the ways in which possible worlds have been used as a framework for considering problems in logic and argument analysis. There are chapters that introduce the absolutely minimal amount of logic required for a logical perspective on possible worlds. These are followed by chapters with possible worlds and modal logic based discussions of questions of meaning, epistemic possibility, temporal logic, metaphysics and impossibility. The focus has been on underlying assumptions and doctrines, rather than on the consequential problems that come out of alleged solutions. It is quite surprising to find in some areas that, although the writers base their work on modal logic, very little use is actually made of possible worlds. Again and again I have come back to the questions of existence, quantification and impossibility. The text is deliberately, and perhaps rashly, provocative. I hope it will provide a good stepping-off point for vigorous discussion.

There is a vast literature in this area. Many excellent books and papers are never mentioned. I have restricted myself to what I see as "classic" or "provocative" material. The annotated bibliography tries to indicate where readers might find further material on each of the topics.

I acknowledge the help I have received from discussions with a subset of graduate students – that perennial source of debate and information – in this case at the University of Auckland. There are also my colleagues – Jerry Seligman, Fred Kroon, Denis Robinson and Jonathan McKeown-Green.

They may have tried to set me right, but I have persisted in idiosyncratic views that are not to be attributed to them.

Rod Girle
Auckland 2003

CHAPTER 1
Introduction

1.1 What might have been

Possible worlds – the very phrase can set the speculative imagination alight.
Leibniz suggested that this world was the *best of all possible worlds*. The
suggestion has enraged some, bewildered many, satisfied some and set others
to pondering. What is this idea of *possible worlds*?

Many works of narrative fiction, such as novels, films and even television
programmes, describe *possible worlds*. Such worlds usually have some sort of
internal consistency, or some sort of internal logic, even when they are quite
unrealistic. Although realism is not always important, it can be. This is
particularly so with the genre of historical novels and films. Works such as
Pride and Prejudice and *No Barrier* are highly realistic and depend on a setting
that is historically accurate. By contrast, some novels, and the films derived
from them, such as *The Lord of the Rings* and *Harry Potter and the Philoso-
pher's Stone* are works of sheer fantasy. Their setting is quite unlike the real
world in crucial ways. They are valued just because they are not realistic. But
there is an internal logic to the possible worlds described in these works.

In the television series *Sliders* there is explicit use of the idea of possible
worlds. The series is built on the idea of possible worlds parallel to ours,
worlds to which the heroes can "slide". The heroes have their adventures in
these possible worlds, in a different one each episode. In one of the possible
worlds the French conquered North America, in one the British still rule all
the North American "colonies", in one there are Cro-Magnon humanoids
instead of *Homo sapiens*, and in another almost everything is the same except
that the Golden Gate Bridge in San Francisco is painted blue.

There are limitations in *Sliders* on the variations from possible world to
possible world. The environment remains the same and allows the heroes to

live on the alternative planet Earths. The alternative planet Earths remain in the same solar system. The sun and moon remain the same. The geography of the planet is much the same. Some things are different, some things are the same from world to world.

The differences are the ways in which things *might have been* or *might have turned out*. The samenesses include the laws of nature and a wide range of natural phenomena. It might even be said that, in *Sliders*, the laws of nature remain the same from possible world to possible world *of necessity*. In fact, it would be quite difficult to understand what is going on if the laws of nature were different.

It has also been argued that the worlds of *Sliders* are not, in fact, *distinct* possible worlds. They are worlds between which there can be traffic, worlds that can be connected by the slide hole through which the heroes and villains can slide. They might at first look distinct, but they must all be part of one huge multi-universe in several dimensions. The worlds to which one can slide are some fifth or sixth dimensional distance away from the real world. There is a machine that allows people to link to one and to travel to it.

It has been argued that one of the key features of possible worlds is that they are utterly and completely distinct from each other from a causal and spatiotemporal point of view across all spatiotemporal dimensions. Lewis writes that things in the same possible world are "worldmates". And further that "whenever two possible individuals are spatiotemporally related, they are worldmates. If there is any distance between them – be it great or small, spatial or temporal – they are parts of one single world".[1] And that "there isn't any trans-world causation . . . if there is no trans-world causation, there is no trans-world travel. You can't get into a 'logical-space' ship and visit another possible world."[2]

Whatever the finer, and even crucially important, philosophical points here, the worlds of *Sliders* are at least very like possible worlds. I will return to some of these points, especially in Chapter 9.

The use of possible worlds to account for what goes on in fiction has been challenged. It might look like the way to go, but it does not really give a satisfactory account. For example, in the case of a child's pretending that a tree stump is a bear, "the real world circumstance that Johnny has put a rope around the stump makes it fictional that a bear has been lassoed".[3] It is not that there is a possible world in which Johnny lassoed a bear; Johnny has lassoed a "pretend bear" in the real world. So we need to bear in mind that possible worlds might not give a good account of exactly what we think they will.

Quite apart from fiction like *Sliders*, we find no difficulty in considering what might have been, and in thinking about what might be. Each *might be* and each *might have been* is a possible world. Many everyday activities depend on being able to consider the many things that might be: several future possible worlds. When someone plans a dinner, looks at clothes, organizes a meeting or decides what courses to take at university, they are considering a range of possible worlds. They ask themselves about the possibilities, the possible worlds, and then set about trying to make one of them become actual.

A person can look back on things that have happened, and regret that other possibilities were not realized. They think about what might have been had they acted differently. They can be pleased that they avoided some of things that might have happened, and satisfied with the way things actually turned out. They can even be astonished and elated at the unexpected outcomes, outcomes that had not even been considered as a reasonable possibility.

There is another side to this coinage of mights and possibles: the musts and necessities. A person will consider these also when they are looking back or looking forwards. There will be some things that *must* be done when they organize a dinner, buy clothes, call a meeting or enrol at university. They can look back and see that, however much they would have wished otherwise, there are some things that just had to happen no matter what. Some things happen *of necessity*.

1.2 Possible worlds technology

What are these possibilities and necessities? The basic tenet of possible worlds logic and of possible worlds metaphysics is that possibilities are to be seen as *possible worlds*. At the heart of the technical and the philosophical use of possible worlds is the simple idea that something is possible if it is so in at least one possible world and something is necessary if it is so in all possible worlds. We can express these ideas in terms of the truth of possibility and necessity statements or propositions. In terms of truth:

- *possibly P* is true if *P* is true in *at least one* possible world
- *necessarily P* is true if *P* is true in *every* possible world.

For example, if proposition *P* is a trivial logical truth, a tautology, a logical necessity such as *if it's raining then it's raining*, then *P* will be true in every possible world, and so *necessarily P* is true. If *P* is a contingently true proposition, such as *Wellington is the capital of New Zealand*, then *P* is in fact true in at least one possible world, the actual world, and so *possibly P* is true.

The actual world, the one in which we live and move and have our being, is one of many possible worlds. Other possible worlds are unactualized possible worlds. The technical use of possible worlds, based on the simple ideas just set out, has had an enormous impact on the study of the logical systems known as *modal logics*. Modal logics can be understood without reference to possible worlds, but possible worlds provide one of the easiest ways of understanding modal logics.

It turns out that possible worlds are seen as useful for helping people to think about a wide range of things. Reality and actuality, possibility and necessity, action and process, knowledge and consciousness, obligation and permission and identity and essence, have all been considered from the perspective of possible worlds.

The first clear detailed technical and formal use of *possible worlds* is in the work of Saul Kripke.[4] His account appeared in the middle of the twentieth century. Kripke's account of *possible worlds* spilled over from formal logic into philosophy. It has provided philosophers with a powerful explanatory apparatus for discussing questions about possibility, necessity, knowledge, time, reality and many other concepts. There has been much argument, discussion and debate about the idea of *possible worlds*, and the explanations that use possible worlds. Our main task in this book is to look at some of those ideas and explanations and the many faceted debate that they have generated.

It will turn out that possible worlds, and the detailed technical apparatus that has been generated by using them (the possible worlds "technology", as I will call it), are not an unmixed blessing. Not everyone sees possible worlds as useful or helpful. This volume will urge that possible worlds be considered more critically than has been the recent tendency.

1.3 From arguments to logic and back again

In this chapter I consider some of the argument analysis background to the development of the formal notion of possible worlds. I use this as a background for subsequent discussion. I look at some of the logical concepts embedded in ordinary language and their relationship to logical ideas in elementary classical formal logic.[5] There are problems about the relationship between elementary classical formal logic and language, particularly with respect to *if *** then +++* conditionals, quantifiers, singular terms and identity.

Some logicians have sought solutions to these problems by constructing logical systems that are not the same as classical formal logic. Modal logics are a case in point. It is important to realize that there is not just one system of formal logic. One system might be dominant, but there is more than one. That is why we keep talking about *modal logics* in the plural. Anyone who talks about formal (or symbolic) logic as if there were just one monolithic system is seriously misguided or ignorant, or both.

In the next three chapters I look at attempts to use modal logic to provide solutions to a variety of problems. Possible worlds have become central to the standard way of understanding the many modal logic systems and the solutions they offer to a range of problems in logic and philosophy.

Possible worlds have been of use in building formal accounts of possibility and necessity in modal logic, but possible worlds are not the only mechanism available. There are other mechanisms that are of equal use. For example, Hintikka's *model sets*,[6] or sets of consistent sentences, are perfectly serviceable, and there is also a range of mathematical structures that can be used, but these have not captured the high ground, and the use of possible worlds has become dominant in the world of modal logics. It may well be part of the case that possible worlds have become dominant because they are so useful in philosophy.

I will not be trying to instruct the reader in elementary, let alone advanced, modal logics. That has been done in many places.[7] My approach will be to consider modal logics in a way that centres on the logics' analyses of both single propositions and premise–conclusion arguments in ordinary language. The emphasis will be on the way that possible worlds have assisted, if at all, in the analysis of problems. I discuss the ways in which possible worlds modal logic has failed to cope with the subtleties of everyday language, and ways in which it has illuminated, or even obscured, difficult concepts.

1.4 Logic and language

My approach to the discussion of possible worlds means that we need to have a fairly clear idea of the relationship between formal logic and ordinary language. There are many views about this relationship. But, for the moment, we assume that logics are independent *artificial languages* with carefully stipu- lated syntax, proof systems and semantics. In what follows we assume that a *logic* is an *artificial language with a semantics*. The semantics is said to provide an *interpretation* of the language. Logics are not the only artificial languages. Programming languages for computing, for example, are also artificial lan- guages.

Artificial languages relate to ordinary languages in the same way that ordinary languages relate to each other. The first obvious relation is transla- tion. One can translate from Arabic to Greek, from Maori to Spanish, or from English to Pitjantjatjara. There are translation dictionaries to smooth the way. We usually assume that what can be said in one natural language can be said in other natural languages, at least most of the time. The same propositions can be asserted in both, the same questions can be asked in both, the same commands can be given and the same promises can be made in both.

Most logics deal with only the assertion of propositions. Although there are some systems that attempt to deal with questions and commands, they are rare. More often than not, logicians try to turn everything into a proposition. Given this harsh restriction to propositions, we can translate from proposition- expressing English to each of several logics. Many students in the twenty-first century are taught first to translate from English to classical propositional logic, and then to classical predicate logic. There are also a substantial number who are first taught to translate from English to some modern version of Aristotle's Syllogistic.

The process of translation from one natural language to another is some-times difficult because there are ideas that are easily expressible in one language but not in another. Nevertheless, even when we cannot find a neat matching word or phrase we can usually find some circumlocution to give expression to ideas from another language. This is not always possible when translating from a natural language to the artificial languages of formal logic.

Although translation is the first port of call when looking at the relationship between a logic and ordinary language, the final arbiter of the relationship is the semantics of the artificial language. The semantics of a logical language is almost always a set of definitions in terms of truth-values. If you look back to what was said about the possible worlds technology (§1.2), you will see that the simple definitions for *possibly P* and *necessarily P* are truth-value definitions. We return to this in §1.5.

Artificial languages usually give expression to a very restricted range of concepts. Programming languages in computer science, for example, contain only a limited number of concepts to do with control, processing and the storage and manipulation of information. They also have quite precise and spartan definitions for the concepts they express. Circumlocution is often not possible. Natural languages are rich, almost beyond belief, in the range of concepts they express and the flexibility of expression. Terms, phrases and sentences sometimes have pre-cise meaning, sometimes not. Sometimes they are deliberately vague. This flexibility is not a handicap; it is an advantage. Meaning can depend on all sorts of factors such as context, rhetorical import, social standards of politeness and the relative social status of speaker and hearer, to name but a few.

Logics are almost always context-free, impoverished languages with strict and unambiguously defined meanings. Some logicians have argued that transla-tion to a logic, such as classical first-order logic, is simply a process of making clear what was really meant in natural language.[8] But many have argued that it is sometimes impossible to capture in a given logic, especially if it is classical first-order logic, the meaning of what has been asserted in ordinary language.[9] It has been argued that the semantic definitions of classical first-order logic make it incapable of expressing vitally important dimensions of what is meant in arguments involving negation, or disjunction, or *if *** then +++* con-ditionals, or assertions of existence, or assertions of identity.

I do not have the space to pursue this debate. I will simply adopt the stance that logic is neither a symbolization, nor a regimentation, of ordinary language. It is a distinct artificial language.

It has also been argued that logic should provide a model, or an explanation, of the logical concepts expressed in ordinary language.[10] This can be so only if we agree that the logic is able to express the logical dimensions of arguments involving the concepts mentioned. It is not clear that this is always so. But logicians continually strive to make logic better able to express the logical concepts in ordinary language. This inevitably means reconsideration of the semantics of logic.

1.5 Syntax, proof and semantics

Given that logics are artificial languages, we consider what constitutes a formal logic and what can be done with such a system. A formal logic will have a carefully stipulated syntax, proof system and semantics. Logics are based on sets of sentences.[11] The syntax, or grammar, of any logical system will set out the symbols and the ways in which the symbols can be put together to make sentences. Proof systems for logic show how sentences might be proved to be theorems, and how to prove that an argument is valid. Our interest in possible worlds will direct us to semantics, not to systems of proof.

In a semantics, the sentences can be assigned meaning, usually by means of *truth-value semantics*. The objective of truth-value semantics is assigning truth-values, such as *true* and *false*,[12] to sentences of the system. The assignments are based on the truth-values assigned to the simplest sentences. The simplest sentences are often called "atomic" sentences. The assignments are worked out by means of stipulated semantic rules, or definitions, which show how to take the truth-values of atomic sentences and calculate the truth-values for more complex sentences.

For example, we might have a word in the artificial language used to translate the negative "not" in English. Say we use the same word but in a different font for the artificial language: **not**. Then **not** might be defined as a truth-value swapper. Let **P** stand for any sentence, no matter how complex, expressing either a truth or a falsehood.

If **P** is true then **not P** is false; and if **P** is false then **not P** is true.

That's it. So **not not not not P** just means the same as **P**, at least as far as truth-value goes.

In some cases, such as propositional logic, there is no "logical" interest in how truth-values are assigned to the simplest sentences. When there are just two truth-values, the main interest is just that every atomic sentence can be either true or false. So for one atomic sentence there are two possibilities, for two there are four, for three there are eight, and so on. The complete set of possibilities is the main interest.

In some cases, such as predicate logic, there is a standard account of how the atomic sentences are assigned truth-values. The standard account makes reference to sets of items and their properties and their relations to each other. In the light of the properties and relations, truth-values are assigned. There is usually no recourse at all to everyday entities in the real world.[13] Non-standard accounts of truth in predicate logic just treat the atomic sentences in the same way as in propositional logic. It is possible for them to be either true or false. The reason, in terms of items to refer to, is bypassed.

There are various mechanisms for working out assignments of truth-value to more complex sentences in propositional, predicate and modal logic. Our main interest centres on truth-value semantics that invoke possible worlds in their definitions for the semantics of any modal logic.

It certainly looks as if the semantics are unlike what we usually expect from semantics. Semantics are supposed to tell us the meanings of terms and phrases. In everyday life we rarely explain meaning in terms of truth and false-hood. We usually make use of other meanings, ones that are well understood, just as a dictionary does. In modern logic the standard starting place for accounts of meaning is truth-values, or truth-values and abstract sets of entities. Because of this non-typical starting place, the semantics of modern logic are sometimes referred to as "formal semantics".

1.6 The logic in ordinary language

The standard motivational rhetoric for logic in philosophical circles is that logic is the best instrument for assessing the quality of premise–conclusion arguments.[14] Translating from natural language to logic is part of the argument assessment process. Logic is used to decide whether the translated argument is valid or invalid, whether the premises are consistent or inconsistent, and, if the argument is not valid, what a counter-example would be. The quality of argument is often assessed by considering the overall pattern of argument, a pattern that places logical concepts in a key role.

The received view[15] is that the main logical concepts in both natural and artificial language argumentation are negation, conjunction, disjunction, impli-cation, quantity and identity. Recently, possibility and necessity have been added to this list. It is often assumed that the concepts expressed in natural language are so close to those defined in the artificial language that there is no real problem with this whole process. That assumption is not correct. There are real problems, and they are mostly ignored.

Let us take a careful look at the first four of these logical concepts in natural language, and the way they are seen as applying.

We take two simple propositions expressed by:

1.6.1.　*Al is a woman.*
1.6.2.　*Chris is a man.*

The first can be abbreviated to *A* and the second to *C*. This is not a move into the artificial language; it is just abbreviation in the natural language context.

In what follows we will sometimes use just "the sentence" for the longer phrase "the proposition expressed by the sentence" when there is no ambiguity. If there is a contrast to be drawn between sentence and proposition, the full expressions will be used.

When *A* is negated we get:

1.6.3.   *Al is not a woman.*
1.6.3 is the *negation* of *A*, and can be abbreviated to: *not A.*

When *A* is *conjoined* with *C* we get:

1.6.4.   *Al is a woman and Chris is a man.*
1.6.4 is the *conjunction* of two conjuncts, *A* and *C*, and can be abbreviated to: *both A and C.*

When *A* is *disjoined* with *C* we get:

1.6.5.   *Either Al is a woman or Chris is a man.*
1.6.5 is the *disjunction* of two disjuncts, *A* and *C*, and can be abbreviated to: *either A or C.*

Disjunction can be either *inclusive* or *exclusive*. We borrow "and/or" from the lawyers and "xor" from computer science to give unambiguous abbreviations of the inclusive and exclusive disjunctions of *A* and *C* – inclusive: *either A and/ or C*; exclusive: *either A xor C.*
    Some philosophers claim that there is only one kind of disjunction expressed in ordinary English but I have disputed this claim elsewhere.[16] We will just use "either . . . and/or . . ." for unambiguous inclusive disjunction, because that is just what "and/or" does mean.
    We now consider the most difficult of logical concepts: the concept of implication.
    When *A implies C* we have:

1.6.6.   *If Al is a woman then Chris is a man.*

In this *implication*, expressed by a *conditional, A* is the *antecedent* and *C* is the *consequent*. The conditional can be abbreviated to: *If A then C.*
    Implications are often referred to as "conditionals" because conditional sentences are used to express implication.[17] There is considerable disagreement about how to understand conditionals. One view is that 1.6.6 is logically equivalent to 1.6.7:

1.6.6.   *If Al is a woman then Chris is a man.*
1.6.7.   *Either Al is not a woman and/or Chris is a man.*
or   *Either not A and/or C.*

When 1.6.6 is taken to be equivalent to 1.6.7, the implication in 1.6.6 is said to be a *material implication* and the conditional a *material conditional*.
    The expression of these four logical notions – negation, conjunction, disjunction and implication – in ordinary language is not always clear and precise.

For example, let us consider conjunction in English:

1.6.8.   *Susan is enrolled in Introductory Logic and Stage 2 Statistics.*

The word "and" has a quite straightforward and simple conjunctive role. It expresses the conjoining of the propositions *Susan is enrolled in Introductory Logic* and *Susan is enrolled in Stage 2 Statistics*. It would not really matter very much if the speaker had said:

1.6.8a.   *Susan is enrolled in Stage 2 Statistics and Introductory Logic.*

Each of 1.6.8 and 1.6.8a expresses a conjunction of the same two propositions. For all practical purposes the conjunctions "say the same thing". This means that conjoining expressed by the "and" is *commutative*. It does not matter which is first and which is second.

But, consider:

1.6.9.   *Susan ran upstairs and jumped out of the window.*

This does not mean the same as:

1.6.9a.   *Susan jumped out of the window and ran upstairs.*

The "and" in both 1.6.9 and 1.6.9a expresses not only conjoining, but also temporal sequencing. The "and", given the content of the conjuncts, is saying the same as "and then". There is conjoining in 1.6.9 and 1.6.9a, but it is *non-commutative* conjoining.

English words and phrases that express logical concepts do not always express the same logical concepts. Thus "and" can express both commutative and non-commutative conjunction. Context and content are important. The words and phrases of ordinary language are, as computer programmers might say, "overloaded": in different contexts they can mean different things.

Premise–conclusion arguments are regularly expressed in English. To evaluate them as "valid" or "invalid" we need the a definition of validity. A standard definition is:

> An argument is *valid* if, and only if, it is not possible for the premises to be all true and the conclusion not to be true.

The definition gives expression to the idea that a valid argument is one where the truth of the premises guarantees the truth of the conclusion. We look at three simple examples to see how the definition is applied to evaluating arguments:

1.6.10.   *If Auckland is less than 200 km from Hamilton, then Auckland is less than 400 km from Hamilton. Auckland is less than 200 km from Hamilton. It follows that Auckland is less than 400 km from Hamilton.*

Let *T* be an abbreviation for *Auckland is less than 200 km from Hamilton* and let *F* be an abbreviation for *Auckland is less than 400 km from Hamilton*. Then the abbreviated argument, in standard form,[18] is:

1.6.10a.   *If T then F*   Premise
            T   Premise
       So   *F*   Conclusion

It is not possible for the premises both to be true and the conclusion not true, so argument 1.6.10 is valid.
    The second example is:

1.6.11.   *If Tom is a dog then Tom is a mammal. Tom is a mammal. So, Tom is a dog.*

If we let *D* abbreviate *Tom is a dog*; and *M* abbreviate *Tom is a mammal*, then we have:

1.6.11a.   *If D then M*   Premise
            M   Premise
       So   *D*   Conclusion

Now, it is possible for the premises to be true and the conclusion to be false. If Tom were a cat, then the premises would certainly be true, and the conclusion certainly false. So this is not a valid argument.
    A more difficult example is this variation on 1.6.10:

1.6.12.   *If Auckland is less than 400 km from Hamilton, then Auckland is less than 200 km from Hamilton. Auckland is less than 200 km from Hamilton. It follows that Auckland is less than 400 km from Hamilton.*

With the same abbreviations as for 1.6.10, the abbreviated argument is:

1.6.12a.   *If F then T*
            T
       So   *F*

In 1.6.12 it is not possible for the premises both to be true and the conclusion not true, simply by virtue of the meanings of the propositions T and F. So, the argument is valid. Yet, many logicians would say, in some cases carelessly, that argument 1.6.12 is invalid, and commits the *fallacy of affirming the consequent*. It just happens to have true premises and a true conclusion.

I would argue that the argument *is* valid. But it is that *particular* argument, 1.6.12, that is valid. It is valid because of the mathematical *content* of the premises and conclusion. But its validity tells us nothing *in general* about arguments with two premises, a conditional for one and the consequent of the conditional for the other, and the antecedent of the conditional as the conclusion. We saw that 1.6.11 was invalid, yet it has the same pattern as 1.6.12.

To find out about arguments in general we have to consider common patterns or *forms* of argument. I come to this later. But keep this validity problem in mind.

1.7 The logic in classical propositional logic

The first, and most important, thing to note is that there are many formal logics. One of the many is "classical propositional logic".

Classical propositional logic has its own version of negation, conjunction, disjunction and material implication, and logical notions that can be defined purely in terms of these.[19] The logical notions set out in classical propositional logic work with complete propositions. There is no attempt to give any account of, for example, the negation of concepts like "redness" to give "non-redness", or of "spatial" to give "non-spatial."

In what follows I will not use the usual formal logic symbols. I will use readable words and phrases in a font that will mark them out as readable substitutes for the symbols often used. If you want to see a typical set of symbols they are in the appendix at the end of this chapter. One advantage of using symbols is that it is at once clear that they are not just abbreviations or symbolizations of English. We sacrifice that advantage for ease of recognition. But remember that propositional logic has its own defined versions of these logical ideas.

Logic negation is represented by **not** (in a different font). So the logic negation of A is **not** A. Logic negation is defined by:

If A is true then **not** A is false, and if A is false **not** A is true.

Logic conjunction is commutative, and is represented by **and**. The commutative conjunction of A and C is (A **and** C). Commutative conjunction in logic is defined by:

If A and C are both true then (A **and** C) is true, otherwise it is false.

Logic inclusive disjunction is represented by **or**, and exclusive disjunction by **xor**.

The inclusive disjunction of *A* and *C* is (*A* **or** *C*).
The exclusive disjunction of *A* and *C* is (*A* **xor** *C*).

Their definitions for logic are:

If either *A* or *C* or both are true then (*A* **or** *C*) is true, otherwise it is false.
If just one of *A* and *C* is true then (*A* **xor** *C*) is true, otherwise it is false.

Material implication is represented by **imp**. The material implication of *C* by *A* is (*A* **imp** *C*). The definition for logic is:

If *A* is false or *C* is true, or both, then (*A* **imp** *C*) is true, otherwise it is false.

These definitions are completely stipulative, and make reference only to the truth-value of the constituent propositional parts of logical negations, conjunctions, disjunctions and material implications.

Context and content are not important in classical propositional logic. There is no ambiguity. Classical propositional logic does not contain any symbols that mean different things in different contexts, or that mean different things depending on the content of propositions. In classical propositional logic there is never any ambiguity about its negation, conjunction, inclusive disjunction or implication.

In the sentences above we have used the letters "*A*" and "*C*". They were first introduced as shorthand for sentences of English that express propositions. We can certainly use such letters in our propositional logic. And we can have them mean just what they meant when first introduced as abbreviations.

Given the definitions of the propositional logic symbols (words), it is easy to see how the following translation table could be generated.

Standard translation table		
1. *not A*	is translated to	**not** *A*
2. *both A and C*	is translated to	(*A* **and** *C*)
3. *either A and/or C*	is translated to	(*A* **or** *C*)
4. *either A xor C*	is translated to	(*A* **xor** *C*)
5. *if A then C*	is translated to	(*A* **imp** *C*)

It is absolutely crucial to see this as a translation table, and not as a table of the "real" meanings of the English sentences. If we ignore this distinction between translation and explaining real meanings, then all sorts of utterly silly nonsense can be forthcoming. For example, there is nothing in classical propositional logic for translating non-commutative sequential conjunction. But it is not correct to represent the situation as Hunt does. He writes:

> Nor does formal logic accommodate temporal or causal relationships, yet the human mind cannot make sense of the world without them. Consider these two statements:
>
> She inherited a fortune and he married her.
> He married her and she inherited a fortune.
>
> In formal logic, say Johnson-Laird and Watson, *the two are identical*, but there is, to say the least, a great difference between them in real life.[20]

These two are *not identical* "in formal logic". It is clear that Hunt just does not observe the distinction between translation and meaning explanation. He does not translate the two English sentences in his text to classical propositional logic. He just sets them out in English. However, if we translate them to commutative conjunction and *ignore the sequential aspect*, then the *translations* of the two are equivalent. But why assume that such a translation means that the English sentences are identical? The translation ignores the sequential aspect of the English. If, in conversation or argument, the sequential difference in English is important, then we have immediate recourse to denying that translations to commutative conjunction are acceptable. We could say that the two are, respectively:

> After she inherited a fortune he married her.
> After he married her she inherited a fortune.

Then these can be translated into propositional logic as independent atomic propositions. Translation is not simple symbolization; and it is not meaning explication even if it helps us understand something of the meaning of the original.

And, by the way, there are some formal propositional logics that contain operators for temporal relations. So, in formal temporal logic, the two English sentences can be translated to quite distinct formal sentences. It may well be essential that, for some arguments to be properly analysed, a temporal logic is used. But it is quite misleading to lump all formal logics together.

For implication there is only material implication available in classical propositional logic for the translation of "if . . . then . . ." conditionals. It is again quite incorrect to say, as does Hunt,[21] that "logic says" that all implication *in ordinary language* is material implication.

Some philosophers have claimed that indicative conditionals in English are best understood as expressing material conditionals,[22] but this claim has been strongly contested, and has been roundly rejected by many logicians. There are some well-developed logics, notably relevant logics, where implication operators are definitely not material implication.

The classical propositional logic operators: **not, and, or, xor** and **imp** (in our notation) have *stipulated* meanings, and those meanings are not always the same as the ordinary language meanings of the expressions they are used to translate.

To these stipulations about the logical words in propositional logic is usually added some standard definition for the *validity* of an argument:

> An argument is *valid* if, and only if, it is not possible for the premises to be all true and the conclusion not to be true.

Consider the following argument:

1.7.1. (A **imp** C) Premise
        A Premise
So C Conclusion

The truth-value definitions show that, irrespective of what A and C mean, if both (A **imp** C) and A are true, then C will be true. So the argument is valid. The validity assessment of 1.7.1 is based purely on the truth-value definition of (A **imp** C).

On the other hand, consider:

1.7.2. (A **imp** C) Premise
        C Premise
So A Conclusion

The truth-value definitions show that if both (A **imp** C) and C are true, and we consider only the truth-value definition of (A **imp** C), then there is no guarantee that A will be true. It is possible for the premises to be true and the conclusion false. So the argument is not valid. But this assessment ignores the content of both A and C.

1.8 Translation and reliable argument evaluation

We begin by looking at the three simple arguments 1.6.10, 1.6.11 and 1.6.12. We will make use of the abbreviations 1.6.10a, 1.6.11a and 1.6.12a. The abbreviation of argument 1.6.10 above was:

1.6.10a.	*If T then F*	Premise
	T	Premise
So	*F*	Conclusion

This can now be translated to propositional logic on the basis of the translation table above, with "So" replaced with the therefore symbol, "∴" :

1.8.1.	(*T* imp *F*)	Premise
	T	Premise
∴	*F*	Conclusion

The translation of the argument, in propositional logic, is valid. From this logic-based evaluation we would usually claim that the original ordinary language argument is also valid. But, you might say, we have already seen that 1.6.10 is valid.

Our original assessment was based on our intuitive understanding of conditionals and their logical relationship to their antecedents and consequents. The assessment of 1.8.1 is based purely on the truth-value definition of **imp**. The basis for assessment is radically different. So if we are to rely on the assessment of 1.8.1 for a reliable assessment of 1.6.10, we had better be sure that nothing logically relevant has been lost, or added, during translation.

We now consider the abbreviation of argument 1.6.11:

1.6.11a.	*If D then M*	Premise
	M	Premise
So	*D*	Conclusion

The typical translation will be:

1.8.2.	(*D* imp *M*)	Premise
	M	Premise
∴	*D*	Conclusion

This is invalid in propositional logic, for the same reasons that showed that 1.6.11 was invalid. This brings us to the third case, the abbreviation of 1.6.12:

1.6.12a.	*If F then T*	Premise
	T	Premise
So	*F*	Conclusion

The translation is:

1.8.3.	(*F* imp *T*)	Premise
	T	Premise
∴	*F*	Conclusion

This also is invalid, as was 1.8.2. But it does not follow that 1.6.11 is invalid. The evaluation of 1.8.3 does not take into account the arithmetical *content* of *T* and *F*, and considers only the logical definition of **imp**. But if we take the content of both *T* and *F* into account, then 1.6.12 is valid. If it suggested that the first premise must be false, then it can be responded that someone could have asserted that premise so as to make a rhetorical point that if the distance is below 400 km then it will be in the range below 200 km as well. So if we transfer the propositional logic evaluation of invalid from 1.8.3 to 1.6.12a and so to 1.6.12, a serious mistake could be made.

The standard response to this point is that while the validity evaluation of the translation can reliably be transferred to the original, the invalidity assessment cannot. Invalidity assessments can only make the original suspect. Propositional logic does not consider the propositional content of the atomic sentences. Arguments are evaluated only in terms of the defined logical terms. This problem is dealt with in some formal detail in several places.[23]

Given the reservations about invalidity assessment, we turn to validity assessment. The problem here is that, if we rely completely on the assessment in propositional logic of translations in order to evaluate the arguments couched in English, then we need to be sure that the translation process is not faulty in any logical sense. So we need to consider the translation process in more detail.

When arguments are translated from English to classical propositional logic, the translator must ensure that the translation is as accurate as possible. Each premise and the conclusion are separately translated and we focus on the sentence pairs. There are four grades of translation.[24] The best is where the English and its translation are synonymous: they mean exactly the same thing. This will happen rarely. Second best is logical equivalence: they always have the same truth-value. When a sentence being translated is either synonymous with its translation or logically equivalent to its translation, then it *entails*[25] its translation and *is entailed by* its translation.

Third is where there is a clear notion of the logical relationship, other than mutual entailment, between pairs of sentences. For example, the sentence being translated might entail the translation, but the translation might not entail the translated. In the case of conjunction above, if the non-commutative sequenced conjunction *Susan ran upstairs and jumped out of the window* is true, then the commutative conjunction *Susan ran upstairs **and** jumped out of the window* must also be true. So the non-commutative conjunction in English entails the commutative conjunction in classical propositional logic. But the commutative conjunction in classical propositional logic does not entail the sequenced conjunction. Something is lost in translation.

The fourth, and failing, grade is where none of the other three apply.

If the translation quality is of first or second grade, then there are no problems with the reliability of the validity assessment of the natural language argument by means of its formal logic translation. There are problems when the quality is of third grade, but the situation is fairly clear. In some cases the assessment will be reliable, in others not.

I now set out an important principle that applies to the translation of an argument. The necessary conditions for a reliable assessment of validity are that:

- the English (natural language) premises of the argument entail or are equivalent to their translation; and
- the translation of the conclusion entails the English conclusion or is equivalent to it.

Negations and commutative conjunctions are standardly taken to be equivalent to their translations.[26] Sequencing conjunctions entail their translations. Inclusive disjunctions are standardly taken to be equivalent to their translations.[27] Conditionals are standardly taken to entail their translations.

Here is a (controversial) table with English abbreviations to the left, and propositional logic to the right, where the propositional logic is the standard translation of the English.[28] The more controversial cases are indicated with an asterisk. The entailment relations are inserted. If the entries are synonymous, mutual entailment is shown. I use "$X \Rightarrow Y$" for "X entails Y", "$X \Leftarrow Y$" for "X is entailed by Y" and "$X \Leftrightarrow Y$" for "X entails Y and Y entails X".

A	$\Leftrightarrow$	A	
not A	$\Leftrightarrow$	**not** A	*
both A and C	$\Leftrightarrow$	(A **and** C)	
either A and/or C	$\Leftrightarrow$	(A **or** C)	*
either A xor C	$\Leftrightarrow$	(A **xor** C)	
if A then C	$\Rightarrow$	(A **imp** C)	*
A and then C	$\Rightarrow$	(A **and** C)	
either A xor C	$\Rightarrow$	(A **or** C)	
either A and/or C	$\Leftarrow$	(A **xor** C)	
A unless C	$\Rightarrow$	(A **or** C)	*
necessarily A	$\Rightarrow$	A	
possibly A	$\Leftarrow$	A	

Note that atomic propositions are equivalent because they are synonymous. If the translation dictionary says that $A = Al$ *is a woman* then the " $=$ " should be taken quite seriously. The most serious problems arise with conditionals and implication.

We consider in detail an example that involves conditionals, because it shows a problem that is directly relevant to the discussion of modal logic and the development of the notion of possible worlds.

Consider the following argument:

(A) *If the diagram on the wall is a hexagon then it has exactly six sides.*
If the diagram on the wall is a rectangle then it has exactly four sides.
Therefore one, at least, of (a) and (b) follows. (a) If the diagram on the wall is a rectangle then it has exactly six sides. (b) If the diagram on the wall is a hexagon then it has exactly four sides.

We can use the following abbreviations: *H* abbreviates *The diagram on the wall is a hexagon*; *R* abbreviates *The diagram on the wall is a rectangle*; *S* abbreviates *The diagram on the wall has exactly six sides*; and *F* abbreviates *The diagram on the wall has exactly four sides*.

With these abbreviations the argument can be abbreviated to:

(Aa) *If H then S*
If R then F
So *either if R then S, and/or if H then F.*

This argument has premises that are true (by standard geometrical definition) and a conclusion that is false (by standard geometrical definition). The argument is invalid.

The standard translation of Aa, based on the translation table above, into classical propositional logic gives the argument Ap:

(Ap) (*H* imp *S*)
(*R* imp *F*)
∴ (*R* imp *S*) or (*H* imp *F*)

According to the definitions of propositional logic, Ap is valid.[29]

We know at once that Aa and Ap cannot be logically the same or logically equivalent. We also know that either the standard translation process is unreliable, or that propositional logic is internally defective with respect to assessing the validity of arguments couched in the propositional logic language. There is nothing to indicate the latter. So the standard translation process must be unreliable.

There are two logical operations expressed in A. They are implication, expressed by "If . . . then . . .", and inclusive disjunction, expressed by "one, at least, of (a) and (b)". The inclusive disjunction is made unambiguously clear in the abbreviation Aa. When inclusive disjunction is translated to propositional logic the quality of the standard translation is almost always of first or second grade. There is no problem here. The major translation problem lies with the implication. The premises create no real problem if we accept that conditionals in English entail their material implication translations in propositional logic. The real problem is with the translation of the conclusion. The translated conclusion does not entail the original conclusion. One of the necessary conditions for reliable assessment is that the translated conclusion entails the original English or natural language conclusion. So even before we go through the processes of assessing the validity of the translation of the original in the logical system, we know that the result of a validity assessment of argument A in the logic will not be reliable.

In fact, classical propositional logic is never reliable for the assessment of natural language arguments with conditional conclusions. This is a harsh stricture on the reliability of classical propositional logic. The impact of this restriction might be ameliorated if, before translation, we can be sure that the conditionals in the conclusion of an argument are simply material conditionals. But this is often hard to judge.

The fact that the material conditional translation of the conditionals in A gives a patently wrong assessment of validity shows that the material conditional translation has lost something crucially important. If the conditionals in A were material conditionals then the assessment in classical propositional logic would be reliable, and the argument would be valid. The assessment in classical propositional logic is wrong for the original ordinary language argument, because the original argument is invalid. If it is wrong then it is not reliable. So the conditionals in A cannot be material conditionals.

Unfortunately, unless we take it that conditionals are generally not material conditionals, we will be tempted always to say that they are material conditionals. If we do this for argument A, we will be in a mess. Reliability is crucial if we are to use translations into formal logic for the evaluation of argument.

Cases like A have prompted a search for a better account of conditionals than the material conditional account. One of the earliest searches in modern logic generated modal logics. The early modal logics contained not only material implication, but also what was called "strict implication". If we assume that, in general, *If . . . then . . .* conditionals express strict implication, then argument A translates to an argument in modal logic that is not the same as Ap.

At this point we represent the translation of A into modal logic with strict implication, using "**strimp**" for the strict implication of modal logic, as:

(Am) H **strimp** S
R **strimp** F
∴ (R **strimp** S) or (H **strimp** F)

This form is invalid[30] in typical modal logics with strict implication. In this case the modal logic has turned out to be more reliable than non-modal propositional logic. But, it is not clear that strict implication entails "If *** then +++". So modal logic may well be unreliable also.

There are many modal logics with slightly different accounts of strict implication. The immediate question is, "Which is the best?" Even more important is the question, "Which is the most reliable?" To answer this question we need to be able to understand each of the modal logics in such a way that we can compare them. One good means of comparison is based on possible worlds; or so the story goes.

1.9 The forms of arguments

There are many arguments in both English and logic that have the same pattern of propositions and logical operations across the premises and the conclusion. The common pattern of both 1.6.11a and 1.6.12a can be set out as:

1.9.1a.　*If p then q*　　　Premise
　　　　　q　　　　　　Premise
　So　*p*　　　　　　Conclusion

This pattern translates to propositional logic as:

1.9.1t.　(*p* **imp** *q*)　　Premise
　　　　　q　　　　　　Premise
　∴　*p*　　　　　Conclusion

These, 1.9.1a and 1.9.1t, set out the *form* of the arguments. The small letters, *p* and *q*, are propositional "spaces" in the forms. The technical name for them is "propositional variables". By analogy we say that the forms of 1.6.10a and its translation will be:

1.9.2a.　*If p then q*　　　Premise
　　　　　p　　　　　　Premise
　So　*q*　　　　　　Conclusion

This pattern translates to propositional logic as:

1.9.2t.　(*p* **imp** *q*)　　Premise
　　　　　p　　　　　　Premise
　∴　*q*　　　　　Conclusion

The capital letters we have been using are not variables. They have meanings fixed by translation dictionaries. They can be called "translation constants".

The question for each of 1.9.1a and 1.9.1t and 1.9.2a and 1.9.2t is, "Is this *form* valid?" To answer that question we have to consider all possible combinations of the truth-values of the propositions that might go in the spaces represented by the propositional variables. In all four there are four combinations. Truth-tables set out all such combinations explicitly. The specific meanings and factual truth-values of propositions that might go into the spaces is ignored. Assessment of the form will have to be based purely on the logical operations expressed in the arguments. There is a sense in which the definition of validity becomes:

> An argument *form* is valid if, and only if, there is no combination of truth-values such that the premises are all true and the conclusion false.

Because we are considering forms, not actual arguments, the content of atomic propositions occurring in the argument is irrelevant. Purely in virtue of the nature of material implication, inclusive disjunction and negation, the forms of 1.6.9 and 1.6.10 are valid. Any arguments, expressed in logic, that have those forms will be valid, because the logical operations alone will guarantee that when the premises are true so is the conclusion.

Argument 1.6.12 was valid, but not purely by virtue of the nature of implication. It was valid because of an entailment between its basic elements. But if we take 1.6.12 to have the *form* 1.9.1a, then we can show that this *form is invalid*, in spite of the argument's being valid. There are arguments with this form that have true premises and a false conclusion. So the form alone cannot guarantee that the premises cannot be true without the conclusion being true.

There is an asymmetry between what a valid form can guarantee and what an invalid form can guarantee. If a form is valid, then any argument that has that form will definitely be valid. But if a form is invalid, then that does not guarantee anything about arguments having that form. Assessment of the form of an argument is a way of assessing all the arguments with that form.

Many advanced logic texts have only propositional variables, and only deal in logical form. In this way they are only dealing in the generality of argument. The question of form means that the relationship between logical form in logic and in language is one of the keys to assessing the role of possible worlds in logic and argument analysis.

1.10 A reflection on method

Two things should be noted. First, our discussion has been firmly based in argumentation theory. We have been looking at the relationship between logic and language in terms of argument analysis, its reliability and failings. This will drive much of our subsequent discussion. It is interesting to see that major possible worlds authors continually revert to arguments analysis to back up their theories and to give counter-examples to other theories.

For example, David Lewis has page after page of cases. There is a whole section in *Counterfactuals*[31] in which he sets out fallacious arguments from ordinary language, and shows how these are rejected by his logic for counter-factuals. Robert Stalnaker, another major author in the possible worlds debate, continually resorts to arguments to show the viability of his *Theory of Conditionals*.[32]

Secondly, there is an important distinction to note for what follows. At the simplest level there is a distinction between saying things *in* a language and saying things *about* a language. When a small child says, "There are three mouses in the cage" then we know they are saying things about the world *in* an infantile dialect of English. When the parent says, "You don't say 'mouses', you say 'mice'" then the parent is making a statement *about* language. The child was speaking *in* the *object language*: English. The parent was speaking in the *metalanguage*, which happens to be English used metalinguistically. The parent was saying something about the syntax and vocabulary of English. Metalinguistic statements are *about* language or languages. They can be about the syntax, the semantics or any other feature of the language we want to discuss. Natural languages, like English, can be used as either an object language or as a metalanguage.

But as soon as anyone starts to raise questions about translation from one language to another, they are discussing relationships between languages. This requires the assumption of some sort of overview, and they are working in a metalanguage. The metalanguage for logical systems, the language in which we talk about such systems, can be more or less formal. The statements are often described as "metalogical" statements. As soon as someone says, "Your argument is not valid" then they are talking about the argument itself, and have made a metalogical evaluation of the argument.

The discussion above has been metalinguistic and metalogical. We have been discussing, from outside, the operations of both logic and language. We have been discussing the meanings of logical terms in both logic and language. We have been discussing the way translation works between ordinary language and classical propositional logic.

1.11 Formal and philosophical

I have already pointed out that not all of our concern will be for modal logic. Modal logic is not the final arbiter when it comes to possible worlds and modality. Some philosophers claim that possible worlds defined and used for the semantics of the artificial languages of modal logic are not adequate for dealing with many of the issues that the "real" notion of possible worlds can well and truly deal with. The formal metalogical notion is very restricted, and boxed around with limiting features. David Lewis writes:

When I say that possible worlds help with the analysis of modality, I do not mean that they help with the metalogical "semantical analysis of modal logic". Recent interest in possible worlds began there, to be sure. But wrongly . . . Metalogical results, by themselves, answer no questions about the logic of modality. They give us conditional answers only: if modal operators can be correctly analysed in so-and-so way, then they obey so-and-so system of modal logic We must consider whether they may indeed be so analysed; and then we are doing metaphysics, not mathematics.[33]

Modal operators, referred to by Lewis in this extract, are the operators expressed in ordinary language, albeit ordinary language as used in a disciplined philosophical way. Lewis is raising much the same question as the question to which we referred earlier: the question of the reliability of formal systems. If these questions are much the same, then there is a very strong sense in which a formal system gives an analysis of the concepts that its logical operations implement.

The classical propositional logic gives, in its conjunction operator, an analysis of propositional commutative conjunction. That analysis has not caused any problem so long as it is seen as just that. But, propositional logic does not give any analysis of temporally sequenced, non-commutative, conjunction. On the other hand, its analysis of implication as material implication has generated deep disputation, a vast literature and many logical systems.

We shall see that there are many modal logics. They offer analyses of implication, disjunction, negation, and possibility and necessity. Their formalities and analyses can be explained in terms of possible worlds, but possible worlds interpreted in a particular way for each modal logic. The differences in interpretation are crucial.

Our beginning is with modal logic understood in terms of possible worlds, but we will not remain there. Possible worlds will take us beyond formal systems. In further chapters we consider some of the problems that arise from the idea itself, and consider how the notion can be and has been applied to a wide range of questions.

Because the formal systems are clear and precise in their use of possible worlds, we will begin with them. There are many uses. The scene is rich with variations. But it will only be a beginning. We must resist the temptation to be overcome with the neatness of formal systems, and especially resist making the mistake of thinking that the neat formal uses of possible worlds in logic must be telling us about the real meaning of modal operators in ordinary language.

People working in artificial intelligence are well aware of a neatness–scruffiness contrast. It is often useful to begin with neat alleged solutions to a problem, even if we finish up with the more scruffy approach. There are virtues in being scruffy at times, despite the blandishments of the paragons of neatness: some of the formal logicians.

Despite the comments quoted, Lewis is not averse to neatness. His counterpart theory,[34] to which we will come later, is set out formally in first-order logic, and drives much of what he has to say about the way in which possible worlds are to be used to solve certain problems to do with identity and possibility.

We will certainly look at the uses to which various philosophers put the notion of possible worlds. We will also look at the maze of related notions expressed in ordinary language. We will move backwards and forwards between formal and philosophical. All in one book? This book can only be a beginning. The intention is to open up this incredibly rich area for your consideration. It is a fascinating area to explore.

Appendix: Formal symbols

Negation is often represented by tilde, "∼". Sometimes use is made of either corner, "¬", or minus, "–". Conjunction (commutative) is usually represented by ampersand, "&", dot, "·" or hat, "∧". Conjunction in classical logic is also associative and idempotent. Inclusive disjunction is represented by vel or wedge, "∨". Material implication is often represented by hook or horseshoe, "⊃". Sometimes an arrow, "→", is used, but the hook was used in *Principia Mathematica* specifically to indicate the material conditional rather than just any conditional. Strict implication is represented by fishhooks, "⥽". Those who call the material conditional symbol "hook" will usually call the strict implication symbol "fishhook", while those who call the material implication symbol "horseshoe" will often call the strict implication symbol just "hooks".

- The negation of A is ∼A.
- The commutative conjunction of A and C is (A & C).
- The inclusive disjunction of A and C is (A ∨ C).
- The material implication of C by A is (A ⊃ C).
- The strict implication of C by A is (A ⥽ C)

CHAPTER 2
Possible worlds

2.1 Modal logics

In this chapter we will consider the way in which possible worlds came to the aid of logicians working with modal logic. Modal logic is generally seen as the logic of possibility and necessity. Possible worlds have made formal modal logic quite clear and precise. In order to see possible worlds and modal logic in clearer perspective we will consider a little of the historical context.

Modern formal logic began with Frege's first-order logic.[1] First-order logic is now seen in philosophy, mathematics, linguistics and computer science as the stepping-off point for virtually all work in logic.[2] First-order logic includes classical propositional logic, which we looked at in Chapter 1, together with predicate logic. We have already said that we take first-order logic to be an artificial language that gives a precise and unambiguous account of logical concepts that are very like, but not exactly the same as, the logical concepts expressed in ordinary language.

We have seen that some of the logical concepts expressed in ordinary language are negation (standardly expressed with "not"), conjunction ("and"), disjunction ("or") and implication ("if . . . then . . ."). We now turn to possibility and necessity. I have introduced special font expressions for the propositional logic operators used to translate these ordinary language logical operations: **not** for negation, **and** for conjunction, **or** for disjunction and **imp** for implication. Standard modal logic adds to these the diamond, ◊, for possibility and the box, □, for necessity.[3] I will bow to the prevailing symbolism for modal logic.

Much of the focus of interest in modal logic is divided between modal propositional logic and modal predicate logic. In texts, there is usually far more material about modal propositional logic than about modal predicate logic. We will begin with modal propositional logic in this chapter, and turn to modal predicate logic in Chapters 3 and 4.

2.2 Modal propositional logic

Our intention is to look at modal logic from the point of view of interpretation and of translation based on interpretation. We begin with modal propositional logic. But before we launch into those details there is one point to make. We have already seen how we might use translation constants such as *A* and *C* as abbreviations for basic propositions, and propositional variables such as *p* and *q* as "spaces" for any complete propositions. When we use translation constants we get *closed sentences*. The sentences in which there are propositional variables are *open* sentences. Open sentences are sometimes called "forms". They display the *logical form* of propositions.

The standard basic translations to modal propositional logic, given that *p* and *q* are spaces in which to put complete propositions, are:

Standard translation table		
1. *not p*	is translated to	**not** *p*
2. *both p and q*	is translated to	(*p* **and** *q*)
3. *either p and/or q*	is translated to	(*p* **or** *q*)
4. *either p xor q*	is translated to	(*p* **xor** *q*)
5. *if p then q*	is translated to	(*p* **imp** *q*)
6. *possibly p*	is translated to	◇*p*
7. *necessarily p*	is translated to	□*p*

We note one thing about the last two sentences on the right, and four things about this very standard translation table.

In the sentences ◇*p* and □*p*, the *p* is known as the *scope* of the modal operator. The *p* could be any sentence, some being quite complex. For example:

((*R* **and** *S*) **imp not** *T*)

With a box to the left it becomes:

□((*R* **and** *S*) **imp not** *T*)

In this sentence the *scope of the box* is ((*R* **and** *S*) **imp not** *T*).

In the sentence:

$((R$ and $S)$ imp $\square$ not $T)$

the *scope of the box* is **not** T.
The scope of the box (or diamond) is often said to be a "modal context". So in

$\square((R$ and $S)$ imp not $T)$

the material conditional is *in* a modal context, as are the conjunction and negation and propositions R, S and T. In

$((R$ and $S)$ imp $\square$ not $T)$

the negation and the T are in a modal context, but the material conditional is not. The idea of scope becomes very important in modal predicate logic.

Now for matters of translation. First, the number of entries in translation tables differs slightly from text to text. In many texts, there will be no entries for 3 and 4. The legalistic "and/or" is not well regarded and the computer science "xor" is just too technical to be considered. The entries for 6 and 7 take no notice of the difference between "possible for" and "possible that", and the difference between "necessary for" and "necessary that". We look at these differences and other ordinary language modalities in Chapter 5.

Secondly, the expressions on the left side of the table carry their usual meaning in English. The expressions on the right side of the table are very precisely defined in terms of the truth-value semantics for classical propositional logic.

Thirdly, this basic translation table is often supplemented by an extended table with entries like:

8. *p in spite of q*	is translated to	$(p$ and $q)$
9. *p only if q*	is translated to	$(p$ imp $q)$
10. *p is sufficient for q*	is translated to	$(p$ imp $q)$
11. *q is necessary for p*	is translated to	$(p$ imp $q)$

It is not always clear that the expressions on the left, such as in 10 and 11, mean the same thing, even though they translate to the same thing in propositional logic. At best, authors will argue that the expressions on the left of 5, 9, 10 and 11 have the "same logical content". But in most texts the authors just present the directions for translation with no argument. It is a standard list, widely accepted, and not seen as being in need of justification. *Mea culpa,* I have done the same in an introductory logic text.[4]

Fourthly, the most problematic area for translation and understanding is the translation of conditionals. There are two discernible areas of difficulty. One is where modality and the conditional are combined. The other is just the conditional itself.

Difficulties with modalised conditionals can be seen with:

2.2.13. *If Socrates is human then he must be mortal.*

The "must" in the consequent of 2.2.13 makes it look as though the modality operates on the consequent. It turns out that the modality operates on the whole conditional, and that 2.2.13 is best understood as:

2.2.14. *Of necessity, if Socrates is human then he is mortal.*

We will return to this later, and why it turns out to be best to take the modality as being for the whole conditional rather than just the consequent.

The difficulties with the bare conditional are many. The reason for the difficulties are many, not least of which is the variety of conditionals in ordinary language. But there is a long history of controversy about how implication is to be understood. We now turn to one modern manifestation of the problem, a manifestation that had a great deal to do with the generation of modern modal logic.

2.3 The problem with implication

We begin with the development of modal logic in the late nineteenth and early twentieth centuries. The development is instructive because modern modal logic did not begin with possibility and necessity as the main focuses of interest. Logicians constructed modal logic because they were dissatisfied with the way in which first-order logic used material implication to deal with implication and conditionals.

There are several reasons for looking askance at material implication. The most obvious was displayed in Chapter 1, where we saw an example of the incorrect classification of an argument that followed from the use of material implication for translating conditionals. There are other examples to be found in a voluminous literature to do with this problem.[5]

Negated conditionals are another important problem area for conditionals. Negated conditionals show that the material implication translation of conditionals is intuitively and logically unsatisfactory. As a general rule, if X is equivalent to Y, then the negation of X should be equivalent to the negation of Y. The material conditional translation of *If A then C* is based on the notion that *If A then C* is equivalent to *Either not A and/or C*. Under the general rule about equivalence, it should follow that the negation of *If A then C* is equivalent to the negation of *Either not A and/or C*. The negation of *Either not A and/or C* is

Neither not A nor C. Neither not A nor C is equivalent to *A and not C.* So, according to the material implication account, the negation of *If A then C* is equivalent to *A and not C.* In practice this would mean that someone who claims *It's false that if Germany had invaded Britain in 1940 then Germany would have won the Second World War* is claiming the equivalent of *Germany did invade Britain in 1940 and did not win the Second World War.* But this is not what the negation of the conditional amounts to.

There are two responses to the counter-intuitive outcomes of the material conditional account of conditionals. The first response is that the negation of a conditional such as *If A then C* is equivalent to *It's possible that if A then not C.* So someone claiming *It's false that if Germany had invaded Britain in 1940 then Germany would have won the Second World War* is claiming the equivalent of *It's possible that had Germany invaded Britain in 1940 then it would* not *have won the Second World War.* This response makes use of a modal notion of negation. Negating a conditional becomes a quite complex thing, unlike the negation of conjunctions or disjunctions.

A second response was suggested by McColl in 1906. It is based on a rejection of the material conditional account of *If A then C* conditionals. An *If A then C* conditional is to be taken as asserting *It's impossible for A to be true and C false.* The negative is *It's not impossible for A to be true and C false.* This is equivalent to *It's possible for A and not C.* So, someone claiming *It's false that if Germany had invaded Britain in 1940 then Germany would have won the Second World War* is claiming the equivalent of *It's possible for Germany to have invaded Britain in 1940 and not to have won the Second World War.*

In general, if the negation of *If A then C* is equivalent to *It's possible for A and not C,* then the positive of the conditional is equivalent to *It's impossible for A and not C.* McColl's account makes use of the notions of possibility and impossibility, and led to a *modal* account of implication and its negation.

2.4 The Lewis systems

McColl's suggestion eventually lead to C. I. Lewis's work on providing an axiomatic account of implication. Lewis's first account, in the form of a logical system in *A Survey of Symbolic Logic,*[7] was eventually to be labelled S3.[8] Lewis eventually developed five systems[9] of modal implicational logic, and hinted at others.[10] The logics are said to provide logic for *strict implication* as distinct from logic for *material implication.*[11] Lewis eventually constructed a series of five axiomatic systems for strict implication. The systems were simply called system 1, system 2,[12] system 3, system 4 and system 5. The shorthand for the logics became S1, S2, S3, S4 and S5.[13]

It is often difficult for logicians and philosophers who have truth-value semantics at their disposal, including possible worlds semantics, to understand how logicians like Lewis and McColl understood logical symbols and operations. As far as I can understand the approach, their understanding was based on what they took to be an intuitive insight into *axiom systems* and *proofs* based on them. It was common for them and their contemporaries to set out logical systems as axiomatic logics with a view to expressing basic principles that revealed the nature of logical operations such as negation and implication.

In constructing a logic axiomatically, the logic's creator is trying to select a possibly minimal list of axioms and inference rules that reflect their ideas of what principles of reasoning should be included in the logic.[14]

For example, suppose that we think that a very important principle about implication is that it is *transitive*. In other words, we think that it is valid to argue:

> *If p then q*
> *If q then r*
> _____
> So *If p then r*

This might seem so basic that we have an axiom of our logic give expression to this principle. So we have an axiom that reads as:

> *If (if p then q) and (if q then r), then (if p then r)*

Lewis used just such an axiom in S1. This shift from valid argument to axiomatic principle was seen as a natural way of proceeding. Most of the discussion of Lewis's systems by William and Martha Kneale[15] is based on this way of understanding the relationship between argument and axioms. Kneale and Kneale are writing, at least on the matter of modal logic, from within the axiomatizer's perspective. It is also clear that Lewis had this kind of view.

But the question can then be asked, "How do you justify the principle behind the axiom?" You might reply, "It's just obvious." You might reply, "Logicians through the ages have agreed to it." You might argue that without this principle you cannot show that certain obviously valid arguments are valid. The first two responses are not strong. The third involves the indirect approach of searching through comparative consequences. But this is not how logicians approach such questions today.

We now work with a quite different approach. The present, and (we think) more powerful, approach to answering the question is to make use of semantics. The axiomatic approach alone is seen, more and more, as impractical and obscure. The semantic approach is based on trying to decide what are the truth-conditions for conditionals. Then we look at what would make the transitive implication principle true, and what would make it false. We place our reliance on truth-value semantics.

Logicians in the first part of the twentieth century made some use of truth-value semantics[16] for implication logics, but not for setting out the underlying logical nature of logical operations. It was only in the second half of the twentieth century that there was a substantial shift to making semantics the most important basis from which to argue about the nature of logical operations.

The idea behind Lewis's axiomatic systems was that some quite basic features of conditionals could be set out directly and intuitively. Even without any formal symbols we will see, in some intuitive way, that the axioms and rules of inference of S1, set out below, are a reasonable expression of the kind of implication expressed in *If . . . then . . .* conditionals. In fact, the original axioms of S1 set out a complete propositional logic with negation, conjunction and possibility as the basic logical notions. *If p then q* is *defined* as *It's not possible for p and not q*. This use of the notion of possibility is a crucial turning point in the history of modern logic.

There are more details of the five Lewis systems in the appendix to this chapter.

2.5 From implication to necessity

During the 30 to 40 years after the publication of the first edition of Lewis's *Symbolic Logic* (1932) there was an increasing interest in possibility and necessity among modal logicians and philosophers. There was also a decrease in interest in constructing a modal logic for implication.

Any explanation of this shift would have to include at least three things.[17] First, there was focus on the paradoxes of strict implication. Secondly, there was an increasingly held view that the perceived problems with the material implication account of implication were more apparent than real. Thirdly, the development of alternative formal approaches to Lewis's five systems shifted the focus of attention. Let's look at each of these in turn.

The first factor in the shift of emphasis was the increasing realization that strict implication is simply necessary material implication. The basic notions in Lewis's approach were negation, conjunction and possibility. Strict implication was defined in terms of these three:

> *p strictly implies q*   is defined as   *It's not possible for both p and not q*

In formal symbols:

> *p* **strimp** *q*   is defined as   **not** $\Diamond$(*p* **and not** *q*)

Necessity is also defined in terms of possibility and negation:

> *It's necessary for p*   is defined as   *It's not possible for not p*

In formal symbols:

$\Box p$ is defined as   **not ◊ not** p

By simple substitution of equivalences and definitions it is clear that:

p *strictly implies* q is equivalent to *It's necessary for p to materially imply q*

or p *strictly implies* q is equivalent to *It's necessary for either not p and/or q*

In formal expressions:

p **strimp** q is equivalent to $\Box(p$ **imp** $q)$

or p **strimp** q is equivalent to $\Box(\text{\bf not } p \text{ \bf or } q)$

These equivalences drove the focus of attention to necessary material implication. Strict implication in the Lewis systems is simply necessary material implication. The more this was noticed, the more that logicians went looking for analogues in strict implication of the paradoxes and problems of material implication. Analogues were soon discovered. The paradoxes led to the vague intuition that strict implication could not be a good account of implication. This vague intuition was reinforced by the lack of any widely accepted semantics for strict implication. The important point here is that modal logic was no longer seen as a fruitful area of investigation for a solution to the problems of implication.

The second factor in the shift of emphasis follows from the first. Given the perceived failure of modal logic to solve the problems of implication, several philosophers and logicians began to question the notion that there were serious problems with material implication as an account of implication. Although they did not say that the supposed problems were completely spurious, they questioned their status. The critics were much aided by the fact that the material conditional seemed to create no problems in the area of mathematical logic and foundations of mathematics: "If it works for mathematics, what's the problem?"

If the problems are nowhere as serious as suggested by McColl, Lewis and their followers, why bother? The "problems" of implication can be put on the back burner while more serious problems are dealt with. This approach helped shift the emphasis away from implication.

The third factor flows from the other two. There was a shift of formal emphasis in modal logic away from implication towards necessity. The publication of *Symbolic Logic* prompted vigorous investigation of the Lewis systems and of a myriad of other modal logics. There was a boom in modal logic, a boom that continues to the present. This boom was marked by an increasing emphasis on the use of necessity, rather than implication, as a basic notion in modal logic.

For whatever reason, twentieth-century logicians seem to have developed a love for basing their axiomatic logics on the notions of negation and material implication. When this preference is translated to modal logic it soon leads to a bias in favour of taking negation, material implication and necessity as basic. This can be seen in the classic modal logic text of Hughes and Cresswell, *An Introduction to Modal Logic*, published in 1968, nearly 40 years after Lewis's *Symbolic Logic*. Although Hughes and Cresswell say that their formal systems are to be based on negation, disjunction and necessity, by the time we reach page 31 the symbols that dominate the text are of negation, material implication and necessity. Above all, necessity is dominant, and strict implication is not. This dominance persists for the rest of the text, except, of course, for the chapters devoted to an account of Lewis's systems.

In the work of E. J. Lemmon,[18] one of the great systematic axiomatizers of modal logics, the same three notions are utterly dominant. Formal modal logic was becoming more and more focused on necessity. By the 1960s, the quest for a better account of implication and a modal logic language to give expression to the account was petering out. That quest was moving more and more to non-classical and relevant logic. The formal logic emphasis on necessity in modal logic was just what was needed to provide a very warm welcome indeed for Kripke's development of the technical notion of possible worlds.[19] Possible worlds are just the thing for a technically precise and intuitively appealing account of necessity.

2.6 Possible worlds

The ideas behind the *possible worlds* semantics for modal logic are quite simple. First, possible worlds are used as part of a *truth-value semantics* for modal notions. Secondly, in the possible worlds semantics, propositions are either true or false *in* or *at* possible worlds. This principle needs to be double underlined. In possible worlds semantics there is no truth outside possible worlds. In some discussions of possibility and necessity, where there is apparent appeal to possible worlds, there is almost no recognition of this principle.

If someone asks, "Is *It's possible that p* true?", then we must first find out what world they are asking about. If they respond, "In world *W*" then we change the question to, "Is *It's possible that p* true in world *W*?" If they respond, "What do you mean, 'What world'? I just mean what I said; is it true?", then we have to say, "Possible worlds semantics cannot tell you. Go somewhere else for your answer."

Truth is always relative to a possible world.

We live in one possible world. It is the actual world. A work of fiction can be seen as a description of what is true in a possible world other than the actual world. Some works of fiction are descriptions of possible worlds very like the actual one. Some, such as works of fantasy, describe worlds quite remote from the actual world.

The possible worlds account of logical notions is an account in terms of truth and falsehood. This is what makes it a *semantic* account. Possible worlds semantics is definitely formal semantics. Possible worlds semantics gives an account of what it is for propositions containing modal terms to be true or false in some world or other, or in all worlds.

The explanatory idea in the possible worlds logics is the idea that if someone says "It's possible for giant squid to live in the sea", then this is true, in the world in which it is stated, just in case there is a possible world in which it is true that giant squid live in the sea.

A statement is *possibly true* in some world, say *W, just in case* it is true in at least one possible world, say *U.*

In the possible worlds logics a statement is true-in-a-world rather than just true.

A statement is *necessarily true* in some world, say *W,* just in case it is true in every possible world.

Statements such as "If it's raining, then it's raining" are true in every possible world, so, in any world *W,* it is necessarily true that if it's raining, then it's raining.

The possible worlds semantics for negation and material implication does not require ranging across worlds. So, *not p* is true in a world if, and only if, *p* is false in that same world. Similarly, *p materially implies q* is true in a world if, and only if, either *p* is false in that same world or *q* is true in that same world.

If we take these straightforward accounts of truth for negation, material implication, possibility and necessity, then we get a modal logic that is Lewis's S5. In possible worlds semantics, an argument form is valid if, and only if, in every world in which all the premises are true so is the conclusion is also true. All the argument forms and only the argument forms that are valid in S5 are valid in the simple possible worlds semantics outlined above.

There is one more thing in the formal semantics for S5. Possible worlds occur in what I will call *set-ups*[20] of possible worlds. A set-up of possible worlds can contain any non-zero number of possible worlds. Possible worlds do not just "float around" independently of one another; they occur in collections. Consider a couple of cases. Say we want to consider what is different, in terms of possible worlds, about asserting that *necessarily P* is true (in a world) and that *necessarily not P* is true (in a world). If the first is true, then *P* is true in every possible world; and if the second is true, then *not P* is true in every possible world. The first account requires a set-up of possible worlds in each of which *P* is true, and the second requires a quite different set-up of possible worlds in each of which *not P* is true.

Someone might well respond to this by saying, "But surely, we will only say '*necessarily P*' when it's clear that *P* is a logical truth or a tautology. If that is the case, then '*necessarily not P*' will never be true, because *not P* will be a contradiction, and there just cannot be a set-up of possible worlds in each of which *not P* is true." This response misses the point that the modal operators, in both logic and ordinary language, are often used to operate on propositions that are not logical truths. For example, "It is not possible for Sue to be here in ten minutes." The possible worlds account of this is that if it is true in some world, that world is one of a set-up of worlds in each of which *Sue does not get here in ten minutes* is true. Logical truth is not the only issue.

So, if we use Ω (capital omega) to represent a set-up of worlds, and "iff" for "if and only if", the more accurate representation of the S5 definitions for box and diamond are:

$\Diamond A$ is true in world w in Ω iff A is true in at least one world, say u, in Ω

and

$\Box A$ is true in world w in Ω iff A is true in every world in Ω.

If straightforward possible worlds semantics is the semantics for S5, what do we need for the semantics for S1 to S4? We need various qualifications of the definitions for the truth of possibility and necessity. The working out of these qualifications has yielded a range of mechanisms that have led to an explosion in the number of formal modal logics. The qualifications have the effect of giving *structure* to set-ups of possible worlds. There are many ways of understanding structured set-ups of possible worlds. The five Lewis systems give five different structures to set-ups of possible worlds.

2.7 Qualifications and frameworks

We now look at some of the qualifications of the definitions for the truth of possibility and necessity propositions and how these qualifications give structure to set-ups of possible worlds. Note again the definitions for S5:

$\Diamond A$ is true in world w in Ω iff A is true in at least one world, say u, in Ω

and

$\Box A$ is true in world w in Ω iff A is true in every world in Ω.

The qualifications that give us the semantics for logics other than S5 are introduced by placing a restriction on the "at least one world in Ω" in the definition for possibility, and on the "every world in Ω" in the definition for necessity. To facilitate such qualifications, a special relationship between possible worlds is introduced. This relationship is called "accessibility". Worlds are said to *have access to* other worlds in the set-up to which they belong. At one point Hughes and Cresswell, for pedagogic purposes, describe the relation as "seeing". I like to think of Hughes and Cresswell's "seeing" as "seeing into". One world might be able to *see into* another world. In S5, every world can *see into* every world, or *have access to* every world, including itself.

There is a general change in the truth conditions for box and diamond, a change that incorporates the accessibility relation. We now have the more general rules:

◊A is true in world *w* in Ω iff A is true in at least one world, say *u*, in Ω and *w has access to u*

and

□A is true in world *w* in Ω iff A is true in every world in Ω *to which w has access.*

So long as we understand that the worlds always occur in set-ups of worlds, we can shorten the definitions to:

◊A is true in world *w* iff A is true in at least one world, say *u*, and world *w has access to* world *u*

and

□A is true in world *w* iff A is true in every world *to which* world *w has access*

or

□A is true in world *w* iff A is true in every *accessible* world.

Then, for example:

It's possible for it to rain on Saturday is true in the world of the fine Friday, *f*, iff *It's raining on Saturday* is true in at least one world, say *s*, and the world, *f* of the fine Friday, *has access to s*

and

It's necessary for it to be raining on Saturday is true in the world of the fine Friday, *f*, iff *It's raining on Saturday* is true in every world to which the world of the fine Friday *has access.*

What would make sense of access in our rainy weather example? Well, it might be something like *foreseeing*. On Friday we look forwards and see the possibility of a fine Saturday, or we look forwards and see that there is only one outcome: it must be fine on Saturday. The latter kind of "only one outcome" foresight is just what the weather forecaster wants to have.

One might think, at first anyway, that every world must have access to, or can see into, itself. But, from a purely formal point of view, not even this is to be assumed once we introduce accessibility. But when accessibility includes self-accessibility, then the accessibility relation is *reflexive*. Accessibility is reflexive in all five Lewis systems of logic.

Because access from one world to other worlds is qualified, we get differing structures. Differing structures give differing semantics: the semantics for logics other than S5. From a mathematical point of view, accessibility in S5 is *reflexive, transitive* and *symmetrical*. But that is just a mathematical way of saying, in terms of the properties of dyadic relations, that every world has access to every world (including itself).

In the following pages we look at the contrasts between four modal logics: K, T, S4 and S5. The main point is that accessibility in systems other than S5 is not as simple as it is in S5. If you are not interested in the technical details, skip the rest of this section.

The systems K, T, S4 and S5

It happens to be a very nice coincidence for mathematical accounts that accessibility in S4 is reflexive and transitive, but not necessarily symmetrical. But what does that mean? Let's begin by looking at the difference between S4 and S5 in terms of the differences between the accessibility that worlds have to worlds in S4 and S5.

We look at a diagram that will show us the crucial difference between S5 and S4. Say we have a set-up of three possible worlds: *world n*, *world k* and *world j*. Let us exercise our arbitrary power and insist that *world n* has access to *world k* and *world k* has access to *world j*. These accessibility links are like a scaffolding, or framework, within which the possible worlds of a set-up are suspended. This can be set out as in Figure 2.1.

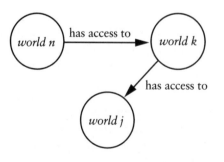

Figure 2.1

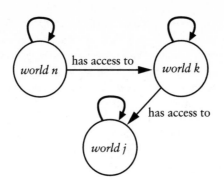

Figure 2.2

In both S5 and S4 each world automatically has access to itself. Accessibility is reflexive. So we can add loopy arrows to get Figure 2.2.

In S4 and S5, because accessibility is *transitive,* and since *world n* has access to *world k* and *world k* has access to *world j,* it follows that *world n* has access to *world j.* We add a new accessibility arrow to get Figure 2.3.

And that's all for S4. A difference now emerges. In S5 every world in a set-up has automatic access to every world. So, for S5, we get double arrows between all worlds. All the S4 arrows are included, but there is more, as in Figure 2.4.

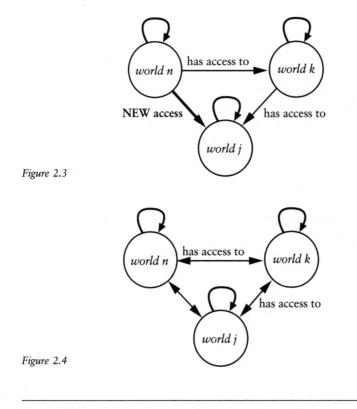

Figure 2.3

Figure 2.4

So we have different kinds of possible worlds structures for S4 and S5. Each structure is like a framework or a scaffolding of accessibility between possible worlds. The framework for S5 can be referred to as an S5-*framework*, and the framework for S4 can be referred to as an S4-*framework*.[21]

The S4-*frameworks* embody the assumptions that accessibility is reflexive (each world can see into itself) and transitive. The S5-*frameworks* embody the assumption that accessibility is universal: all worlds have access to all worlds. But there is a modal logic in which there are no assumptions at all about accessibility. That logic is K. Its lack of any assumptions about accessibility leads logicians to say that it is the *weakest* normal modal logic. Because accessibility is not even reflexive in K, K is the weakest non-reflexive modal logic. In K set-ups, the worlds do not have access to themselves. If one adds the assumption that accessibility is reflexive, but nothing more, then the logic is T. T is said to be the weakest reflexive normal modal logic. It will be useful to know about K and T when we come to modal predicate logic in Chapter 3.

What do the differences amount to? It is common for people to see S5 as the logic for logical possibility and logical necessity, while S4 is seen as the stepping-off point for logics for temporal possibility and temporal necessity. Temporal possibility covers things such as what might happen *in the future*, or what might happen *after* something happens. We look at this question in more detail later, but it is a question about the importance for possibility and necessity of the *framework of accessibility*.

Just as K can be seen as a non-reflexive T, there is a non-reflexive S4. It is known as K4. Accessibility is transitive for K4, and K4 is seen as a stepping-off point for logics for *proof*.

When we turn to the way in which possible worlds feature in the semantics for S1, S2 and S3, there are additional complications over and above the framework of accessibility. The worlds themselves are divided into two kinds of worlds. The technical terminology calls some of them the "normal" worlds, and the remainder of them the "non-normal" worlds. The rules that assign truth-value are different in normal worlds from those in non-normal worlds. In essence this means that possibility and necessity are being described differently in different possible worlds.

These variations on accessibility and the differing kinds of possible worlds give us different frameworks of possible worlds for different modal logics. Another way of putting the key question in modal logic is, "Do these different frameworks match different sorts of possibility and necessity?"

2.8 Set-ups and models and contingent necessity

If we concentrate our attention on the theorems and valid argument forms of a modal logic such as S5, then it is easy to forget that the box and diamond symbols can operate on any proposition, and the result is not necessarily a logical truth. We have already looked at this, and noted that possible worlds, in the semantics for modal logic, come in set-ups of worlds. Assume for the moment that we are working in S5 (where there is a set-up with an S5-*framework* of accessibility).

Take a proposition from the theory of relativity:

1. *No object has a velocity greater than the velocity of light.*

Consider then a modal version:

2. No *object* can *have a velocity greater than the velocity of light.*

This is equivalent to:

3. *It's* not possible *for any object to have a velocity greater than the velocity of light.*

According to standard modal logic equivalences, 3 is equivalent to:

4. Necessarily no *object has a velocity greater than the velocity of light.*

It would be more accurate to have:

3p. *It's* not physically possible *for any object to have a velocity greater than the velocity of light.*

According to standard equivalences, 3 is equivalent to:

4p. *It's* physically necessary for no *object to have a velocity greater than the velocity of light.*

There is nothing logical about the impossibility in 3 and 3p, or the necessity in 4 and 4p. So, from a logical point of view, we can easily find a possible world in which at least one object has a velocity greater than the velocity of light. But such a possible world will not be one in which the theory of relativity is true.

But there will be a set-up of possible worlds such that 4 is true in every one. An even smaller set-up of worlds will have true, in each one, all the propositions that constitute the theory of relativity. If we restrict our considerations to just this set-up of possible worlds then everything true in all the worlds of this set-up will tell us what is physically necessary, and whatever is true in at least one world in the set-up will tell us what is physically possible, given that the theory of relativity is correct.

But physical necessity is, on this account, not logically necessary. It is "contingent necessity", or "physical necessity" where "physical" is determined by the theory of relativity. The necessity is contingent upon the physical theory's being true in all worlds in the set-up. The accessibility relation in this S5 set-up of worlds does not restrict which world has access to which. Since it is S5, every world has access to every world. The accessibility is confined overall by the physical theory, by physical necessity. So, even though it is S5, worlds have access only to worlds in a particular set-up of possible worlds. It is the set-up *in all of whose worlds* the same theory about physical reality is true.

This makes it look as if physical necessity is a restricted form of logical necessity. The restricted set-up of possible worlds have S5 accessibility to each other. The restriction to possible worlds in all of which a certain set of propositions (laws) is true, is a restriction that does not change the S5 accessibility and the S5 structure of worlds.

Particular S5 set-ups of worlds, with their propositional contents, are S5-*models*. So if we think of an S5 set-up of one billion worlds, in every one of which the theory of relativity is true, then we are thinking of one S5-*model*. One of the worlds in the billion-world model might be the actual world, but only if the theory of relativity is true in the actual world.

By contrast, we could have a set-up of worlds in which all the worlds are Newtonian worlds, and the set-up is an S5-*model*. In every world in the model Newton's laws of motion will be true. So in the worlds of the particular S5 set-up, Newton's laws of motion are physically necessarily true.

There are two important features of set-ups of possible worlds: the *framework* of accessibility and normality or non-normality that determines which particular modal logic is being used; and the *content* of the worlds, the propositions true in them. These features give us particular models.

But the same could be done with S4 or T or K. We could have S4-*models* with relativity worlds, or S4-*models* with Newtonian worlds or with relativity worlds, and so on for each of the modal logics available. But what would be the differences between K and T and S4 and S5 relativity set-ups of possible worlds? And what would be the differences between K and T and S4 and S5 Newtonian set-ups of possible worlds? It is important to realize that the box and the diamond do not have to mean logical necessity and logical possibility. They simply mean "in all possible worlds" and "in at least one possible world", where the worlds may be only those worlds in a restricted set-up.

2.9 Worms and instants

In much of the possible-world literature the focus is on the actual world and worlds very like the actual world. There are two ways of looking at worlds, especially at worlds like the actual world, the world in which we live. The worlds can be seen as *worm* worlds, or as *instant* worlds.

When the worlds are seen as worm worlds, then each possible world is understood in terms of a complete history of that possible world. The possible worm worlds are four-dimensional wholes. They have three spatial dimensions. They have a fourth time dimension. The time dimension goes from either the big bang to the big crunch, or from infinitely long ago to infinitely far into the future, or some combination of these temporal durations.

Individuals, say people, are *spatiotemporal worms* that stretch in time from birth to death. They meander around space in accordance with their movements during life. Everything that existed, exists and will exist in the world exists in the worm world. Socrates exists in the worm world, but for an interval along the time dimension that does not overlap with the twenty-first century interval.

The present is a time slice across the whole. You, as you are in the present, are a three-dimensional slice, at the time you are reading this, of your worm. Particular times are slices across the whole four-dimensional world.

There is an alternative view that sees possible worlds as temporal instants. The present world is just a three-dimensional spatial world, the world as it exists *now*, at this present instant. The past does not exist, and the future does not exist, as far as the actual world is concerned.

On the instant view, the past is a sequence of many possible worlds, each world an instant of history. The actual past is just one sequence of many possible sequences. One job of the historian, presumably, is to try to discover which sequence of three-dimensional possible instants is the actual past. For the future, we are faced with many possibilities, many three-dimensional instants in sequences. Eventually we will actually wend our way along just one of the sequences.

The debate about which account of the world is correct is part of the debate about time and reality. We will return to this particular debate later. For the moment we just note that there are these two views. We note that philosophers from both camps who think it sensible to talk about possibilities will agree that the actual present is only one of many possible presents. It matters not whether we see the present as a three-dimensional slice across the four-dimensional worm or the actual instant between past and future; what does matter is that there are other possibilities.

In general, unless we explicitly say otherwise, we will adopt the instant worlds approach. This approach makes it easier to introduce temporal logic and its use of possible worlds. Hopefully our approach can be seen as one of technical convenience, and we will still be able to consider worm worlds sympathetically when we discuss questions of time, reality and existence.

Appendix: The five Lewis systems

We set out the Lewis axiom systems, starting with S1.

Formal axioms for S1

11.1   (p and q) strimp (q and p)

11.2   (p and q) strimp p

11.3 p strimp (p and p)

11.4   ((p and q) and r) strimp (p and (q and r))

11.5 p strimp not not p[22]

11.6   ((p strimp q) and (q strimp r)) strimp (p strimp r)

11.7   (p and (p strimp q)) strimp q

Remember that *If p then q* is understood and translated as (*p* **strimp** *q*). The axioms can be translated to English to read as follows (parentheses used to assist):

11.1   *If (p and q) then (q and p)*

11.2   *If (p and q) then p*

11.3   *If p then (p and p)*

11.4   *If ((p and q) and r) then (p and (q and r))*

11.5   *If p then not not p*

11.6   *If (if p then q) , and (if q then r) , then (if p then r)*

11.7   *If (p and (if p then q)) then q*

Strictly speaking, given the definition of *If p then q*, the first axiom should be read as *It's impossible for both p and q and not both q and p*. The same applies to all the other axioms.

The first, third and fourth axioms give expression to the recognized principles that formal language conjunction is commutative, idempotent and associative, respectively. The second axiom gives expression to the intuitively recognized principle that conjunction is simplifiable, that is, each conjunct is separately implied by the conjunction. The fifth axiom gives expression to the intuitively recognized principle that a proposition implies its double negation. This leads eventually, with the other axioms and the rules of inference, to proof of the principle that a proposition is equivalent to its double negative. This is not, by any means, an uncontroversial principle. The sixth axiom, the first of the principles directed specifically to implication, gives expression to the intuitively recognized principle that implication is *transitive*. The seventh axiom, the second directed to implication, gives expression to the intuitively recognized principle that truth of the antecedent of a true conditional implies the truth of the consequent. This last is, perhaps, one of the least controversial of all the principles to do with implication.[23]

The rules of inference for S1 are *substitutivity of strict equivalences* and *modus ponens*. The latter is often called *detachment*.

There are two versions of *modus ponens*. Hughes and Cresswell[24] call them *strict detachment* and *material detachment*.

$$\frac{\begin{array}{c} p \\ p \ \textbf{strimp} \ q \end{array}}{\therefore \ q} \qquad\qquad \frac{\begin{array}{c} p \\ p \ \textbf{imp} \ q \end{array}}{\therefore \ q}$$

Lewis uses strict detachment in his axiom systems. But material detachment is a derivable rule in all those systems.

Lewis also shows that the strict implication expressed in *If . . . then . . .* conditionals implies the material implication analogue:

If (if p then q) then (either not p and/or q)

Further details of other systems

If you are not really interested in more details of the systems S2 to S5, skip the rest of this section.

Having set out principles for implication, Lewis then looks at a principle that he calls the "Consistency Postulate". He sees this as more directly related to the notion of possibility. (The numbering in what follows is Lewis's.)

19.01   *If it's possible for both p and q, then it's possible for p.*

If this principle is added to S1 as an axiom, then the logic becomes S2.

We have seen that Lewis's first published system, in *A Survey of Symbolic Logic*, was S3. This system is gained from S1 and S2 by either the addition to S1 of A8, as Lewis did,[25] or the addition to S2 of AS3.

A8.   (p **strimp** q) **strimp** (**not** $\Diamond q$ **strimp not** $\Diamond p$)

AS3.   (p **strimp** q) **strimp** ($\Box p$ **strimp** $\Box q$)

On the prompting of Becker, Lewis added C10[26] to construct S4.

C10.   **not** $\Diamond$ **not** p **strimp not** $\Diamond$ **not not** $\Diamond$ **not** p

By definition C10 is the same as C10L.

C10L. $\Box p$ **strimp** $\Box\Box p$

Lewis then added C11 to get S5.

C11. $\Diamond p$ **strimp not** $\Diamond$ **not** $\Diamond p$

By definition this becomes C11L.

C11L. $\Diamond p$ **strimp** $\Box\Diamond p$

These additions for S4 and S5 were first constructed to reduce the number of modalities. The most interesting case is S5. Consider the proposition:

DP.   *It might be possible for Chris to find the book.*

On the surface, it looks as if it should be translated with a diamond for "might" and a diamond for "possible", and if F is for *Chris finds the book*:

$\Diamond\Diamond F$

In S5 this is strictly equivalent to the sentence with just one diamond.

$\Diamond F$

In fact, in S5, any uninterrupted sequence of modal operators is equivalent to just the last in the sequence. For example, the following pairs are equivalent:

$\Diamond F$ and $\Diamond\Box\Box\Box\Diamond F$

$\Box F$ and $\Diamond\Box\Diamond\Box\Diamond\Box F$

This means that there are really only three modalities[27] in S5. They are *no modality*, *possibility* and *necessity*. If a proposition has what appears to be several layers of modality, then that is not necessarily so. The double possibility in DP above, if possibility is understood in S5 terms, is logically the same SP:

SP.   *It's possible for Chris to find the book.*

The simplification to three modalities in S5 and to seven[28] in S4 was not altogether welcomed by Lewis. Lewis seems to have preferred the first three of the five systems, and to have viewed S2 with particular favour. In the 1959 edition of *Symbolic Logic* he added Appendix III, "Final note on system S2", and shows his preference for S2.[29]

The question for us is, how do we decide about the relative merits of these systems, or if any of them have any merit at all? Just looking at axiom systems and using intuition is not seen as adequate today. In fact, it never was really adequate. Without some reasonable semantics, deciding is virtually impossible. Possible worlds offer a basis for deciding: a basis that is semantic.

CHAPTER 3
Possible worlds and quantifiers

3.1 Predicate logic

We begin with the extension of propositional logic to predicate logic and then to modal predicate logic.[1] We look first, from a logical perspective, at what happens when we translate from ordinary language to predicate logic without modal operators. We focus on a very small fragment of both ordinary language and predicate logic: a fragment large enough to show the impact of possible worlds semantics on a range of topics and problems. We then turn to what happens when possible worlds semantics is added to predicate logic.

The first thing about translating from ordinary language to predicate logic is that there is far more to consider than when translating to propositional logic. Predicate logic forces us to understand what is said in ordinary language in a way that does not always accord with our simplistic intuitions. Our intuitions have to be informed and changed. We have to look for features, expressions and underlying meanings in natural language that match the structures and meanings in predicate logic. Here we see clearly that ordinary language and predicate logic are quite different languages. Fortunately, we do not have to begin with complex sentences to see what is important.

3.2 Basic logical features

Consider the simple sentences:

3.2.1.   *Kermit is a frog.*
3.2.2.   *Kermit is green.*

These sentences contain a *singular term* and two *general terms*. The singular term is "Kermit". It is a naming term that we take to refer to just one entity. Even if there were several entities with the same name, "Kermit", in these sentences we take the reference to be to just one entity. The general terms are "is a frog" and "is green". They are used in each sentence to say what property Kermit has. The general terms say what properties are *predicated of* Kermit.

Now consider the sentences:

3.2.3.   *Every frog is green.*
3.2.4.   *At least one frog is green.*

Each sentence contains a quantity word or phrase. The first contains "every", and the second "at least one". These words and phrases are *quantifiers*. Aristotle called the first quantifier "universal" and the second "particular". Modern logicians, for reasons we come to later, call the second quantifier "existential". Universal and existential are the only quantifiers to be recognized in predicate logic. In ordinary language there are many more, such as "a couple", "a few", "many", "most" and "the minority of"; as in "Most frogs are green", "A couple of frogs are green" and so on.

The quantifiers indicate a *quantity of* items in some *domain* of items. The domain is known as the *domain of quantification*. Sometimes the domain is called "the universe of discourse". We will use the word "item" as a catch-all term for whatever is in the domain. Domains are often restricted to some particular set of things. The domain might be restricted to existing things, or to people, or physical objects, or beliefs, or numbers.

The quantifiers are taken to be quite logically distinct from the terms to which they intuitively attach in the sentences. So in 3.2.3, "every frog" is taken as being in two quite distinct parts: the universal quantifier "every", distinct from the general term "frog". In 3.2.4, the existential quantifier, "at least one", is distinct from the term "frog". This can be made clearer with:

3.2.3a.   *Every frog item (in the domain) is a green item.*
3.2.4a.   *At least one frog item is a green item.*

Sentences 3.2.3 and 3.2.4 have the following logical structure:

3.2.5.   Quantifier: general term [is] general term.

One of Aristotle's most important contributions to logic was detecting structure or form like this.[2] But for our purposes, and in the context of modern logic, 3.2.5 shows what we want to show.

As well as the general terms and quantifiers in 3.2.3 and 3.2.4, there is the *logical operation* represented by the "is". In predicate logic, the operation in the universally quantified sentences is taken to be implication; and the operation in the existentially quantified sentences is taken to be conjunction.

To understand 3.2.3 so as to translate it to predicate logic, we have to see the content of the proposition as being:

3.2.6.   For each and every item in the domain, *if* it is a frog *then* it is green.

For 3.2.4 we have:

3.2.7.   For at least one item in the domain, it is a frog *and* it is green.

In predicate logic the quantifiers are taken to be saying things about the items in the domain, but the items are considered, as it were, one by one. Take each item and say the same thing of each one, and we have universal quantification. In 3.2.3 the same thing said of each and every item is that *if it's a frog, then it's green*. In what follows we will use "every" for universal quantification rather than the more popular "all"; and the "every" is to be understood as "each and every".

We have existential quantification if something is true of at least one item in the domain (not saying which specific one). In what follows we use "some" in the singular for "at least one", because it's less clumsy. But we use it with the "at least one" sense. The way the quantifier works in 3.2.4 is that it says that at least one item has the two properties, but the specific item is not nominated. So 3.2.4 says something about a *range* of items, the range being the whole domain. At least one *of the range* has the two properties.

Both quantifiers are said to "range over" the domain of quantification. The universal ranges over the domain in order to indicate that the same thing is said of each member of the domain. The existential ranges over the domain in order to indicate that something is said of at least one of the individuals in the domain.

There is a perennial philosophical question about whether the domain of quantification contains only items that exist. Can the domain also contain items that do not exist? We can and do speak about nonexistent things. We talk about all the Greek Gods, some imaginary cities and every crime solved by Sherlock Holmes. Recently there have even been questions about quantities of impossible objects such as round squares and numbers that both are and are not equal to zero. Should the domain of quantification include nonexistent entities, and even impossible entities? We return to this question later in the discussions of existential import and possibility import. For the moment we leave it as an open question.

In this chapter we will focus our attention on *general terms, quantifiers* and *logical operations*. We return to *singular terms* in Chapter 4.

3.3 Symbols and translations

In this text we have been trying to avoid the special symbols of symbolic logic while using expressions that will do the same work. It turns out that we do not need the full apparatus of predicate logic in order to explore the impact of possible worlds semantics on predicate logic. We can continue with our non-symbolic approach. Symbolic versions of some predicate logic sentences are to be found in an appendix to this chapter.

For our purposes in this text we do not even have to use sentences as complex as the ones in the previous section. We can cover most of what we want to discuss by considering sentences as simple as:

3.3.1.   *Everything is physical.*
3.3.2.   *Something is physical.*
3.3.3.   *Everything is non-physical.*
3.3.4.   *Something is non-physical.*

We can get these half way to predicate logic by re-writing:

3.3.1l.   Every item, x, in the domain, x is physical.
3.3.2l.   At least one item, x, in the domain, x is physical.
3.3.3l.   Every item, x, in the domain, x is not physical.
3.3.4l.   At least one item, x, in the domain, x is not physical.

The translation of these to predicate logic is based on using:

"**(Every x)**" for "for every item, x, in the domain", sometimes read as "all x"
"**(Some x)**" for "for at least one item, x, in the domain".

We also use "**Px**" for "x is physical". The logical convention places the "**x**" *after* the general term "**P**", and much as I would like to have "**xP**", that might be too much of a departure from convention.

We also use the logical operators of propositional logic: negation, conjunction, material implication and inclusive disjunction. Our quantifiers have parentheses around them to emphasize that each of them is a logical operator. So we get:

3.3.1t.   **(Every x) Px**
3.3.2t.   **(Some x) Px**
3.3.3t.   **(Every x) not Px**
3.3.4t.   **(Some x) not Px**

With little extra complication, we could use these sorts of sentences to translate something such as:

3.3.5.   *Some things are physical and some are not.*
3.3.5t.   (Some x) Px and (Some x) not Px

These simple formal sentences will be very useful in seeing what happens when modal operators are added to predicate logic.

There is a set of important logical equivalences that hold in predicate logic. They are the quantifier negation equivalences. We set out just one, in both predicate logic and ordinary language translation:

QN: (Every x) Px   *is equivalent to*   not (Some x) not Px
      Every item is *P*   *is equivalent to*   Not even one item is non-*P*

The QN equivalences show how the quantifiers are inter-definable.

Those of you who have completed a course in predicate logic will at once ask, "What about the more complex sentences of predicate logic, especially those with relational terms and multiple quantification?" I am happy to say that we will not be looking at these complexities. This text is not a text from which one can learn a full and comprehensive predicate logic for use in detailed argument analysis.[3] Nevertheless, we assume that our discussion takes place against a background of the full predicate logic. For our purposes, we only need to look at a small fragment of the full modal predicate logic. We return now to the simpler sentences.

Now we look at what happens when the □ and ◊ are added to predicate logic with just quantifiers, general terms and logical operations. There are two key issues. We have mentioned that one key issue for predicate logic without modal operators is the nature of the items in the domain of quantification, especially as far as existence is concerned. For modal predicate logic this key issue becomes one of the nature of the domain of quantification from possible world to possible world. We begin with this issue in §3.5.

The second key issue concerns the relationship between the scopes of quantifiers and the scopes of modal operators. To understand what is at issue, we need to discuss scope.

3.4 Scope of two kinds

We met the *scope of modal operators* in Chapter 2. It is now time to meet the *scope of quantifiers*. The idea of scope does not, at first, make much sense in English, but it is of considerable importance. Scope can be more easily explained by looking at the scope of quantifiers in predicate logic. In the sentence:

3.4.1.   (Some x) Px

the *scope* of the existential quantifier is:

3.4.2. **Px**

In the sentence:

3.4.3. **(Some y) not Py**

the *scope* of the existential quantifier is:

3.4.4. **not Py**

The existential quantifier in 3.4.1 is an existential quantifier *with respect to* **x**, simply because **x** occurs in **(Some x)**. The existential quantifier in 3.4.3 is an existential quantifier *with respect to* **y**, because **y** occurs in **(Some y)**.

Where there is a quantifier with respect to **x**, as in 3.4.1, the occurrence of **x** in the *scope* of the quantifier is *bound* by the quantifier. Similarly, in 3.4.3, the **y** in the scope, **not Py**, of the existential quantifier is bound by the existential quantifier with respect to **y**. [4]

When □ and ◊ are added to get modal predicate logic, there will be interesting and important overlaps of the scopes of the modal operators and the scopes of the quantifiers.

3.5 Existential import and the domain

Predicate logic can be assumed to have or lack *existential import* with respect to two things. It depends on the way we interpret the logic. The quantifiers can have or lack existential import, and non-descriptive singular terms can have or lack existential import. These different kinds of existential import are related, but will be looked at separately. In this chapter we consider existential import for quantifiers. In Chapter 4 we will consider existential import for singular terms. When quantifiers have existential import, then the domain of quantification consists of all and only *existing* items, entities or things.

With existential import for quantifiers we have:

3.5.1. **(Some x) Px** translates as *At least one* existing *item is P*
                             or as *At least one P exists*
                             or as *There exists at least one P*
                             or as *There is a P*

Also

3.5.2.   **not (Some x) Px**   translates as   *Not even one* existing *item is P*
                     or as   *There are no Ps*
                     or as   *Ps do not exist.*

We have seen that the following are logically equivalent:

(Every x) Px	::	**not (Some x) not Px**
Every item is P	::	*Not even one item is not P*

If the quantifiers have existential import then it would be more accurate to translate the pair above as:

Every existing *item is P*   ::   *Not even one* existing *item is not P*

The problem that arises out of the quantifiers' having existential import concerns translating the quantifiers of English. If quantifiers have existential import then there is no way that predicate logic can translate:

3.5.4.   *Some things do not exist.*

This seems to be a reasonable enough thing to say in English. But there has been a view among some philosophers, dating back some millennia, that 3.5.4 is self-contradictory or even nonsensical. Such a philosophical view seems quite puzzling. We will return to it.

If quantifiers in predicate logic have existential import, then translating the quantifiers in English in a direct way to predicate logic quantifiers assumes that the English quantifiers also have existential import. If English quantifiers have existential import, then *Some things do not exist* "really" means:

3.5.4r.   *At least one existing thing does not exist.*

This is clearly self-contradictory. But most uninitiated readers, and quite a few who are well appraised of predicate logic, would probably say that 3.5.4 does not *really mean* 3.5.4r. It follows that, for the uninitiated, quantifiers in English do not have existential import. The orthodox view, for twentieth-century philosophers and logicians anyway, is that quantifiers in predicate logic always have existential import.[5] And that assumption is transferred to English.

There is a non-standard view that agrees with the uninitiated view. The non-standard view is that quantifiers, at least in ordinary language, do not have existential import. The domain of quantification can contain items that do not exist, and even items that could not exist. Some speakers of English would not object that the following is (outrageously) inconsistent:

3.5.5.   *Some things, such as round squares, are impossible.*

The assumption of existential import rules out 3.5.5 as utterly self-contradictory. But, even if we rule out 3.5.5 as contradictory, we still have 3.5.4 as a perfectly sensible (and true) proposition.

The assumption of existential import is simply an assumption that the quantifiers have a restricted domain of quantification. It is not unusual to restrict the domain of quantification to some "universe of discourse" when arguments are being evaluated. Life can be simpler if the universe of discourse is limited to persons. Natural language quantifiers often have such restrictions built into them: *someone, everyone, somebody, everybody, sometime, something* and so on. When quantifiers are so restricted, then they are sometimes said to be "sortal" quantifiers. The domain of quantification contains all and only entities of one sort, such as persons, things, times and so on.

When a quantifier is so restricted, then the relevant property is absorbed into the quantifier. If we used "**(SomeP x)**" for "somebody, x", where the letter "**P**" stands for the restriction to persons, then we would not have to worry about explicit mention of the property of being a person outside the quantifier. So, we have a personalist particular quantifier. We could translate:

3.5.6.   *Somebody is honest.*

as

3.5.6t.   **(SomeP x) Hx**

We could, in this way, be rid of most properties, by absorbing them into the quantifiers. But, when we do that, we don't get "rid of most properties". We just hide them, suppress them. They are still there. Existential import simply suppresses existence, but it does not get rid of it. What happens if we drop the assumption of existential import?

The universal quantifier is then more truly universal, and the *exist*ential quantifier is really a *particular* or *partial* quantifier.[6] McGinn writes:

> In the orthodox notion expressed by [the existential quantifier] we have conflated two distinct linguistic functions into the [existential quantifier] symbol – the function of saying how many and the function of implying existence . . . And this fits the linguistic data, because we do use "some" in contexts in which existence is not implied, even conversationally. Thus we can say, "some of the things you are talking about don't exist", "some superheroes are entirely fictional", "some cities are purely imaginary". In these sentences "some" expresses a proportion, but it does not imply that this proportion exists – quite the opposite, since the predicates negate existence.[7]

In this view there is no *logical* distinction between existent and nonexistent items. So, how does the logic deal with existence without existential import? In a sense, it doesn't. Existence is treated, for the purpose of formulating sentences, like any standard property. From a grammatical or syntactical point of view, no distinction is drawn between **"Sx"** for *"x sings"* and **"Ex"** for *"x exists"*. If we add **"Px"** for *"x is a person"*, then we get the following two pairs. In each pair, the sentence of predicate logic is a translation of the English sentence.

3.5.7.   *Some people do not sing.*
3.5.7l   For at least one item in the domain, it is a person *and* it does not sing.
3.5.7t. **(Some x)(Px and not Sx)**

3.5.8.   *Some people do not exist.*
3.5.8l   For at least one item in the domain, it is a person *and* it does not exist.
3.5.8t. **(Some x)(Px and not Ex)**

Although this grammatical approach to "exists" gives an intuitively acceptable approach to translation, there are many philosophers who have strong objections to treating "exists" like "sings", "walks", "is a person" or "is green".

Our claim is that the demand for existential import is a demand for a logic that is unable to deal with a range of sensible propositions because it has a strong metaphysical bias built into it. The logic we seek is a logic that is neutral, as far as possible, with respect to important philosophical questions such as existence. We prefer a logic that is able to quantify over all the things (items, individuals, entities) about which we can and do talk. Since we do talk sensibly about things that do not exist, it follows that our logic should be able to quantify over both existent and nonexistent items.

When we talk about things that do not exist, or have beliefs about things that do not exist, it is said that the objects of our talk or belief are *intentional* objects. One of the applications of modal predicate logic is in the logic of belief: *doxastic* logic. So, in as much as the objects of belief are intentional, the quantifiers of doxastic logic should be able to range over intentional objects.

Our domain of quantification can be quite unconstrained. We sometimes talk about impossible objects such as round squares, as in 3.5.5. Should we allow for such entities to be denizens of our domain of quantification? If we want our logic to deal with propositions such as *Some things cannot exist, namely round squares*, then we will have to consider allowing impossible objects into the domain; otherwise our logic will not allow unbiased argument about whether round squares can possibly exist. Even if they cannot exist, we should be able to argue about whether they do in an unprejudiced logic.

But some philosophers will be aghast at such permissiveness. Nevertheless, one would hope that modal predicate logic would at least allow us to consider entities that *might* exist. Consider the proposition:

3.5.8.   *There might be a planet beyond Pluto.*

We can certainly envisage a possible world in which there exists a planet beyond Pluto, and also a possible world or worlds in which no such planet exists. We might require that, in each possible world, the quantifiers range only over existing items, but some items that exist in one world do not exist in another.

In this approach we change the domain of quantification from world to world, depending on what exists in each world. So the quantifiers have existential import, but in a world-relative way. The logic required for this picture has *actualist* quantification. This sort of logic has mechanisms for coping with *Some things do not exist*, but they are quite complex and require numerical identity. We introduce numerical identity in Chapter 4.

It may well be argued that if quantifiers are totally unconstrained then there is the risk that a range of paradoxes will emerge to bedevil our logic. If that is a major concern then we can resort to a constraint suggested by Fitting and Mendelsohn. But before we explain that constraint we should note that the whole idea of a fixed domain of quantification might be far too inflexible to allow us to deal with a wide range of argumentation:

> "some" only acquires existential force as a matter of conversational implicature. But this implicature can be cancelled without contradiction, as when one annoyingly says "some of the things I've just been referring to don't exist" or (less annoyingly) "some of the gods are tempestuous, but of course no gods exist" . . . most of the time the implicature is in force, since generally we mean to be speaking of existing things, and this is common knowledge between us; but the general implicature can in principle be cancelled, and then "some" shows its true semantic colours as a device of pure quantification, with no existential entailments.[8]

So for pure quantification we should be most careful about what is built in to our quantifiers. Existential import is just too much for quantifers in modal logic. But there is a half-way house that does not, at least, beg the existential questions.

The half-way house rejects full existential import but accepts weak existential import (WEI). Weak existential import uses an inclusive domain of quantification, so that every item in it exists in at least one possible world, but not necessarily in all worlds. So, the quantifiers quantify over items that *might exist*. This is what Fitting and Mendelsohn describe when they write of the case where "quantifiers range over what does and what might exist. Now

[(Some x)] . . . can be read, 'there is something, x, that could exist, such that . . .'".[9] The logic for this picture has *possibilist* quantification. There is a sense in which, although every item in the domain does exist in some world, the quantifiers do not have existential import. In any one world they quantify over both existent and nonexistent items. The domain of quantification is the same from world to world; it is a constant domain of items that might exist.

An even more radical view would be that the domain of quantification could contain even impossible objects such as round squares, so that we could say, quite sensibly, that some of the things about which we have discussions are impossible. Not only should we be able to assert 3.5.4 but also 3.5.9:

3.5.9.   Some things are not possible.

Even if we free quantifiers of existential import by accepting WEI, then there still remains possibility import. This import will be discussed in Chapters 9 and 10. At the moment we focus on existential import and WEI.

To see how these different logics work, we need to know what happens to the domain of quantification from possible world to possible world. In particular, we need to know whether the domains of all possible worlds contain the same items, or whether some possible worlds contain or lack items from other possible worlds, or whether each possible world has a distinct domain of quantification. We consider this in §3.6.

3.6 The domain from world to world

There are three major options for the domain from possible world to possible world. First, the domain of quantification is exactly the same in all possible worlds. Semantics based on this option are known as *constant domain* semantics. Secondly, the domain of quantification in each possible world is separate from the domain in every other possible world. Semantics based on this option are known as *distinct domain* semantics. One important version of distinct domain semantics is *counterpart* semantics.[10] Thirdly, there is a mixture of relationships. Some possible worlds have the same domain as others, some domains include the domains from other possible worlds or are included in the domains of other possible worlds, some domains overlap the domains of other possible worlds, and some domains are distinct from domains of some worlds, but overlap or include domains of other possible worlds. Semantics based on this option are known as *varying domain* semantics. Semantics for the first and second options can be subsumed under varying domain semantics, but it is convenient to keep them separate.

Three viewpoints

The three main viewpoints, with two additional variations of the third, can be pictured in Figures 3.1–3.5.

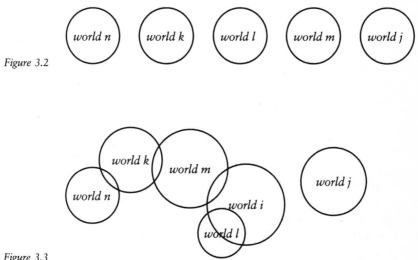

Figure 3.1

Figure 3.2

Figure 3.3

Figure 3.3 is meant to show that all sorts of relationships can hold between the varying domains. But there are two more regimented versions: an ascending chain of domains (*world n, world m, world l, world k, world j*), and a descending chain of domains (Figs 3.4, 3.5).

What, then, is the real difference between the ascending and descending chains of domains? It is that in both diagrams *world n* has access to *world m*, *world m* has access to *world l*, and so on. In the ascending chain the access is to worlds with ever larger domains, and in the descending chain the access is to worlds with ever smaller domains.

We adopt the phrase "world domain" for the "domain of quantification in a world" and "*world n* domain" for "the domain of quantification in *world n*."

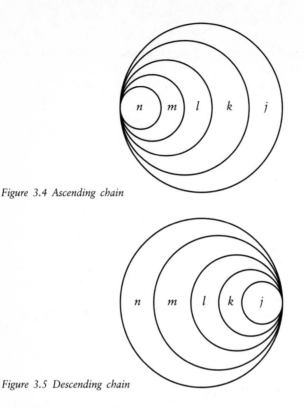

Figure 3.4 Ascending chain

Figure 3.5 Descending chain

There are, it could be said, three dimensions to the options. One dimension is the variety of frameworks of accessibility. The options here are for K, T, S4, S5 or whatever. The second dimension is the relationship between world domains. The third dimension, which is essentially a philosophical dimension, is the dimension of existential import.

Finite set-ups

Although set-ups can contain infinitely many worlds, and world domains infinitely many items, in what follows we will often resort to finite set-ups with finite world domains in order to show in what set-up something might be true or false. For example, given possibilist quantification and a constant domain we have Figure 3.6.

Figure 3.6 represents a finite set-up of three worlds. The world domains contain the same three items, so we have finite world domains. We could have **P** representing "exists"; then *item 1* exists in *world n*, *item 2* exists in *world k*, and *item 3* exists in *world j*. If we also assume that each world has access to itself, then this is a finite T set-up. If we do not assume self-access then it represents a finite K set-up.

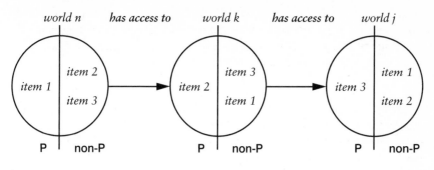

Figure 3.6

Adopting the simplest viewpoint

The details of the technical implications for these options can be retrieved from Fitting and Mendelsohn. But it is clear that the viewpoints can, with great complexity, all be generated out of each other. From a formal point of view it just does not matter which one we use. So, given that *possibilist* quantification with a constant domain is by far the simplest, and because I agree with McGinn that existential import is quite unacceptable, I adopt possibilist quantification from here on. In this case, existence will have to be treated separately from quantification.

For my purpose in this book I do not need to explore all the possible variations for quantification in modal predicate logic. I will use the possibilist viewpoint for most of what is discussed, and occasionally refer to the other options.

Since I am going to use possibilist quantification, I will stop referring to the particular quantifier as an "existential" quantifier. From now on I will call it what it is: the "particular quantifier".

3.7 Sentences and world domains

When we add □ and ◊ to predicate logic to get modal predicate logic, there is nothing unexpected in the sentences themselves. Wherever a negation expression can go in a predicate logic sentence, a modal operator can go. Here are eight relatively simple sample sentences of modal predicate logic.

3.7.1.	◊ (Some x) Px	3.7.2.	(Some x) ◊ Px
3.7.3.	□ (Some x) Px	3.7.4.	(Some x) □ Px
3.7.5.	◊ (Every x) Px	3.7.6.	(Every x) ◊ Px
3.7.7.	□ (Every x) Px	3.7.8.	(Every x) □ Px

Note that the eight sentences have □ and ◊ in different places with respect to the scope of the quantifiers. In the odd numbered cases the □ and ◊ are outside the scope of the quantifiers, but in the other four the □ and ◊ are *inside the scope* of the quantifiers. The scopes of quantifiers are:

◊ **Px**   and   □ **Px**

So the open sentence, **Px**, is the scope of the modal operator. The **Px** is a modal context. In a sentence such as **(Every x)** □ **Px** the quantifier is outside the scope of the modal operator, but it binds an *x* inside a modal context. In this situation the quantifier is said to *quantify into a modal context* (from outside). In all of what follows we will not attempt to give independent sense to open sentences[11] of predicate logic. We will always give sense to them as part of a quantificational context.

In this section we will begin with options in modal T. Although there are three major domain viewpoints – constant domain, distinct domain, and variable domain – we will look at only the first when working out the differences in meaning of the key sentences.

We will call the modality in the even numbered sentences a "quantifier main" (QM) modality. These sentences contain a quantifier that quantifies into a modal context. We call the modality in the odd numbered sentences a "modal main" (MM) modality. The scope of the modal operator contains no free occurrences of variables. The MM sentences, on the left, pose no real problems for interpretation and translation in any of the three domain viewpoints. The QM sentences, on the right, are seen as posing some problems. But these are not problematic if we look for a possible worlds account.

Constant domain

The first viewpoint is where the domain of quantification is the same for all possible worlds. The world domains all contain the same items. Consider a finite set-up in which there were three worlds, *world n*, *world k* and *world j*, and a constant domain of three items. In *world n* the first of the three items is *P* and the other two are not, in *world k* the second of the three items is *P* and the other two are not, and in *world j* the third item is *P* and the other two are not. Each of the three worlds has access to itself (T), and *world n* has access to *world k*, and *world k* has access to *world j*. There is no access from *world n* to *world j*, and *world j* has access only to itself. Figure 3.7 sets this out.

Each world is divided into **P** and **non-P** areas. So, in this finite three-world set-up, from within *world n* we can talk about the possibility that some item which is **P**, *item 1*, might not be **P**, and that another item which is not **P**, *item 2*, might be **P**.

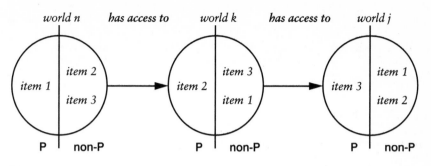

Figure 3.7

Since the sentences with MM modalities are not particularly problematic, we will consider them first. Consider the sentence:

3.7.1.   ◊ (Some x) Px

A swift intuitive translation would be:

3.7.1t.   It's possible for something to be **P**.

In the constant domain viewpoint this means:

3.7.1s.   In at least one accessible possible world, at least one item is **P**.

So 3.7.1 will be true in *world n*, in some set-up, if some item, say *item 1*, in the world domain of at least one accessible world is **P**. Since the domain is constant, *item 1* will be in every world domain. One way to realize this is the finite domain and finite set-up in Figure 3.7.
Consider the next sentence:

3.7.3.   □ (Some x) Px

A swift intuitive translation would be:

3.7.3t.   It's necessary for something to be **P**.

In the constant domain viewpoint this means:

3.7.3s.   In every accessible possible world, at least one item is **P**.

So 3.7.3 will be true in *world n*, in some set-up, if some item, in the world domain of every accessible world, is **P**. There are many ways in which to realize this. One of them is the finite domain and finite set-up in Figure 3.7.

The third sentence is:

3.7.5.　◊ **(Every x) Px**

A translation would be:

3.7.5t.　It's possible for everything to be **P**.

In the constant domain viewpoint this means:

3.7.5s.　In at least one accessible possible world, every item is **P**.

So 3.7.5 will be true in *world n*, in some set-up, if every item in the world domain of at least one accessible world is **P**. Sentence 3.7.5 will be true in *world n* in the T set-up in Figure 3.8, because *world n* has access to *world k*, and in *world k* everything (both *item 1* and *item 2*) is **P**.

Without further ado we can see that □ **(Every x) Px** will be false in *world n* in Figure 3.8 and true in *world k*, because *world k* has access only to itself, and so **(Every x) Px** is true in every world accessible from *world k*.

Now for the first of the sentences with a QM modality:

3.7.2.　**(Some x) ◊ Px**

Since we are considering what the truth conditions for 3.7.2 are in some world, say *world n*, and since the particular quantifier is *not in the scope* of a modal operator, we must take it that the "at least one item" is an item from the domain of quantification *in world n*. Given that we are considering constant domain set-ups, the item from the world domain of *world n* will be in all world domains. In at least one accessible possible world that item will be **P**. So we have the exposition:

3.7.2s.　At least one item (from this world) is, in at least one accessible possible world, **P**.

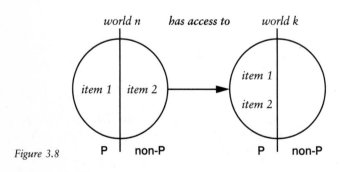

Figure 3.8

This would translate, for a person in *world n*, as:

3.7.2t. At least one item is possibly **P**.

Sentence 3.7.2 will also be true in *world n* in Figure 3.8 because *item 1* from *world n* is also in *world k*, because of the constant domain, and *world n* has access to *world k*, and *item 1* in *world k* is **P**.

In Chapter 2 I pointed out that one needs, when looking at plausible accounts of what something might mean, to consider not only truth, but also falsehood. Sentence 3.7.2 is false in *world n* in the finite domain finite set-up in Figure 3.9.

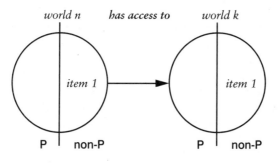

Figure 3.9

Every item in the *world n* domain is **non-P** in every world to which *world n* has access. So the negation of 3.7.2 is true, and 3.7.2 is false. Figure 3.9 also gives a set-up in which sentence 3.7.1 is false in *world n*.

Now consider the second QM modality sentence:

3.7.4.   **(Some x) □ Px**

Given our approach to 3.7.2, we can go straight to the account:

3.7.4s. At least one item (from this world) is, in every accessible possible world, **P**.

This would translate, for a person in *world n*, as:

3.7.4t. At least one item is such that it is necessarily **P**.

Sentence 3.7.4 will be true in *world n* in the set-up in Figure 3.8. The "at least one item" from *world n* that is necessarily **P** (**P** in all accessible possible worlds) is *item 1*.

This sentence will not be true in *world n* in the set-up in Figure 3.7, because there is no one item from *world n* that is **P** in all accessible possible worlds.

Consider the third QM modality sentence:

3.7.6.   (Every x) ◊ Px

Given our approach to 3.7.2, we can go straight to the account:

3.7.6s.   Every item (from this world) is, in at least one accessible possible world, **P**.

This would translate, for a person in *world n*, as:

3.7.6t.   Every item is possibly **P**.

Sentence 3.7.6 will be true in *world n* in the set-up in Figure 3.8 because *world n* has access to *world k*, and in *world k* everything (both *item 1* and *item 2*) is **P**. Sentence 3.7.6 will be false in Figure 3.7, because, although *world n* has access to both *world n* and *world k*, in neither of these is every item from *world n* **P**.

I leave the reader to work out the details for 3.7.8.

Finally, I point out that the complexity of predicate logic is such that some sentences will contain both QM and MM modalities. A slightly mind-boggling example is:

3.7.9.   □ (Every x)(Px imp (Some y) ◊ (Qy and xRy))

In cases like 3.7.9, the sentence contains both MM and QM modalities. It contains an MM necessity and a QM possibility. We will focus discussion on simpler cases.

The Barcan formula and the converse Barcan formula

There are two important logical principles that highlight the differing domain viewpoints. They are the Barcan formula (BF) and the converse Barcan formula (CBF). There are at least two equivalent ways of formulating the BF. We set out an example of each of the two ways:

(BF)   ◊ (Some x) Px imp (Some x) ◊ Px

(Every x) □ Px imp □ (Every x) Px

Any discussion of such sentences must observe the principle that sentences are true or false *in some world*, and that quantifiers give quantities from world domains. Truth is not off somewhere beyond worlds, and quantifiers do not refer to some unidentified domain. We will use the letters *n, k, m* and *l* as terms to refer to worlds. The first (BF) expands in English to:

If in at least one possible world, say *k*, accessible from *n*, at least one item is **P**, then at least one item from *n* is, in at least one possible world accessible from *n*, **P**.

There are at least two equivalent ways of formulating the CBF. We set out an example of each of the two ways:

(CBF) □ (Every x) Px imp (Every x) □ Px

(Some x) ◊ Px imp ◊ (Some x) Px

The first expands in English to:

If, in every possible world accessible from *n*, every item is **P**, then every item from *n* is, in every accessible possible world, **P**.

Both of these are valid from the constant domain viewpoint. Neither are valid from the distinct domain viewpoint. The CBF alone is valid from the ascending chain viewpoint, and the BF alone is valid from the descending chain viewpoint.

If both the BF and the CBF are logical principles of modal predicate logic, then **(Every x)** □ **Px** is logically equivalent to □ **(Every x) Px**, and ◊ **(Some x) Px** is logically equivalent to **(Some x)** ◊ **Px** . So these are equivalent from the constant domain viewpoint.

Quantifying into modal contexts

The exposition in the subsections above shows that the real difference between the four MM modality sentences and the four QM modality sentences has to do with the relationships between world domains. The interpretation of the QM modality always requires that, for truth in some world, we consider at least one or every item from that world domain to be in at least one or every accessible world's domain.

There are two ideas that provide an important insight into the complex area of quantification into modal contexts: the idea of possible worlds and the idea that the domains of quantification could be different from world to world. These give us a way of providing a clear interpretation, or range of interpretations, of quantification into modal contexts.

According to our exposition, based on these two ideas, the special requirement for the interpretation of QM modality sentences is *not* to do either with general terms (predicates) or with the way properties are predicated of items. It is to do with quantification from world to world. The focus is on quantification, not on predication.

3.8 *De dicto* and *de re*

Medieval logicians were aware of ambiguities in ordinary language statements in which necessity and possibility were used. In Chapter 2 we looked at the use of necessity with conditional statements. It was clear that we have to be careful not to follow our immediate intuitions about the logical role of necessity in conditionals. There are also cases involving quantifiers, predicates and necessity (and possibility) operations where we also have to be careful in the analysis of the logical structure of the statements.

A case in point is the ordinary language:

3.8.1.   *Some things are necessarily physical.*

This might mean either of the following two statements:

3.8.2.   *Of necessity, some things are physical.*
3.8.3.   *At least one item is such that it is necessarily physical.*

Medieval logicians explained the difference between these two by means of the *de dicto–de re* distinction. Hughes and Cresswell write:

> These terms are often explained by saying that in a modality *de dicto* necessity (or possibility) is attributed to a proposition (or *dictum*), but that in a modality *de re* it is attributed to the possession of a property by a thing (*res*); thus in asserting a modality *de dicto* we are saying that a certain proposition is bound to be (or may be) true, while in asserting a modality *de re* we are saying that a certain object is bound to have (or may have) a certain property.[12]

The logicians of the Middle Ages did not have modern symbolic methods at their disposal. We can use modal predicate logic to translate 3.8.2 and 3.8.3 to get:

3.8.2t.   □ **(Some x) Px**
3.8.3t.   **(Some x)** □ **Px**

Sentence 3.8.2t is 3.7.3 in the previous section, an MM modality sentence. In accordance with the *de dicto–de re* distinction, 3.8.2t contains a *de dicto* necessity, because it can be seen as saying that **(Some x) Px** is "bound to be" true. All MM modality sentences can be taken as containing a *de dicto* modality.

In the second, 3.8.3t, the scope of the modal operator is just **Px**. It seems to introduce the notion of an item's being *necessarily* P. There is quantification into a modal context. This is a QM modality sentence. All QM modality sentences can be taken as containing a *de re* modality. We have seen that the complexity of predicate logic is such that some sentences will be both QM modality and MM modality sentences. In those cases the sentences will contain both *de dicto* and *de re* modalities. Sentence 3.7.9 in the previous section contained a *de dicto* necessity and a *de re* possibility.

There are at least three ways of looking at the *de dicto–de re* distinction. First, it can be seen as a purely syntactic distinction and the difference in syntax is mirrored, in a simple and straightforward way, in the possible world semantics. And that is all that there is to it. Secondly, it can be seen as a distinction that tells us about the nature of predicates and predication. The distinction might be seen as raising logical problems for which unmodified and unextended modal predicate logic cannot provide an analysis. Thirdly, it can be seen as an inadequate or misleading explanatory distinction that is best set aside with notions such as the distribution of terms.

First, the distinction can be defined in a purely syntactic way. Hughes and Cresswell give a definition:

> A sentence, α, containing a modal operator (◊ or □) will be said to express a modality *de re* iff the scope of some modal operator in it contains some free occurrence of an individual variable; otherwise α will be said to express a modality *de dicto*.[13]

This syntactic distinction is not "substantial" in the way in which the *de dicto–de re* distinction is usually seen to be. This possible worlds account of the difference in meaning between 3.8.2t and 3.8.3t is often dismissed as too shallow.

It is often claimed that the *de dicto–de re* distinction highlights predication and predicates. Hughes and Cresswell have suggested in a footnote that there is an ambiguity about the scope of the box in □**Px**. It might be just the predicate **P** or all of **Px**.[14] A similar suggestion occurs in Fitting and Mendelsohn.[15] This approach raises the question of whether for every predicate **P** there are two others, *necessarily* **P** and *possibly* **P**. These two, if there are such, are *modal predicates*. Modal predicates are predicates then of things, and have an "internal" *de re* modality.

If there are such modal predicates, it may well turn out that it is best to consider them in the context of a logic of predicate modifiers.[16] There are some analogies with negation. Predicate modification is sometimes appealed to when logicians wish to distinguish between **not Px** and **non-P x**. Two quite different kinds of negation are called for if a distinction is to be maintained. If we distinguish, analogously, between **necessarily(Px)** and **(necessarily-P) x**, then we may well need two quite different kinds of modality. For the moment we will bypass this issue. We will return to this question in Chapter 4, when we look at singular terms.

There is a view that some items have *essential* properties. It is sometimes pessimistically suggested that human beings are *essentially greedy*, or optimistically suggested that they are *essentially rational*. But it is not clear that these suggestions are that there are special properties of essential greed or essential rationality. On the one hand, the properties could be said to be straightforward properties – greed and rationality – properties without which a creature could not be human. On the other hand, it might be claimed that individuals have essential properties in some special way, they have them "essentially".

If there are either modal properties or properties that are essential, then the question is, "Is there some special modal logic for these properties, or can standard possible worlds modal logic provide an account of them?" There is a sense in which this problem will simply dissolve if the *de dicto–de re* distinction, as commonly described, and distinct from the possible worlds account, just does not exist. So, we need to consider whether or not there is a substantial *de dicto–de re* distinction.

This brings us to the third way of seeing the distinction. The distinction is seen as a failure in explanation, and best set aside.

The first point is that the status of *de dicto* modality is itself somewhat problematic. Consider, by way of an analogy, the status of negation. The following sentences are usually taken to express that same negation.

3.8.4.   *Susan is not at the dentist.*
3.8.5.   *It's not the case that Susan is at the dentist.*

Both are usually taken to express the same proposition: the proposition *Susan is not at the dentist*. They are not assumed to express the metalinguistic proposition: *The proposition that Susan is at the dentist is false.*

When the truth conditions for 3.8.4 are set out one might have: *The proposition that Susan is not at the dentist will be true iff the proposition that Susan is at the dentist is false.* But this does not mean that 3.8.4 expresses the metalinguistic assertion that the proposition that Susan is at the dentist is false. Sentence 3.8.4 is about Susan and where she is (Where is Susan? Well, she's not at the dentist.), not about propositions. We do not usually take it that there is a distinction between *de dicto* and *de re* negation.

Similarly, 3.8.2 is not about propositions. Of necessity, at least one item (thing) is *P*. It is not about the *proposition* that at least one item is *P*. Sentence 3.8.2 says that, whatever the possibilities, there will be at least one *P* item. This is about items, properties and possibilities. And again, this is not to deny that we may want to set out truth conditions for 3.8.2 in terms of truth conditions for the proposition that at least one thing is *P* and a set of possible worlds. But that does not mean that 3.8.2 contains an "about propositions" modality: a *de dicto* modality.

If we want to read the modalities expressed by box and diamond to be *de dicto* modality, then we will have to see modal sentences, and modal sentences of ordinary language, as metalinguistic, at least in some sense stronger than a metaphorical sense. Some logicians such as Quine[17] would see this to be an excellent way of interpreting modal logic and modality in general.

This way of understanding 3.8.2t is to interpret the box as a universal quantifier ranging over possible worlds – In every possible world: at least one item is *P* is true. But even this interpretation could be spelled out as either:

> *The proposition that at least one item is* P *is true in every possible world.*

or:

> *In every possible world at least one item is* P.

If possible worlds are seen as a technical term for "possibilities", then the latter does not seem to be strongly *de dicto*, even though the former does.

We are left with the puzzle about why we should not take 3.8.3t to be about the possibilities for things to be this way or that.

Secondly, there are arguments in White[18] that the *de dicto–de re* distinction is not substantial. It is a distinction, he claims, built on a mistake. He describes the distinction made in modern philosophy as a distinction between how "modals qualify what is said about something" and how modals "qualify the something . . . it is said about".[19]

White claims that the distinction is based on two assumptions.

> The first, and correct, assumption is that modal qualifications can apply either to the whole or to the part of something. The second, and incorrect, assumption is that what is qualified when the whole is qualified is a proposition, that is, something which is said.[20]

An example of the whole/part contrast is "between e.g., 'He possibly (necessarily, certainly) gave a misleading answer' and 'He gave a possibly (necessarily, certainly) misleading answer'." White denies that the latter gives any "evidence for a peculiar composite property being possibly (necessarily, certainly) misleading in addition to the property being misleading."[21]

Finally, we saw at the end of the last section that the important thing about the interpretation of QM (syntactically defined *de re* modality) modality sentences is not predication, but quantification. There might be some other source for some kind of *de dicto–de re* distinction, but it is not at all obvious that it gives a reasonable explanation of what is going on when there is quantifying into modal contexts.

Appendix of formulas

3.3.1t. $(\forall x)Px$

3.3.2t. $(\exists x)Px$

3.3.3t. $(\forall x)\sim Px$

3.3.4t. $(\exists x)\sim Px$

QN: $(\forall x)Px$ *is equivalent to* $\sim(\exists x)\sim Px$

3.7.1. $\lozenge(\exists x)Px$ 　　　　　　　3.7.2. $(\exists x)\lozenge Px$

3.7.3. $\square\,(\exists x)\,Px$ 　　　　　　3.7.4. $(\exists x)\,\square Px$

3.7.5. $\lozenge(\forall x)Px$ 　　　　　　　3.7.6. $(\forall x)\,\lozenge Px$

3.7.7. $\square\,(\forall x)\,Px$ 　　　　　　3.7.8. $(\forall x)\,\square Px$

3.7.9. $\square\,(\forall x)(Px \supset (\exists y)\lozenge(Qy \,\&\, xRy))$

(BF)　　$\lozenge(\exists x)Px \supset (\exists x)\,\lozenge Px$
　　　　$(\forall x)\,\square\,Px \supset \square\,(\forall x)Px$

(CBF)　$\square\,(\forall x)\,Px \supset (\forall x)\,\square\,Px$
　　　　$(\exists x)\,\lozenge Px \supset \lozenge(\exists x)Px$

CHAPTER 4

Possible worlds, individuals and identity

4.1 Singular terms and identity

We begin with the addition of singular terms to predicate logic. Consider again the following two sentences:

4.1.1. *Kermit is a frog.*
4.1.2. *Kermit is green.*

"Kermit" is a proper name. Proper names are *singular terms*, not general terms. They are terms that, in everyday discourse, refer to one and only one individual, one and only one entity in the domain. Proper names like "Emma", "Socrates", "Pickwick", "Pegasus" and "Excalibur" are singular terms. If I say "Emma is a student," then I am not taken to be talking about all the people who are named "Emma", but only about one individual named "Emma". This is so even though we know that there are many individuals called "Emma". Similarly when I say, "Excalibur was cast into the lake," I am taken to be talking about just one sword: the sword named "Excalibur".

There are other words and phrases that we normally take to be singular terms as well. Some of these are singular pronouns like "I" and "she". Some are descriptive singular terms like "the King of France", "the Lord Mayor of Brisbane" and "the fountain of youth". The definite article, "the", in English usually gives indication of a descriptive singular term.

Individual constants and proper names

It is not unusual to translate all singular terms in English to *individual constants* in predicate logic. If this is done then the descriptive content of some singular terms is lost. We will look further at descriptive singular terms later. In this text I reserve the individual constants for the translation of proper names.

Individual constants are the proper names of predicate logic. Singular terms are assumed to *designate* just one entity in the domain. So, if **"k"** is the predicate logic term for "Kermit", 4.1.1 and 4.1.2 are translated to:

4.1.1t. **Fk**
4.1.2t. **Gk**

The lower case single letters, such as **"k"**, for singular terms in predicate logic are often called individual *constants*, because they refer in a constant way, like proper names, to items in the domain.

Some philosophers would prefer to have a predicate logic in which there were no individual constants, no logically proper names. But, those who are prepared to accept, or even welcome, individual constants into predicate logic will certainly agree that each individual constant designates just one entity in the world domain. There is considerable philosophical debate about just how individual constants designate entities in the world domain.

Identity

The idea of simple or numerical identity is added to basic predicate logic for *predicate logic with identity*. Although identity is usually seen as non-essential to basic predicate logic, it is very important for our considerations. Consider the statements:

4.1.3.   *Hesperus* is *Phosphorus*.

"Hesperus" is the proper name of the morning star, the planet Venus; and "Phosphorus" is the proper name of the evening star, which is also the planet Venus.

4.1.4.   *Cicero* is *Tully*.

The "is" in these statements connects singular terms. This is not like "Kermit is green", where the "is" seems to act as if it connects a singular term to a general term. Some might even say that the "is" in "Kermit is green" is part of the general term "is green"; this "is" is known as the "is" of predication. There are general terms in English that do not have an "is". For example, "Kermit sings" could easily be translated to predicate logic as **"Sk"**, with **"Sx"** for "*x sings*". There is no "is" of predication in the English sentence "Kermit sings." But when the "is" does occur, as in "Kermit is singing", then it is the *"is" of predication*.

The "is" in 4.1.3 and 4.1.4 is the *"is" of identity*. Those identity statements are translated, with appropriate individual constants, to:

4.1.3t. h = p
4.1.4t. c = t

The truth of an identity statement (formula) is determined by the facts about the entities to which the names (individual constants) refer.

There are some very difficult philosophical problems generated by identity, which we will look at later in this chapter. For the moment we focus on the additional facilities that identity gives to predicate and modal predicate logic.

Once we have identity, then predicate logic can deal with what is sometimes called "numerical quantification". Predicate logic can give a precise formulation of propositions such as "There is exactly one frog", "There are at most two frogs", "There are at least two frogs" and "There are exactly two frogs." For any whole number, n, predicate logic with identity can accurately formulate *there are at least n F's, there are at most n F's* and *there are exactly n F's*.[1] The "exactly n" formulation is built by conjoining "at least n" and "at most n". Numbers do not have to appear explicitly in these formulations in predicate logic with identity.

Logical principles

Once identity and individual constants have been added to predicate logic there are some important logical principles to note. Some principles are logical truths, but one principle is a valid argument form.

First there are the logical truths that involve individual constants in an important way. Consider:

4.1.5. *If a is P, then something is P*

It is a logical truth.

If quantifiers were to have existential import then 4.1.5 would really mean:

4.1.6. *If a is P, then some existing thing is P*

So if we were to assume the quantifiers have existential import, and 4.1.5 is a logical truth, then the singular term, a, must name an existing entity. Singular terms have existential import if the quantifiers do and if 4.1.5 is a logical truth.

Under the possibilist viewpoint, where quantifiers do not have existential import, 4.1.5 remains a logical truth, but 4.1.6 is not the appropriate reading of it.

In standard predicate logic with identity the following is a logical truth:

4.1.7. **(Some x)**(x = c)

With existential import for quantifiers, 4.1.7 is most accurately translated back to English as:

4.1.8. *At least one existing item is Cicero.*

or

4.1.8s. *Cicero exists.*

On this reading, with explicit existential import, you might think, then, that the way to say that Cicero does not exist would be to negate 4.1.8:

4.1.9t. **not (Some x)(x = c)**

Unfortunately, given the assumption of existential import for quantifiers, 4.1.9t is the negation of a logical truth, 4.1.7, and is self-contradictory.

Say we want to use singular terms in such a way that both 4.1.8 and 4.1.9t are contingent, and are true or false depending on whether Cicero exists. We will either have to use *free logic*, or have yet another good reason to give up existential import for quantifiers. We look at free logic later in this chapter.

Our assumption of possibilist quantification in predicate logic with identity, and giving up existential import for quantifiers means that 4.1.7 remains a logical truth, but it translates into English as:

4.1.10. *At least one item that could exist is Cicero.*

or

4.1.10. *Cicero might exist.*

This means that 4.1.9t is still contradictory, since it is the negation of a logical truth. It would translate the English:

4.1.9. *Cicero cannot exist. (It is impossible for Cicero to exist.)*

Items that could not exist – impossible-to-exist objects – cannot be designated by individual constants in possibilist semantics. Singular terms have *possible existence import* under the possibilist viewpoint.

The other logical symbols are specific to identity. There is the *self-identity principle*, *symmetry* and *transitivity*. Self-identity is:

4.1.11. *Everything is identical to itself.*
4.1.11t. **(Every x)(x = x)**

Secondly, there is the principle expressed in the valid arguments below. We begin by noting the definition of validity:

> An argument is valid if and only if, in every world in which all the premises are true, so is the conclusion.

This definition has the important feature that the truth of premises and conclusion are assessed, for every world, internally to that world.

Consider the argument:

4.1.12.   *Cicero is Tully.*
            Cicero was a writer.
            So Tully was a writer.

This translates to:

4.1.12t.   c = t
            Wc
            ─────
            ∴ Wt

This argument has the valid form known as the *substitutivity of identicals*. We will return to this argument form when we discuss the contrast in doctrine between necessary and contingent identity.

4.2 Descriptive singular terms

Singular terms come in at least two varieties; there are non-descriptive singular terms and descriptive singular terms. Proper names in ordinary language, and certainly individual constants in predicate logic, are understood to be non-descriptive singular terms. Although ordinary language proper names often have some descriptive content, that is not essential to their logical status. For example, names like "Chris Smith" carry a certain amount of descriptive connotation. Chris Smith is probably human, but even that is not certain. "Chris Smith" might be a funny name to give to a platypus, but it could be done. Chris might be either male or female, tall or short, or whatever. "Jack Smith" would almost certainly have the connotation of maleness, and "Shirl Smith" the connotation of femaleness. But, such connotation might be misleading. There used to be an Australian male popular singer with "Shirl" as his first name. The name "Chris Smith" carries some Anglo-Saxon connotation, in contrast to a Dutch or Germanic connotation for "Kris Schmidt". In the logical sense, a proper name should be without connotation, like an Army serial number, which usually has no numerical meaning. Individual constants in predicate logic are "pure" proper names.

On the other hand, singular terms like "the Lord Mayor of Brisbane" or "the second planet from the sun" or "the tallest woman in Te Awamutu" carry considerable descriptive content. These terms are *definite descriptions*.

They can be dealt with in predicate logic so that their descriptive content is explicit, and yet they remain singular terms. They have the general form *the F*. They occur in sentences like *The F is G*. There are two ways of dealing with them. One is to introduce a new independent quantifier: a singular quantifier for the "*the*". The other is to define definite descriptions "in context".

New singular quantifier

The first way is with a new independent singular quantifier. The singular quantifier in standard symbols is (ιx) "*iota x*". We will use **(The x)**. Let us use **Lx** for *x is a Lord Mayor of Brisbane*. The singular quantifier is used in expressions such as

4.2.1.   **(The x)Lx**

to mean "the *x* such that *x* is a Lord Mayor of Brisbane", or, more felicitously, "The Lord Mayor of Brisbane"

The definite description expression is not a complete sentence. It can occupy the space *in* a sentence that would normally be occupied by an individual constant. So just as we might have **Pk** for *Kermit is a person,* we could have

4.2.2.   **P(The x)Lx**

for *The Lord Mayor of Brisbane is a person.*

It is usual with the independent quantifier to have the logical truths

4.2.3.   **F(The x)Fx**

for *The F is F,* and

4.2.4.   **(The x)Fx = (The x)Fx**

for *The F is the F.*

Contextual definition

The second way of dealing with definite descriptions is by contextual definition. The same notation is used as above. The most common contextual account is called the *theory of definite descriptions*. It was first proposed by Russell.[2] This way of dealing with definite descriptions has become the most widely accepted way of dealing with definite descriptions.

The theory of definite descriptions has the general rule that *The F is G* is to be defined as, or is shorthand for, *There is one and only one F and it is G.* Predicate logic needs identity to formulate the numerical quantity "one and only one" in the theory of definite descriptions. So

4.2.5.   *The F is G.*
4.2.5t. G(The x)Fx

is shorthand for

4.2.6.   *There is one and only one F and it is G.*

which translates to the far more complex predicate logic formula:

4.2.6t. (Some x)(Fx and (Every y)(Fy imp x = y) and Gx)

There is no need for us to worry too much about the details of this complex formula, but the *italics* in the following display of the formula is the "There is one and only one *F*" part:

4.2.6t. *(Some x)(Fx and (Every y)(Fy imp x = y)* and Gx)

and the *italics* in the following is the "and it is *G*" part of the complex formula.

4.2.6t. (Some x)(Fx and (Every y)(Fy imp x = y) *and Gx*)

What, then, are the semantics for the contextually defined definite descriptions? They are derived from standard predicate logic. There is a problem with the standard symbols that is best considered from the point of view of the theory of definite descriptions. It is a "scope" problem, and becomes obvious when even a simple statement is negated. It goes like this. We know the contextual definition of *The F is G*, but there are two options for the contextual definition of:

4.2.7.   *The F is not G.*

The two options are:

4.2.7a. not (Some x)(Fx and (Every y)(Fy imp x = y) and Gx)
         It's not the case that there is one and only one *F* which is *G*.

4.2.7b. (Some x)(Fx and (Every y)(Fy imp x = y) and not Gx)
         There is one and only one *F* and it is *not G*.

This problem is really about an ambiguity in the notation **(The x)Fx**. It can be avoided if we use a symbolism for the singular quantifier that does not allow for such ambiguities. There is a standard complex way of modifying the notation to make it unambiguous, and there is a non-standard simple way. We will not explore the details; we just note that it can be done.

Apart from the (fixable) scope problem, there are many other interesting technical questions to do with the theory of definite descriptions. For example, the two logical principles with which we concluded the previous subsection are not logical principles when we adopt the theory of definite descriptions. But these problems and their detailed discussion are far beyond the scope of this text.

In most of what follows we will default to the theory of definite descriptions. If we use the theory, then we do *not* have to provide a new account of the new singular quantifier. We simply use the standard semantics for quantifiers and identity. Definite descriptions "pick out" a single item in the domain of quantification by reference only to properties. This facility has led many to suggest that individual constants are not needed. This suggestion has already been mentioned, and will be considered in §4.3.

With the addition of identity and singular terms we have five things to consider when understanding and translating to predicate logic: singular terms, general terms, identity, quantifiers and logical operations. The additional features of predicate logic, over and above those of propositional logic, are singular terms, general terms, identity and quantifiers. The semantics for all four are directly related to the domain of quantification. For modal predicate logic, as we have already seen, the issue becomes the nature of the domain of quantification from possible world to possible world.

We have already taken a policy stance about quantification from world to world. We discuss this further in §4.3.

4.3 Existential import

We have seen that predicate logic can have or lack *existential import* with respect to two things. The quantifiers can have or lack existential import, and non-descriptive singular terms can have or lack existential import. These different kinds of existential import are related. We considered existential import for quantifiers in Chapter 3, and argued for abandoning it.

Recall that with existential import for quantifiers we have:

4.3.1. **(Some x) Px**   translates as   *At least one* existing *thing is P*
4.3.2. **(Every x) Px**   translates as   *Every* existing *thing is P*

We turn to the second kind of existential import. The individual constants, the simplest singular terms of predicate logic, can have or lack existential import. In §4.1 I mentioned that if quantifiers have existential import and the following is accepted as a logical truth, then singular terms will also have existential import.

4.1.5. *If a is P, then something is P*

There are four options for existential import: (a) both singular terms and quantifiers have existential import; (b) quantifiers have existential import but singular terms do not; (c) the reverse of the second option, singular terms have existential import but quantifiers do not; and (d) neither singular terms nor quantifiers have existential import. Option (d) is the totally possibilist option. Of these four options, (c) has no substantial following.

Option (b) has a considerable following that finds formal expression in a version of predicate logic called *free logic*.

Since we have already adopted possibilist quantification, our policy runs contrary to (a) and (b). But we will discuss (b) because free logic has been extensively used in the possible worlds logics for knowledge and belief.

4.4 Free logic

There is a predicate logic in which the quantifiers do have existential import, but the individual constants do not have existential import. The predicate logic of this kind is free logic. Free logic uses exactly the same symbols as does predicate logic with identity. Identity is essential. In free logic, 4.4.1 and 4.4.1r are not logical truths: not tautologies of free logic.

4.4.1. *If a is P, then something is P*
4.4.1r. *If a is P, then some existing thing is P*

Since the quantifiers of free logic have existential import, if 4.4.1 had been a logical truth then 4.4.1r would have been a logical truth also. The crucial point is that 4.4.1r is not a logical truth in free logic. But the following is a logical truth of free logic:

4.4.2. *If a exists and a is P, then some existing thing is P*

This is formulated in free logic as 4.4.3:

4.4.3. ((Some x)(a = x) and Pa) imp (Some x)Px

In free logic is easy to say that *c* exists or does not exist. In free logic, 4.4.4 is not a logical truth and nor is 4.4.4n a contradiction.

4.4.4. (Some x)(x = c)
4.4.4n. not (Some x)(x = c)

The proposal that singular terms can refer to nonexistent entities is not welcomed by many philosophers. It is clearly contrary to the Parmenides' principle:

Things which do not exist cannot be referred to or mentioned; no statement can be about them.[3]

Common sense tells us that Parmenides' principle is plainly false. But common sense will find it difficult to explain *how* we are able to refer to things that do not exist. The enduring problem is that there exists nothing to which to refer. But when we look more closely at the description of the enduring problem, "there exists nothing to which to refer", we soon discover that this is equivalent to "there is no existent thing to which to refer". This description of the enduring problem seems either to be unproblematically true, because we just don't want to refer to existent things, or to be going around in a question-begging circle where the assumption is that quantifiers and singular terms must have existential import.

What does free logic do with the domain of quantification? The domain of quantification is a subset of the set of entities to which reference may be made by the proper names of the logic: the individual constants. So there is a large set of entities to which reference is made, and the quantifiers inform us only about the quantities of existent entities. It is often said that there is an *inner* and an *outer* domain (Figure 4.1).

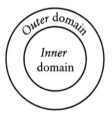

Figure 4.1

The quantifiers range over the inner domain: the domain of existing entities. So the particular quantifier is an existential quantifier. The outer domain contains the nonexistent entities. But, of course, there is a totality of both domains.

We note at this point that free logic looks absolutely tailor-made for fictional and mythical entities. We can put Sherlock Holmes, Harry Potter, Pegasus, Cair Paravel, Excalibur and all such entities into the outer domain. So we can say that there has never existed a pipe-smoking detective who lives in Baker Street, and this is not contrary to the assertion that no existent detective has ever lived in Baker Street. But there are other problems of logical consistency to which we return.

Despite the apparent additional flexibility in free logic, there are some features that need to be noted. Above all, although the individual constants are able to refer to nonexisting entities, the quantifiers still have existential import. This means that free logic lacks the mechanism for translating our pet proposition: *Some things do not exist.*

Three questions arise. What happens to definite descriptions? Why not have some sort of quantifier to range over the totality of entities? If the outer domain contains all the nonexistent entities to which we refer, do the propositions about entities "out there" have to be strictly consistent?

The first question has an unfortunate answer. If quantifiers still have existential import, then the contextual theory of definite descriptions will not allow definite descriptions to refer to entities in the outer domain. Yet this is precisely how we usually pick out entities such as Vulcan, Sherlock Holmes or Cair Paravel. If someone asks "What is Vulcan?", then we would reply that it is *the* planet that was supposed to be between Mercury and the Sun. "Who is Sherlock Holmes?" is answered by asserting that he is *the* detective who lived in Baker Street. In each case it is common to resort to definite descriptions.

But if definite descriptions are understood in accordance with the theory of definite descriptions, and quantifiers have existential import in free logic, then our response to the question about Sherlock Holmes becomes: "There exists one and only one detective who lived in Baker Street, and he was named 'Sherlock Holmes'." This false proposition is certainly not what the response would be intended to convey.

One way around this impasse would be to abandon the theory of definite descriptions and to introduce the one-and-only-one quantifier, but it would have to be a quantifier without existential import, and it would have to be able to range over both the inner and outer domains. And we are back to square one, or we need to move on to our second question, the question of a general quantifier.

On the surface, it looks as if all we need to cope with *Some things do not exist* is a pair of general quantifiers that range over everything. Just such was suggested by Routley[4] when he proposed the addition of two quantifiers, analogous to the universal **Every** and the existential **Some**. They are Π for *every* (with no existential import) and Σ for *at least one* (with no existential import). With these we get a straightforward formulation of *Some things do not exist*:

4.4.5. $(\Sigma x)(\text{Every } y)(x \neq y)$
4.4.6.   At least one x is not identical to any existent y.

The universal **Every** and the existential **Some** are "existential" quantifiers, and the Π and Σ are "possibilist" quantifiers.

If we introduce these new general quantifiers without existential import, then the theory of definite descriptions is rescued, but only by use of Π and Σ. We can go back to using definite descriptions to identify Sherlock Holmes and the planet Vulcan. But this form of rescue would be most unwelcome to Russell and Quine and all supporters of existential import for quantifiers.

If the Π and Σ quantifiers are added to free logic then the usual quantifiers, **Every** and **Some**, become what are known as *sortal quantifiers*. They range over individuals of just one sort: existent individuals. Sortal quantifiers are not on our agenda.

But predicate logic with sortal quantifiers is no longer free logic. It looks, from the history of free logic, as if its constructors were trying to abide by the dominant philosophical opinion about quantifiers having existential import, and break away only from the view that individual constants have existential import. The introduction of quantifiers with no existential import takes us to option (d), where neither quantifiers nor singular terms have existential import.

But we have seen that under the possibilist viewpoint the use of individual constants is restricted to possible-to-exist items. This raises a "what if " question: what if we had a free logic in which the quantifiers **Every** and **Some** carried possible existence import, but the individual constants could designate anything at all, impossible-to-exist items and even impossible items? Impossible-to-exist objects might not be impossible objects, although it is difficult to conceive of what they might be.

Impossible objects would be those objects that both have and lack some property. So, for some property **R**,

4.4.7. Rc and not Rc

would describe the impossible object **c**.

Any free logic that allowed impossible objects into its outer domain would be a *possibility free logic*.

The outer domain could contain inconsistent objects in possibility free logic. This is really stretching the logical boundaries, and brings us to the third of our questions, the question of logical consistency in the outer domain. This is the problem to which we referred earlier. This question arises even before we get to impossible objects.

Say we have two distinct stories, both fictions. One story is about the world in which the Aztecs conquer Europe, and the other is where they do not. In the first story, *a* is the Aztec King who lives in Paris and has never been to Mexico, and in the second story the Aztec King lives in Mexico and never visits Paris. "*a*" refers to an individual in the outer domain. In one story, *a lives in Paris* is true, and in the other *a does not live in Paris* is true. If "*a*" refers to just one individual, then *a* has contradictory properties.

To cope with these fictions we might cut the outer domain up into separate stories or novels or scenarios. Maybe we should do that, and then export each scenario to a possible world of its own. If so, we abandon the outer domain. Nonexistent entities are sent off to other possible worlds. This would mean that references to entities in the outer domain become converted to reference to "possible entities", possible individuals like Sherlock Holmes, possible planets like Vulcan, possible swords like Excalibur and possible castles like Cair Paravel. Possible entities, in this sense, are just entities in the world domain of a possible world.

This is no longer free logic, but it brings us closer to modal predicate logic. Of course, that might not be good enough. We might want modal free logic, or even modal possibility free logic. Another option is to introduce other ways of dealing with truth in the outer domain. This is discussed at length in several papers.[5] There are at least 16 ways of dealing with this issue, but we will step around them all in this book.

If we have possibility free logic, we cannot resort to exporting impossible objects to other possible worlds, because once the impossible objects "arrive in" or are detected in a world, the world becomes an impossible world. We consider impossible worlds in Chapter 10.

We leave free logic and turn now to the fourth option, (d), for existential import.

4.5 Total possibilism

The fourth option is the option we declared for in Chapter 3. Individual constants can designate either existent or nonexistent entities. The range of the quantifiers **Every** and **Some** becomes a domain that is effectively the combination of both the inner and outer domains of free logic. There is no need to introduce Routley's Π and Σ. The universal quantifier is truly universal, and the existential quantifier is replaced by the particular quantifier. This is quantificational possibilism.

In this option there is no logical distinction between existent and nonexistent entities. So how does the logic deal with existence? In a sense it doesn't. Existence is treated, for the purpose of formulating sentences, like any standard property. "Pickwick does not exist" is understood as and translated to **not Ep**, where **E** is the general term for existing and **p** is Pickwick.

When modality and possible worlds arrive on the scene, we need to know not only what happens to the domain of quantification from possible world to possible world, but what happens to individual constants from world to world. In Chapter 3 we adopted a policy in favour of possibilist quantification with a constant domain. We now consider what quantificational possibilism entails when married to modal operators.

4.6 Adding necessity and possibility

We have already seen that when we add □ and ◊ to predicate logic to get modal predicate logic there is nothing unexpected in the formulas themselves. Wherever a negation term **not** can go in a predicate logic formula, a box or a diamond can also go. Our interest in this section will be with formulas with singular terms such as ◊ **Fa** and □ **Fa.**

We begin with:

4.6.1. ◊ **Fa**

At first sight 4.6.1 might reasonably be translated to:

> *Possibly, a is F.*
or *It's possible for a to be F.*
or *It's possible that a is F.*
or *a is possibly F.*

According to the possible worlds account of diamond, 4.6.1 means that:

4.6.1s. ◊ **Fa** is true in some world, say *world n*, if **Fa** is true in some accessible possible world, say *world k*.

If one adopts the actualist varying domain viewpoint, an immediate question is, "Does **a** exist in *world k*, or does **a** exist in both *world k* and *world n*?" This question raises all sorts of technical complications,[6] which can be completely avoided by going the possibilist way where individual constants have no existential import.

Now, we do not automatically know about the status of **a** in either *world n* or *world k*: **a** might exist in both, neither or in just one. We set out Figure 4.2 to represent what is said in 4.6.1s. Since **a** might exist or not in *world n*, we represent those possibilities with a disjunctive line for **a**, which might be at either end of the line.

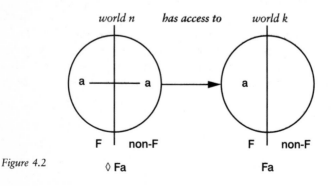

Figure 4.2

These contrasts and cases will apply equally to 4.6.2.

4.6.2.   □ Fa

which means that:

4.6.3.   a *is* F in every accessible possible world.

In the example above, we have assumed that the same item has the same name, **a**, from world to world. This assumption is the assumption of *rigid designation*. This is not an unproblematic assumption. The picture we have of total possibilism opens the way to consider a set of perennial philosophical problems about names from world to world, identity, and the scope of modal operators.

Names

We have made the assumption above that the same item has the same name, **a** in the example, from world to world. One key logical question about names is: can an item change its name from world to world? Could the Socrates of this world be the Plato of another possible world, and the Plato of this world be the Socrates of that other world?

Kripke's answer to this question is "no".[7] His claim is, in brief, that if items change name then the language changes. If we have a modal predicate logic with proper names (individual constants), then the language does not really have its full meaning until we fix the referents of the individual constants. Once those referents are fixed, then we cannot fiddle with them or the meanings of sentences will change, and the language changes. Once we fix the referents of individual constants we cannot change those referents from world to world. Individual constants are rigid designators, and so are the proper names of ordinary language.

Kripke has argued that ordinary proper names are rigid when the modalities are understood alethically.[8] The reference of a proper name is fixed by some arbitrary procedure in which the names are assigned to individuals – a baptismal ceremony perhaps. But once the reference has been fixed, that name refers to the individual it has been assigned to, in every possible world. When we consider whether it is possible (say) for Cicero to be a modal logician, we consider whether there is a possible world in which *that person* who had been baptised "Cicero" is a modal logician.[9]

Read points out, in discussing possible worlds, that

> when we suppose that Edmund might have been brave, it is
> Edmund himself whom we suppose to be brave . . . There are many
> abstract possibilities concerning Edmund: that he be brave or

cowardly, a mountaineer or a squash player or a yachtsman or whatever. One set of these possibilities is exemplified in concrete reality. Through them all it is Edmund who is the recurrent subject.[10]

The important thing is the constancy of the reference to the same Edmund from possible world to possible world. The name "Edmund" must designate rigidly in order to keep this constant reference.

There are logicians who give the contrary answer "yes". They hold that items could change their names from world to world. They argue that changing the referents of individual constants from world to world does not mean that each world has a distinct language. Maybe people (or items) were "baptised" with different names in different worlds. The logical constants (negation, conjunction, quantifiers, identity and modalities) remain the same. We know that a predicate can change its extension[11] from world to world without the predicate changing. Why not the same, analogously, for names?

For example, consider two worlds, *world n* and *world k*. The first is a state of the world in which the 20 lemons on my lemon tree are green and not ready to pick. But the 15 figs, which will form on my fig tree, have not yet formed. In the second state of the world, *world k*, the lemons have all become yellow, and the figs have formed and are green. (I will pick them in *world m* when they are brown.) The number of items in *world n* with the property of being green includes my 20 lemons but not my 15 figs. The number of items in *world k* with the property of being green does not include my 20 lemons, but it does include my 15 figs. Yet the property of being green is still the same in both worlds despite the changes in the sets of things having the property of being green. In each world we assign the greenness predicate to different items, but we do not assume that the language has changed from world to world.

Why should we assume that the language changes from world to world if we assign different referents to the individual constants from world to world?

Those who advocate non-rigid individual constants will have to respond in some way to Read's assertions about Edmund. If there were rigid individual constants, then we would formulate the assertion that Edmund might be brave as:

4.6.4.   ◊ **Be**
"There is an accessible possible world in which Edmund (the "Edmund" of this world) is brave."

With non-rigid constants we would have to have something like:

4.6.5.   (Some x)(x = e and ◊ Bx)

We have to rely on the binding force of the particular quantifier to ensure that it is the "Edmund" of this world who, in some possible world, is brave. And, furthermore, if we want the individual who is named "Edmund" in this world to be so named in that world, then we would have to add some more to get:

4.6.6.   **(Some x)(x = e and ◊ (Bx and x = e))**

Of course, if the individual who is named "Edmund" in this world is named "Hamish" in the world in which the individual who is named "Edmund" in this world is brave, then we would have:

4.6.7.   **(Some x)(x = e and ◊ (Bx and x = h))**

We could also declare that some names were rigid designators by having, for each (say **e**), the following:

4.6.8.   **(Some x)(x = e and □(x = e))**

This says, effectively, "What is named **e** in this world is named **e** in all worlds."

It must be clear by this point that rigid designation greatly simplifies the logical notation with names and speculations about what is possible for any given individual, but the simplicity sacrifices flexibility.

4.7 Identity

The key philosophical question about identity can be asked in the technical form "Is identity contingent?", or in the form "Could **a** be identical with **b** in one possible world, but not identical in some other?" If Aristokles is Plato in this world ("Plato" being the nickname of Aristokles), and Aristokles is not Socrates in this world, is it possible that Socrates might have been Plato and Aristokles not Plato?

Those who answer "yes" to the questions above are said to hold the view that identity is contingent, while those who answer "no" are said to hold the view that identity is necessary. Kripke is the chief proponent of necessary identity.[12] It should be clear that necessary identity follows automatically from the doctrine of rigid designation. If "**a**" designates the same item across all worlds, and "**b**" designates the same item across all worlds, and if they are identical in just one, then they will have to be identical in all worlds. So it is impossible to have rigid designation without necessary identity for identities involving only individual constants.

Conversely, if we want identity to be contingent, then we will have to abandon rigid designation for individual constants. There is an interesting contrast that might be taken, in some sense, to strengthen the case for contingent

identity. The contrast arises out of one of the proof methods for modal predicate logic with identity. The contrast is set out in the formal excursion in the
appendix to this chapter.

Modal scope

We have already looked at the scope of modal operators and the related *de
dicto–de re* distinction. But the question of scope becomes, in some ways,
clearer when we have individual constants at our disposal.

Consider the formula:

4.7.1.   □ Fc

We have seen that some logicians are concerned about the scope of the box.
Fitting and Mendelsohn point out that the scope might be just the **F**, or the
whole **Fc**. In the former, the box is a predicate modifier not a propositional
operator, and that makes it *de re* rather than *de dicto*. In the latter, the box
operates on a closed formula, and that makes it a *de dicto* necessity.

> On the one hand, we can regard the constant as primary: **c** desig-
> nates an object in the actual world and that object is said, in every
> possible world, to be **F**. On the other hand, we can regard the
> modal operator as primary: in every possible world, the object des-
> ignated by **c** in that world is said to be **F**. [13]

In order for the distinction to make any difference it will be important to
have non-rigid designation for individual constants. If **c** designates exactly the
same item in any one world as it does in any other, then **c** is automatically
"primary", to use Fitting and Mendelsohn's term. But if **c** can designate different items from world to world, then the box is primary.

One interesting question is: if there is non-rigid designation, can we somehow ensure that it is the **c** of this world that has the property **F** in every world?
Consider the following:

4.7.2.   (Some x)(x = c and □ Fx)

The quantifier in this formula quantifies into a modal context. Our account of
what this means, as set out in Chapter 3, is that the "at least one **x**" is an item
from this world that, in every world, has the property **F**. The left conjunct, **x** =
c, says that the at least one item is, in this world, **c**. But, if we want that one
item to retain its name, **c**, from world to world, then we would have to have:

4.7.3.   (Some x)(x = c and □ (Fx and x = c))

This tells us that the one item, called **c** in this world, has the property **F** in all accessible worlds and is called **c** in all those worlds. We can distinguish between rigid and non-rigid designation.

Another way to make the distinction is to introduce two kinds of individual constants. We leave that complication aside in this book.[14]

4.8 Mathematical necessity

There is a problem lurking in the wings about mathematical possibility, impossibility and names. The problem is this: in what sense can we say that the truths of mathematics are necessarily true because they are true in all possible worlds, rather than they are true in all possible worlds because they are necessarily true? This might sound like a strange question, but it is no more strange than asking whether the good is good because God commands it, or does God command things because they are good?

This is somewhat like asking whether we need possible worlds at all for the explanation of mathematical necessity or impossibility. Does the proof that it is impossible to trisect an angle with only a compass and a straight-edge require impossibility of the possible worlds kind?

Say we had a set of possible worlds in each of which there were only the tautologies of first-order logic and mathematical truths. These worlds would be partial in the sense that they would have nothing to say about the contingent truths that could be represented in logic. There would be just one world, and necessity would be no more than just being true. We really find it difficult to understand what it would be like for 5 plus 7 to equal 13, or for 42 to equal 6 multiplied by 9, but are these things impossible because they are not true in any but impossible worlds, or are they simply not true in mathematics? We will return to this question in Chapter 9.

Appendix of formulas and an excursion into proof

4.1.7. $(\exists x)(x = c)$

4.1.9. $\sim (\exists x)(x = c)$

4.2.6. $(\exists x)(Fx \ \& \ (\forall y)(Fy \supset x = y) \ \& \ Gx)$

4.2.7a. $\sim (\exists x)(Fx \ \& \ (\forall y)(Fy \supset x = y) \ \& \ Gx)$

4.2.7b. $(\exists x)(Fx \ \& \ (\forall y)(Fy \supset x = y) \ \& \ \sim Gx)$

4.4.3. $((\exists x)(x = a) \ \& \ Pa) \supset (\exists x)Fx$

4.4.5. $\quad (\Sigma x)(\forall y)(x \ne y)$

4.6.10. $\quad (\exists x)(x = e \,\&\, \Diamond Bx)$

4.6.11. $\quad (\exists x)(x = e \,\&\, \Diamond(Bx \,\&\, x = e))$

4.6.12. $\quad (\exists x)(x = e \,\&\, \Diamond(Bx \,\&\, x = h))$

4.6.13. $\quad (\exists x)(x = e \,\&\, \Box\,(x = h))$

4.7.2. $\quad (\exists x)(x = c \,\&\, \Box\, Fx\,))$

4.7.3. $\quad (\exists x)(x = c \,\&\, \Box\,(Fx \,\&\, x = c))$

A formal excursion

In this section we pursue the question of necessary and contingent identity by considering what happens in one of the formal validity assessment methods for modal predicate logic with identity. Readers who are not interested in technicalities of modal predicate logic with identity can skip this section.

One of the proof methods for modal predicate logic is the method of semantic tableaux, or of modal truth-trees. In modal truth-trees the rules for non-modal predicate logic (including the rules for non-modal propositional logic) are taken and converted into "one world" rules. For example, here are three rules from non-modal predicate logic:

$$
\begin{array}{ccc}
(\alpha \,\&\, \beta) & \sim (\forall \eta)\alpha & (\forall \eta)\alpha \\
\vdots & \vdots & \vdots \\
\alpha & (\exists \eta) \sim \alpha & \alpha(\kappa/\eta) \\
\beta & & \text{for any } \kappa, \text{ where } \kappa \text{ is any} \\
& & \text{individual constant and } \alpha(\kappa/\eta) \\
& & \text{is the result of replacing all free} \\
& & \text{occurrences of } \eta \text{ in } \alpha \text{ with } \kappa.
\end{array}
$$

These rules show what follows if one assumes that the formula above the ":" is true. If one assumes a conjunction to be true, then it follows that both conjuncts are true. If one assumes that a negated universal quantifier is true then it follows that a particularly quantified negation is true. If one assumes that everything is α, then each item is α.

When one shifts to modal predicate logic, all the non-modal rules, such as these three, are indexed with world indices, because the non-modal rules are taken to operate only *within* single worlds. So we get the following, where "(ω)" is the "in world ω" index:

$$(\alpha \,\&\, \beta)(\omega) \qquad\qquad \sim (\forall\eta)\alpha\,(\omega) \qquad\qquad (\forall\eta)\alpha\,(\omega)$$
$$\vdots \qquad\qquad\qquad \vdots \qquad\qquad\qquad \vdots$$
$$\alpha\,(\omega) \qquad\qquad (\exists\eta) \sim \alpha\,(\omega) \qquad\qquad \alpha(\kappa/\eta)\,(\omega)$$
$$\beta\,(\omega)$$

for any κ, where κ is any individual constant and $\alpha(\kappa/\eta)$ is the result of replacing all free occurrences of η in α with κ.

If one assumes a conjunction to be true in world ω, then it follows that both conjuncts are true in world ω. If one assumes that a negated universal quantifier is true in world ω then it follows that a particularly quantified negation is true in world ω. If one assumes that everything is α in world ω, then each item is α in world ω.

The only truth-tree rules for modal predicate logic that involve more than one world are the rules for box and diamond. As one might expect, these rules enable truth in one world to entail truth in another. The standard rules for S5 are:

(MN) $\qquad \sim \Diamond\, \alpha\,(\omega) \qquad\qquad\qquad\qquad \sim \Box\alpha\,(\omega)$
$$\qquad\qquad\qquad \vdots \qquad\qquad\qquad\qquad\qquad\qquad \vdots$$
$$\qquad\qquad\quad \Box \sim \alpha\,(\omega) \qquad\qquad\qquad\qquad \Diamond \sim \alpha\,(\omega)$$

($\Diamond$ S5) $\qquad \Diamond\, \alpha\,(\omega) \checkmark\upsilon \qquad\qquad$ ($\Box$ S5) $\qquad \Box\, \alpha\,(\omega) \setminus \upsilon$
$$\qquad\qquad\qquad \vdots \qquad\qquad\qquad\qquad\qquad\qquad\quad \vdots$$
$$\qquad\qquad\quad \alpha\,(\upsilon) \qquad\qquad\qquad\qquad\qquad\quad \alpha\,(\upsilon)$$

where υ is *new* to   where υ is *any* index.
this path of the tree.

Even the modal negation (MN) rules are "one world" rules.

Now we consider the identity rules. There are two rules in truth-trees for identity in non-modal predicate logic with identity. They are:

$$\kappa \neq \kappa \qquad\qquad\qquad\qquad \tau = \sigma$$
$$\vdots \qquad\qquad\qquad\qquad\qquad \Phi(\tau)$$
$$\times \qquad\qquad\qquad\qquad\qquad\quad \vdots$$
$$\qquad\qquad\qquad\qquad\qquad\qquad \Phi(\sigma/\tau)$$

where Φ is an atomic formula or the negation of an atomic formula.

The first shows that non-self-identity is contradictory. The second is simply the rule for the substitutivity of identicals, which we met in §4.1.

One would think that, on strict analogy with what happened to all the other rules from non-modal predicate logic with identity, when these rules are translated into modal predicate logic with identity rules they would be "one world" indexed to get:

$$\kappa \neq \kappa \ (\omega) \qquad\qquad \tau = \sigma \ (\omega)$$
$$: \qquad\qquad\qquad \Phi(\tau) \ (\omega)$$
$$\times \qquad\qquad\qquad :$$
$$\Phi(\sigma/\tau) \ (\omega)$$

where Φ is an atomic formula
or the negation of an atomic formula.

If we adopt this "one world" version of the identity rules, then we have contingent identity. To get necessary identity we have to change the second rule to a rule involving more than one world:

$$\tau = \sigma \ (\upsilon)$$
$$\Phi(\tau) \ (\omega)$$
$$:$$
$$\Phi(\sigma/\tau) \ (\omega)$$

where Φ is an atomic formula
or the negation of an atomic formula
and *where υ and ω are not necessarily distinct.*

So if there is an identity in any world, it applies in all worlds. This is necessary identity. This places identity in quite a different logical category from all the other non-modal logical operations. But if identity is necessary identity, why is negated identity not the possibility of non-identity? The advocates of necessary identity claim that non-identity is necessary non-identity. What we have then is an asymmetry in the logic of identity that is quite unlike any other logical operation.

CHAPTER 5
Possibility Talk

5.1 Language

In this chapter we will consider the ways in which the notions of possibility and necessity, and related notions, are expressed in ordinary language. Ordinary usage[1] will indicate the concepts used, and the interrelations between them. There are also sentences of English that pose considerable difficulties for translation to logics that use possible worlds semantics. At the same time, possible worlds can, in some cases, illuminate the meaning of the propositions expressed by such sentences. Above all, reasoning and arguments involving the notions of possibility and necessity are usually expressed in ordinary language.

We begin with the distinction, in ordinary language, between "possible for" and "possible that". We then move on to consider some difficult cases. We consider whether the idea of possible worlds is effective in explaining the interrelationships between the concepts that surround possibility, correct reasoning and the validity of argument in ordinary discourse.

5.2 "Possible for" and "possible that"

"What's possible?" "What's impossible?" These questions are asked in context. In government the questioner might want to know what is economically possible. In business the questioner might want to know what is financially possible. In academia the questioner might want to know what is politically possible in the academic institution, or what is possible given the regulations for the degree. In physics the questioner might want to know what is physically possible. In chemistry the questioner might want to know what is chemically possible. When we know the context, we know what they are asking. We know how the answer should go. The answer is in terms of what are seen to be the possibilities in that context, and what is seen to be not possible in that context. If we don't know the context, we demur, or should demur, and send the questioner away to interrogate the expert.

When philosophers ask about what is possible, they are very often asking what is *logically* possible – but not always. They could be asking about what is morally possible, or about what is epistemically[2] possible. The possibilities are relative to some context, or to some set of concepts such as moral or epistemological concepts. The possibilities are *qualified* possibilities.[3]

The least qualification of possibility seems to be logical possibility. And even here, there will be argument about what is logically possible.

What is possible often seems to stand in contrast to what is actual, what is real. In everyday life we often look at the possibilities in order to move to the most desirable of the possibilities, the best of all possible outcomes, and to avoid moving to undesirable possibilities. We know we cannot have what is impossible, and try to see opportunities among the possibilities.

Possibility is not only contrasted with the actual, but it is often set in a context where some things are seen to be necessary. It might be morally possible to invest in a company because it pays its foreign workers decent wages, but it is financially necessary for the investment to return a fair dividend to the superannuitants who have put their life savings into the company. The government might think that it is economically possible for them to cut tax rates, but that it is also economically necessary for them to have a balanced budget. Some logicians, not classical logicians, might argue that it is logically necessary for some contradictions to be true, and that it is logically necessary for these to be derived in a particular kind of proof.

So we see that qualified and qualifiable possibility brings with it qualified and qualifiable necessity. It is logically possible for contradictions to be true if, and only if, it is not logically necessary for contradictions to be false (not true). This fits well with the idea that a proposition is logically necessary when it is true in all worlds that are logically consistent.

This is just like what David Lewis[4] describes as *relative* modality when he writes:

> Just as a sentence ϕ is necessary if it holds in all worlds, so ϕ is causally necessary if it holds in all worlds compatible with the laws of nature; obligatory for you if it holds in all worlds in which you act rightly; implicitly known, believed, hoped, asserted, or perceived by you if it holds in all worlds compatible with the content of your knowledge, beliefs, hopes, assertions, or perceptions. These, and many more, are *relative* modalities, expressible by quantifications over restricted ranges of worlds.

We note that Lewis treats logical possibility as if it were unqualified possibility. When he says that a sentence ϕ is necessary if it holds in all worlds, he is implicitly nailing up a classical logic: a sentence ϕ is necessary if it holds in all classically consistent worlds. Some would argue that there are logically possible worlds in which logical consistency is not classical. We will discuss this further in Chapter 10.

Possible for

If we turn to ordinary language we see certain patterns of words and phrases that are regularly used to express qualifiable possibility. Qualifiable possibility is most clearly expressed in English with "possible for": "It is economically *possible for* us to raise the tax rate"; "It is not logically *possible for* any contradictions to be true." But people also use both "to" and "that" to express these propositions: "It is economically possible *to* raise the tax rate"; "It is not logically possible that any contradictions are true." Qualifiable necessity can be expressed the same ways: "It is financially necessary *for* us to return a fair dividend to our investors"; "It is financially necessary *to* return a fair dividend to our investors"; "It is financially necessary *that* the investors receive a fair dividend." The everyday users of English are not limited to just one set of words or phrases for the expression of qualifiable possibility and necessity. Their usage can be quite sloppy. Nevertheless, it is usually clear what is being said.

What light does the possible worlds account of possibility throw on qualifiable possibility? The obvious answer is to be found in Lewis's reference to *relative* possibility. When someone in our actual world, for example, states that it is not physically possible for physical objects to travel faster than the speed of light, then they are talking about what does not happen in any of the possible worlds that have the same physical laws as does the actual world. There is a subset of all possible worlds that contains all the possible worlds that have the same physical laws as does the actual world.

Of that subset there is a further subset of all the possible worlds that have the same economic laws as does the actual world. When we talk about economic necessity we are talking about what happens in all the economically possible worlds. And so we could go on to look at a wide range of what, in Chapter 2, we called "contingent necessities".

Possible that

As well as qualifiable possibility, there is the sort of possibility that people ask about with questions such as: "Just how possible is it?" The answer will be something like: "It is barely possible"; "It is quite possible"; "It is hardly possible." This is *variable* possibility.[5] It is standardly expressed with "possible that". Variable possibility can be varied by terms such as *slightly, hardly, barely, faintly, vaguely, greatly* and *quite*. A person will say, "It is *barely possible that* this project will finish on time." But people will also use "for" and "to": "It is barely possible for this project to finish on time"; "It is quite possible to finish this project on time."

Without such variation to "possible that" statements we might have statements such as:

> *It is possible that Susan is buying a car.*

When varied we have:

> *It is quite possible that Susan is buying a car.*

The terms that go with variable possibility are *definite* and *certain*. We can replace unvaried "possible" with "definite" in the statements above to get:

> *It is definite that Susan is buying a car.*

The varying term can be inserted to give:

> *It is quite definite that Susan is buying a car.*

The logical equivalences here do not accord with possible worlds logics that usually link possible and necessary. But the following link *possible* and *definite*:

> *It is definite that Susan is buying a car iff*
> *it is not possible that Susan is not buying a car.*

It has been argued by White that "certain that" rather than "definite that" pairs with "possible that". But "certain that" brings a psychological dimension that is absent from both "possible" and "definite".

Given that there are these two kinds of possibility expressed in ordinary language, wherein lies the contrast? White describes the contrast between qualifiable and variable possibility:

> To say that it is possible for X to V – where "V" is a variable for any verb – is to stress the actual existence of a possibility, that is, what possibility actually exists; whereas to say that it is possible that X Vs is to stress the possible existence of an actuality, that is, what actuality possibly exists. Hence, I shall sometimes, for convenience, call the former "existential" possibility and the latter "problematic" possibility. In existential possibility nothing prevents X from Ving, while in problematic possibility something allows it. The former possibility indicates what is capable of being so, the latter what is likely to be so.[6]

Given White's emphasis on "what is likely" for variable possibility, what light does the possible worlds account of possibility throw on variable possibility? White also says that a "modal logic can be formulated for possibility and [definitely] corresponding to that for possibility and necessity".[7] But it turns out that the only elements of such a logic, discussed by White, are the inter-definability of *possible that* and *definite that*. That is, it is clear that "It is not definite that not *p*" is equivalent to "It is possible that *p*". This alone is certainly not enough basis for a modal logic, and it tells us nothing about the semantics for *possible that*, let alone about possible world semantics for *possible that*.

It would seem that there is not much help at all unless we introduce probabilities or likelihoods of some kind. Consider the following:

It is barely possible that p is true in ω iff the probability that there is a possible world in which *p* is true is just above zero.

It is absolutely possible that p is true in ω iff the probability that there is a possible world in which *p* is true is 1.

We might scale the probabilities to match the variations.

What, then, are the philosophical questions, if any, about possibility and necessity? There are three sorts of questions. First, what are the logical and conceptual relationships between the different kinds of possibility? Secondly, what are the logical and conceptual relationships between the possible and the actual? Thirdly, do the explanations of the different kinds of possibility, and the conceptual and logical relationships, benefit from the notion of possible worlds?

5.3 Connections

We turn to the first question. White has argued that there is a logical connection between variable and qualifiable possibility. If he is correct that variable (problematic) possibility is "about what is likely to be so", then since being probable entails being possible (if it is impossible then it cannot be probable), we would expect that variable possibility would entail qualifiable possibility. This can be expressed in the entailment:

If it is possible that Susan is buying a car
*   then it is possible for Susan to be buying a car.*

The converse entailment does not hold:

> *If it is possible for Susan to be buying a car*
> *then it is possible that Susan is buying a car.*

If we agree with contraposition and with the logical equivalences between possible, definite and necessary, then we get the following entailment:

> *If it is not possible for Susan to be buying a car*
> *then it is not possible that Susan is buying a car.*

It is not difficult, given double negation equivalence and some logical manipulation to get the entailment:

> *If it is necessary for Susan to be buying a car*
> *then it is definite that Susan is buying a car.*

If the entailments set out above are correct, then there are problems for the possible worlds accounts of possibility and necessity. The first problem is that the pairing of "possible that" with "necessary that" may well be a mistake.

One response to this problem is simply to say that the box and diamond symbols of modal logic are the translations of "possible for" and "necessary for".

> *possible for* p   translates to $\Diamond p$
> *necessary for* p   translates to $\Box p$

At the same time, what is it for it to be possible for *a proposition* p? The swift answer has to be that it is possible for a proposition *to be true*. Then the question arises as to what is it for it *to be necessary for* a proposition to be true? The phrase almost demands a qualification. It is *logically* necessary for *If it is raining then it is raining* to be true.

Some logicians would want to argue that the modality in box and diamond is assumed to be qualified to "logically possible" and "logically necessary". This response would be acceptable if "possible for" worked, in English, in much the same way as the diamond works in modal logic.

For example, suppose someone asked me whether Jill was in her office. Suppose that, as I was being asked, I looked out the window and saw her getting into her car in the car park. I could reasonably respond, "It is not possible for her to be in her office because I can see her, right now, getting into her car in the car park." My response to the query seems to imply that there are two things that are incompatible. They are that Jill is not in her office (because she is in the car park) and that it is possible for Jill to be in her office. Given the "possible for" translation of the diamond, this pair of incompatible statements translates into instances of the general forms *not p* and $\Diamond p$. This supposed incompatibility is quite problematic because it seems to arise from a supposed entailment of which the following is an instance:

> *If Jill is not in her office, then it is not possible for her to be in her office.*

But, if the general form

> *If not* p *then not possible for* p

is the form of a general entailment, and if contraposition and double negation are accepted, then we get:

> *If it is possible for* p *then* p.

But this is clearly false. We could bypass this unacceptable conclusion by rejecting one or both of double negation and contraposition. At this stage that could be seen as a radical solution. A less dramatic way out of the problem might be found by another consideration.

If the contrast between "possible for" and "possible that", so strongly portrayed in White, is not so strictly observed in everyday usage, then the "reasonable" response above should be reconsidered. In everyday English there might not always be a sharp distinction drawn between the two kinds of possibility. So the response might have been better expressed if it had been, "It is just not possible that she is in her office, because I can see her, right now, getting into her car in the car park."

The "because" part of the response can be seen as a way of saying, "Jill is *definitely* not in her office." Given the pairing of "possible that" with "definite that", this gives us the incompatible pair as:

> *It is definite that Jill is not in her office (because I see her in the car park).*

and   *It is possible that Jill is in her office.*

These two are definitely incompatible, especially since the first is equivalent to:

> *It is not possible that Jill is in her office.*

A second response to these kinds of cases would be to say that the possible worlds account of possibility is not intended to clarify either of the two kinds of possibility in ordinary language. It is, in some sense, intended to replace these with a clearer and more easily understood concept. When philosophers and logicians use the phraseology of *It is possible that p* and *It is necessary that p*, or *possibly p* and *necessarily p*, then they are making use of possibility of a possible worlds kind. In a sense, they are resorting to a technical form of words that is definitely not the same as the ordinary language forms. The idea is that modal logic will give us a clearer account of possibility and necessity than can be given in English, because people slide over the many distinctions available in English when using it in everyday conversation.

This response leaves us with the problem of translating arguments from ordinary language into the artificial modal language with possible worlds semantics.

5.4 Translation cases

David Lewis has some interesting cases in *On the Plurality of Worlds*: cases that show that modal *logics* based on possible worlds cannot cope with propositions expressed in English. "In any case, modality is not all boxes and diamonds. Ordinary language has modal idioms that outrun the resources of standard modal logic, though of course you will be able to propose extensions."[8] But the notion of possible worlds, apart from formal languages, can illuminate the meanings of the propositions. These cases are produced with a view to showing that possible worlds stand in no need of modal logic in order to be useful in philosophy.

> There are modalised comparatives: a red thing could resemble an orange thing more closely than a red thing could resemble a blue thing. I analyse that as a quantified statement of comparative resemblance involving coloured things which may be parts of different worlds.
> For some *x* and *y* (*x* is red and *y* is orange and
> for all *u* and *v* (if *u* is red and *v* is blue, then
> *x* resembles *y* more than *u* resembles *v*))
> Try saying that in standard modal logic. The problem is that formulas get evaluated relative to a world, which leaves no room for cross-world comparisons.[9]

We have seen that, in modal logic, the notion of truth is always world relative. But Lewis wants to allow for truth that is "overarching" in some sense. This will certainly take him beyond standard modal logic with possible worlds semantics and truth at (or in) worlds. But all is not lost.

There are other cases in Lewis. He discusses the case of Humphrey, who did not win, but might have won, the United States presidential election. There are difficulties in saying that Humphrey is essentially human and saying that he might not have existed. Being essentially human is to be represented as "necessarily x is human". The case is discussed in terms of Humphrey's satisfying "necessarily x is human", and satisfying "possibly x does not exist", and

> that he does *not* satisfy the modal formula "possibly x is human and x does not exist" since that seems to be the way to say something false, namely that he might have been human without even existing.[10]

The problem is that the standard possible worlds semantics means that "he satisfies 'x is human' at all worlds and 'x does not exist' at some worlds; so he satisfies both at some worlds".[11] But this is not what we (Lewis) want. We want Humphrey to satisfy both without satisfying the conjunction in order to avoid the consequence that he might have been human without even existing.

Although Lewis discusses this in the context of his own idiosyncratic version of modal predicate logic – counterpart theory – he also points out that the same problem will arise in any modal predicate logic. "Shall we dump the method of counterparts? – That wouldn't help, because we can recreate the problem in a far more neutral framework."[12] After discussing the case of wanting to be able to say that Humphrey is essentially human, and also wanting to be able to say the Humphrey might not have existed, and finding it difficult in modal logic to say these things, Lewis writes:

> Maybe, for instance, saying that Humphrey satisfies "necessarily x is human" is *not* the right way to say that he is essentially human. That would disappoint anyone who hopes that the language of boxes and diamonds affords a good regimentation of our ordinary modal thought.
>
> Whichever it is, the friend of boxes and diamonds is in for a disappointment. He can pick his disappointment to suit himself. He can lay down uniform and unambiguous semantic rules for a regimented formal language – and re-educate his intuitions about how to translate between that language and ordinary modal talk. He can discipline himself, for instance, never to say "necessarily human" when he means "essentially human"; but instead, always to say "necessarily such that it is human if it exists". Alternatively, he can build his language more on the pattern of what we ordinarily say – and equip it with outright ambiguities, or else with devious rules that look at what a formula says before they know what it means to satisfy it.[13]

Without some severe modification, the logic of boxes and diamonds is unable to account for both statements of essential nature and statements of possible nonexistence. If one thinks that existence is the problem, then it is not. We can substitute "possibly x is a cat" and get the bad consequence.

5.5 The limits of formality

These cases, and the manifold richness of ordinary language, show that we have to be very careful about our expectations. Artificial languages, and possible worlds semantics for them, might be quite unreliable for the evaluation of a wide range of argumentation. This unreliability will have a great deal to do with the success of the combination of the artificial language boxes and diamonds with the possible worlds semantics as an explanatory model for the meanings of modal expressions.

The more one looks at the overall situation the more it looks as though there are severe limits to what has been accomplished in logic. There are several responses to the unreliability challenge. The foremost response among logicians who agree that there is a problem is the "we are working on it" response. What else could be said except "Let us pack up and quietly depart"? There is not much sign of that.

Unfortunately, there are many logicians who hold that we already have all the answers, and that the fault, if any, is in the many imperfections of ordinary language. This defeats the standard rhetoric for teaching logic. Ordinary language arguments are best ignored, and we should be teaching an applied logic in school and kindergarten instead of natural language skills. So one might argue a *reductio ad absurdam* case. On the other hand, there are those who would have us abandon the programme of using artificial languages for the analysis and evaluation of argumentation.[14] The case is not so strange, although I do not agree with it.

It seems important to me that the "we are working on it" response should be taken as the best and most serious response. Neither logicians, philosophers, computer scientists nor their students should forget the incomplete state of the art.

CHAPTER 6

The possible worlds of knowledge

6.1 Knowledge and belief

One of the common uses of modal logic, apart from use in the discussion of logical possibility and necessity, is to provide a logic for knowledge and a logic for belief. These logics have practical applications in artificial intelligence, especially in knowledge representation.

Logics for knowledge are *epistemic* logics,[1] and logics for belief are *doxastic* logics. Nevertheless, the term "epistemic logic" is often taken to encompass both epistemic and doxastic logics. One of the first twentieth-century suggestions for a logic for knowledge came from Lemmon in his paper, "Is There Only One Correct System of Modal Logic?"[2] We have already noted that Lemmon was one of the great axiomatizers of modal logic, and he presented his epistemic logic in terms of the axiomatic system S0.5 ("S nought point 5").

The first comprehensive text in epistemic and doxastic logic, *Knowledge and Belief*, was published by Hintikka in 1962.[3] This work has become a classic. Hintikka made no explicit use of possible worlds as such in the text. He used *model sets* instead of possible worlds. Model sets are consistent sets of sentences. He set out consistency conditions for these sets of sentences, conditions such as:[4]

(A. ~)   If $p \in \lambda$ and "$\sim p$" $\in \lambda$, then λ is inconsistent.
(A. &)   If λ is consistent and if "$p \& q$" $\in \lambda$ then $\lambda + \{p, q\}$ is consistent.

These conditions would be equivalent, respectively, to:[5]

(C. ~)   If $p \in \mu$ then not "$\sim p$" $\in \mu$.
(C. &)   If "$p \& q$" $\in \mu$ then $p \in \mu$ and $q \in \mu$.

Where μ is a consistent *model set*.

He also used an *alternative* relation between model sets in a *model system* instead of an accessibility relation between possible worlds in a system of worlds. His presentation of the alternative relation did not, at first, even mention the properties of reflexivity, transitivity or symmetry. Nevertheless, his approach is so closely analogous to possible world semantics that *model set–model system* semantics can easily be transposed into possible worlds semantics. Model sets can just be taken to be sets of sentences true in possible worlds, and the alternative relation can be taken to be the accessibility relation. *Model set–model system* semantics can be described as "virtual possible world semantics".

Hintikka is not altogether at ease with possible worlds. In a paper in which he uses possible worlds terminology all the time, he writes "of the basic idea of analyzing knowledge in terms of excluded and admitted alternatives (options, or scenarios, misleadingly called 'possible worlds')".[6] So, we will use the terminology of possible worlds semantics with some reservation, as he does.

It is both interesting and important that Hintikka's methods of presentation of epistemic and doxastic logic are thoroughly semantic. Hintikka provides semantically based justifications for the underlying principles of his epistemic and doxastic systems. He tends to treat epistemic logic as more or less primary, and doxastic logic as secondary. But we have an interest in looking at the doxastic logic in its own right, and will do so in Chapter 7. Also, we delay the treatment of epistemic predicate logic until Chapter 7, because many of the key issues related to quantification are best considered after we have discussed doxastic logic. So we look at epistemic propositional logic alone in this chapter.

We begin by looking at Hintikka's epistemic logic and its virtual possible world (*model set–model system*) framework, and then indicate some of the philosophical issues generated by the logic's virtual possible world semantics. Our main aim is to show the impact of possible worlds in epistemic logic. We will not pursue the many fascinating topics that are generated by epistemic logic, issues that are not generated by possible worlds semantics as such.

6.2 Standard epistemic logic symbols

In what follows this section we will mainly avoid the use of symbolic notation and formulas. Nonetheless, it is important to see how the modal box and diamond are adapted to epistemic logic.

If we interpret the $\Box$ as "It is known that", then we have an *epistemic* interpretation of modal logic. Since knowledge involves some knowledge agent (knower), most epistemic logics use a subscript with the modal operator to indicate the agent. If the agent were a, then we would have $\Box_a$. If several agents were to be considered, then we would have a logic for each agent.

It is usual to replace the □ in epistemic logic with K for knowledge. So we translate:

$K_a p$ as   *a knows that p*

Given agents: $a, b, c, d, \ldots$, there will be a knowledge operator for each agent:

$K_a, K_b, K_c, K_d, \ldots$

Given that the K_a operator is analogous to the box of alethic modal logic, there are diamond-like operators, one for each agent:

$P_a , P_b , P_c , P_d , \ldots$

such that, for any agent x:

$P_x \, \alpha =_{df} \textbf{not } K_x \textbf{ not } \alpha$ [x does not know that not α]

Hintikka translates:

$P_a p$ as   *It is possible, for all that a knows, that p*

From this translation we see that the denial of a knowledge claim,

a does not know that p or, in symbols,   **not** $K_a \, p$

is equivalent to:

It is possible, for all that a knows, that not p P_a **not** p

It is also insisted that the denial of $P_a \, p$ is to be taken as follows:

not $P_a \, p$ reads as   *It does not follow from what a knows that p*

Hintikka is at pains to point out: "From this it is seen that the negation of [$P_a p$] is not expressed by 'It is impossible, for all that a knows, that p'."[7] This translation occurs very early in *Knowledge and Belief*, and sets the stage for several important contentions. Far much more hangs on this rather innocent looking point of translation than might appear, and we will return to consider it later in this chapter.

Hintikka's epistemic logic is straightforwardly an epistemic interpretation of S4. If we assume that epistemic logic is to cope with more than one epistemic agent, then the logic will be a multiply-modal or multi-agent S4. The possible worlds of epistemic logic are often referred to as "epistemically possible worlds" or "epistemically alternate worlds".

6.3 The ideal epistemic agent

Lemmon made the important suggestion that to interpret the epistemic logician's "X knows that": "We may make a start . . . by treating X as a kind of logical fiction, the rational man . . . (A rational man knows (at least implicitly) the logical consequences of what he knows.)"[8] Lemmon is aware of some of the "queer consequences" of the ideal agent view. Lemmon's preferred system has, as one of its rules, the rule that:

If T is a tautology then X knows that T.

He writes: "There are some queer consequences: X knows that T, let us say, where T is some very long tautology containing 396 propositional variables. But this is not to worry us . . .".[9]

Clearly, the "rational man" of Lemmon is very knowledgeable (at least implicitly). The ideal rationality of agents is sometimes exactly what makes these logics attractive to people working in artificial intelligence. Artificially intelligent agents are often taken, automatically, to be rational, logically inerrant, never forgetful and, above all, always able to beat mere humans at chess.

This assumption of ideal rationality has led some logicians to question the viability of the whole area of epistemic and doxastic logic. Ideal agents are unreal agents, and maybe they are too unreal to be considered seriously. We return to this topic later in this chapter.

Given this overarching idealization assumption, there are two ways of looking at epistemic logic: the *axiomatic way* and the *semantic way*. Each of these can help us to understand the model of the knowledge agent that a particular epistemic logic gives. The axiomatic way is explored in other places.[10] We will focus on the *semantic* way because we are mainly concerned with the way in which possible worlds, or virtual possible worlds, have been used as the basis for philosophical discussion and debate.

6.4 The semantic way

We look now at the way Hintikka used his virtual possible worlds semantics to present his logical picture of an epistemic agent. He begins by setting out some quite fundamental principles about consistency and logical truth. Then he goes on to the epistemic logic proper.

The semantic notions of *defensibility* and *indefensibility* are basic for Hintikka. He wants to interpret *consistency* as *defensibility*. Consistency is the notion of, in his words, "immunity to certain kinds of criticism".[11] So if we say that a set of sentences is consistent, then we are saying that it is defensible, because it is immune to certain kinds of criticism. A person might also be persuaded that a set of sentences is consistent or inconsistent by showing them that the set is defensible or indefensible respectively.[12]

Logical truths, that is the tautologies[13] of propositional and predicate logic and the principles of epistemic logic, are "self-sustaining". This gives us a virtual definition:

A sentence is *self-sustaining* if and only if its negation is *indefensible*.

This definition opens the way for *reductio ad absurdum* arguments in the body of the text. The arguments are often presented in a form that is essentially (and virtually) the same as semantic tableaux. Semantic tableaux, or truth-trees, are based almost wholly on *reductio ad absurdum*.

Given these basic notions we can consider the logic. We begin by presenting Hintikka's logic in terms of five principles governing his epistemic agents. This is not the way the logic is presented in *Knowledge and Belief*, but it suits us to take it this way at the beginning of our discussion.

The first principle is that epistemic agents know all the tautologies of both propositional and predicate logic. An agent who has this ability will satisfy the principle known as the weak necessitation principle (WNP):

WNP   *If T is a tautology then x knows that T*

In what follows we will use x as a space into which a, b, c and so on can be inserted. It should be noted in passing that the WNP does *not* mean that if T is a tautology then an agent, a, knows that T is a tautology. Nor, contrary to what Lemmon seems to say in the passage quoted above, does this mean that a formula or semi-logical sentence[14] with propositional variables, which is a tautology, should be known *to be a tautology*. This ability is not about knowing logical definitions or the terminology of logic. The agent simply *knows that T*. For example, *If it is raining, then it is raining* is a tautology. The WNP asserts that any agent, a, would know that *If it is raining, then it is raining*. That's all. The principle does *not* assert that they would know that "*If it is raining then it is raining*" is a tautology.

How does Hintikka justify WNP? Of logical truths Hintikka says:

> Logical truths are not truths which logic forces on us; they are not necessary truths in the sense of being unavoidable. They are not truths we *must* know, but truths which we *can* know without making use of any factual information.[15]

When we apply the defensible–indefensible contrast to the principle that any epistemic agent knows all the logical truths (tautologies) of first-order logic, the following account would seem to pick up on Hintikka's approach:

If *T* is a tautology of first-order logic, and someone says that they do not know that *T*, then, if they are rational, they can be persuaded to retract their statement without anyone imparting to them any factual information.

Hintikka is not just telling us about his epistemic logic. He is telling us something about his view of what knowledge is. Knowledge is not merely being aware of the facts. An agent's knowledge must form a coherent defensible whole, immune from logical criticism. But even that is not all. There is a reverse side of this coin.

If anyone claims *not to know* something, that claim should also be immune from criticism. The logic is also a logic of ignorance. In the case of the tautologies of first-order logic, the claim not to know them is not immune from the sort of "persuasive criticism" that Hintikka outlines.

The second principle is known as the *veridicality principle* (VP).[16]

VP   *If x knows that p, then p*

or

VP   *(x knows that p) only if p*

This principle is one of the very few principles that is universally[17] accepted in epistemology.[18] Something can be known only if it is true. We cannot *know that p* if *p* is false; at best we might *believe that p*. The negation of VP, for example, is quite indefensible. To deny VP would be to argue that

> *a knows that p*
> *not p*

is a defensible set of statements. But it is not defensible, certainly not in terms of our normal understanding, and so VP is immune to criticism.

The third principle is known as *distribution* (Dist):

Dist   *If x knows that if p then q, then if x knows that p then x knows that q.*

Closely related to this principle, and derivative from both it and WNP, is the principle that:

Ent   *If p logically entails q, then if x knows that p then x knows that q.*

The point is that if *p logically entails q* then, in accordance with WNP, all agents know that *p logically entails q*.

Of this derivative principle, Ent, Hintikka writes:

> suppose that a man says to you, "I know that p but I don't know
> whether q" and suppose that p can be shown to entail logically q by
> means of some argument which he would be willing to accept . . .
> If he is reasonable, you can thus persuade him to retract one of his
> statements without imparting to him any fresh information beyond
> certain logical relationships come to know q all by himself if he
> had followed far enough the consequences of what he already
> knew.[19]

There is also an argument for the Dist principle in which possible worlds
feature strongly. We will set that out later. For the time being we simply note
how Hintikka argues for Ent by appealing to the notions of persuasion and
defensibility. But this does mean that the knowledge agent is being described in
a way that makes them deductively omniscient,[20] in some sense at least.

There is also a subsidiary *consistency principle*:

Con.K   *If x knows that p then x does not know that not p*

Denial of Con.K would mean that one would have to claim that, for some a:

> *a knows that p*
> *a knows that not p*

is a consistent (defensible) set of sentences. But as a pair of premises in an
argument, it would be possible, by use of VP, to draw the inconsistent and
indefensible conclusion:

> *p and not p*

Con.K is typically seen as applying to knowledge agents, because it is assumed
that the only defensible bodies of knowledge are consistent bodies of knowledge.

Some philosophers might disagree, especially those who take the *dialethic*[21]
view that reality, and hence knowledge, can be logically contradictory. We will
return to discuss this in Chapter 10. For the moment we will assume the Con.K
is correct because its denial is indefensible.

If we accept WNP, Dist, VP as self-sustaining, then we are effectively accepting
Lemmon's epistemic logic, the S0.5 epistemic logic. Any agent who embodies
such principles can be called an "S0.5 agent".

We can add a fourth ability to the abilities of an S0.5 agent and we get a new,
stronger epistemic agent, the T agent. The new ability gives the T agent the
automatic knowledge of all the tautologies *plus* automatic knowledge of the
principles of epistemic logic. An agent who has this ability will satisfy the

principle known as the *necessitation principle* (NP):

NP   *If L is a logical truth (of this logic), then x knows that L*

Knowledge agents who have the ability asserted by NP are said to be *logically omniscient*.[22] The NP ability includes the WNP ability. The NP principle means that knowledge agents know that Dist and know that VP.

So, KDist and KVP will be self-sustaining for all logically omniscient knowers:

KDist   *x knows that (if x knows that if p then q, then if x knows that p then x knows that q).*

KVP   *x knows that (if x knows that p, then p)*

It is important to distinguish between the knowers, such as T agents, of whom KDist and KVP are self-sustaining and those of whom KDist and KVP are not self-sustaining, such as S0.5 agents.

The agents of whom both KDist and KVP are self-sustaining are knowers who know that both Dist and VP *apply to themselves*. They are automatically *self-aware* in a very profound philosophical sense. They know what governs their own knowing.

6.5 Conditions across worlds

Possible worlds do not obviously come into play when we consider Dist and VP *simpliciter*. But, when we claim that agents *know that* Dist and *know that* VP, then possible worlds come obviously into play. They come obviously into play when someone wants to *deny knowing* that VP or *deny knowing* that Dist. In this context it becomes very clear that epistemic logic is a logic for both knowledge *and ignorance*.

When we look at standard modal logic with box and diamond, we understand it to be the logic of necessity *and possibility*. It is not just a logic of necessity. It is also central to our understanding of epistemic logic that the box is interpreted as "knowing that", and the diamond as "being ignorant that". Epistemic logic is not just a logic of knowledge; it is a logic of knowledge *and ignorance*. The possible worlds of epistemic logic are the worlds of *possible ignorance*.

Hintikka's use of the "epistemic diamond" becomes crucial when dealing with the denial of knowledge. He uses his reading of the epistemic diamond as part of a set of arguments to justify a condition called the "(A.PKK*)" condition. This condition is first set out very early in the work,[23] and, if accepted, must lead to an S4 epistemic logic. It is therefore vital that we look at (A.PKK*) carefully, because the justification of (A.PKK*) uses possible worlds.

It is best to look directly at Hintikka's own case, even though the quotes will be long. I will interpose some comments in square parentheses at one or two points. This is his case:

> Let us suppose that someone makes a number of statements . . . [and] that among the sentences he utters there are the following:
>
> "I know that p_1"
> "I know that p_2"
> . . .
> "I know that p_k"
> "It is possible, for all that I know, that q."
>
> Under what conditions is he consistent? It will be agreed that one condition at least has to be fulfilled, namely, that the following set of sentences is also consistent:
>
> "I know that p_1"
> "I know that p_2"
> . . .
> "I know that p_k"
> "q is in fact the case."[24]
>
> If it is consistent of me to say that it is possible, for all that I know, that q is the case, then it must be possible for q to turn out to be the case without invalidating any of my claims to knowledge; that is, there must not be anything inconsistent about a state of affairs in which q is true and in which I know what I say I know.

[The formal version of (A.PKK*) is then set out.[25] Note also that "It is possible, for all that I know, that q" is equivalent to "I do *not* know that *not q*": a statement of ignorance.]

> The rule (A.PKK*) is perhaps the most important rule with which we shall deal in this essay. It is therefore worth while to examine it somewhat more closely.
> . . . The rule (A.PKK*) may be compared with the weaker rule – we shall call it (A.PK*)[26]

I will set out the rule (A.PK*) in a form analogous to Hintikka's informal introduction of the stronger rule:

(A.PK*) The following will be consistent:
    "I know that p_1"

"I know that p_2"

. . .

"I know that p_k"
"It is possible, for all that I know, that q."
if the following set of sentences is also consistent:
"p_1 is in fact the case."
"p_2 is in fact the case."

. . .

"p_k is in fact the case."
"q is in fact the case."

Let us try out the rules to find out, from a logical point of view, what (A.PKK*) adds that (A.PK*) misses. Formal versions of these arguments, couched in possible worlds terminology, are in an appendix at the end of this chapter. We begin with an investigation of Dist. (not KDist) by using (A.PK*).

Dist   *If x knows that if p then q, then if x knows that p then x knows that q.*

To deny Dist is to claim that it is defensible for some *a* to claim that the following three sentences are consistent: *a knows that if p then q; a knows that p;* and *a does not know that q.* Since there is an equivalence between *a does not know that q* and *It is possible, for all that a knows, that not q,* the denial of Dist becomes the assertion that the following is consistent:

> *a knows that if p then q*
> *a knows that p*
> *It is possible, for all that a knows, that not q*

If we apply the weaker rule (A.PK*) then the set above, let us call it set *n*, is consistent only if the following set, let us call it *k*, is consistent:

> *if p then q*
> *p*
> *not q*

Set *k* is obviously inconsistent. So the original set, *n*, is also inconsistent, and hence indefensible. So Dist is *self-satisfying.*
    What happens if we use the stronger rule? The process goes:

> *a knows that if p then q*
> *a knows that p*
> *It is possible, for all that a knows, that not q*

is consistent only if the following set, say *m*, is consistent:

> *a knows that if p then q*
> *a knows that p*
> *not q*

Set *m* is not, at once, obviously inconsistent unless we apply some other principle. But, to really be clear that *m* is inconsistent, we have to apply VP to both knowledge statements to get:

> *if p then q*
> *p*
> *not q*

as additional members of *m*.

What is going on here? What is the real contrast between the two rules? With rule (A.PKK*) we put all of *a*'s *knowledge*, that is *if p then q* and *p*, and what was allegedly possible for all *a*'s knowledge, *not q*, together in model set *k*. In the application of rule (A.PK*) we include in model set *k*, which contains what is possible for all that *a* knows: the *content* of *a*'s knowledge.

In the case of rule (A.PKK*), the case of the stronger rule, we put all *a*'s *knowing*, that is *a knows that if p then q* and *a knows that p*, and what was allegedly possible for all *a*'s knowledge, *not q*, together in model set *m*. That is, in the application of the stronger rule we include in model set *m*, which contains what is possible for all that *a* knows: *a*'s knowledge *state*. This means that with the stronger rule we have to resort to the VP principle to "clinch" the argument about Dist's self-satisfiability.

We now return to Hintikka's case for adopting (A.PKK*) rather than (A.PK*).

> Why are we justified (as clearly we are) in adopting the stronger rule (A.PKK*) and not only the weaker rule (A.PK*)?
>
> One answer to this question seems to be as follows. That *q* is the case can be compatible with everything a certain person – let us assume he is referred to by *a* – knows only if it cannot be used as an argument to overthrow any true statement of the form "*a* knows that *p*." Now this statement can be criticized in two ways. One may either try to show that *p* is not in fact true or else try to show that the person referred to by *a* is not in a position or condition to know that it is true. In order to be compatible with everything he knows, *q* therefore has to be compatible not only with every *p* which is known to him but also with the truth of all the true statements of the form "*a* knows that *p*." And this is exactly what is required by (A.PKK*).[27]

Consider the two lines of allowable criticism of "*a* knows that *p*" in terms of *q*. The first line is where *q* simply falsifies knowledge claims because what is claimed to be known is inconsistent with *q*. The second line concerns the idea that *q* is incompatible with *a*'s being in a position to know.

The weaker rule, (A.PK*), just requires that *q* be compatible with the content of *a*'s knowledge: knowledge expressed in "*a* knows that *p*". The weaker rule provides a necessary condition for compatibility and, conversely, a sufficient condition for incompatibility.

But being sufficient is not sufficient for Hintikka. Hintikka not only wants the criticism by *q* of "*a* knows that *p*" that *p* is inconsistent with *q*, but more. Even though (A.PK*) delivers a sufficient condition for the incompatibility of "*a* knows that *p*" with *q*, that is not enough. He also wants to have the criticism of "*a* knows that *p*" based on the assessment that "*a* is not in a position or condition to know that *p* is true."

Is this an additional condition when *p* is prima facie consistent with *q*? Well, no – not the way the logic works. The stronger rule, (APKK*), *includes* the weaker. The requirement is that if *q* is compatible with "*a* knows that *p*", then *q* must be compatible with *p* and *also*, in some sense, assure us that *a* is in a position to know that *p*. So what in addition to the (A.PK*) condition does the (A.PKK*) rule generate that shows that *a* is in the position to know that *p*?

It effectively generates the fifth principle in Hintikka's epistemic logic. It generates the *KK-thesis* – the agents' ability to know everything they know:[28]

KK   *If x knows that p, then x knows that x knows that p.*

This principle is shown to be self-sustaining by the following argument, which shows that the denial of KK is not defensible. The denial of KK for an agent, *a*, gives:

> *a knows that p*
> *It is not the case that a knows that a knows that p*

This is equivalent to:

> *a knows that p*
> *It is possible, for all that a knows, that a does not know that p*

By the condition (A.PK*), this is consistent only if

> *a knows that p*
> *a does not know that p*

is consistent. This is clearly indefensible, so KK is self-sustaining, given (A.PKK*).

But, if we use only the (A.PK*) condition, then

a knows that p
It's possible, for all that a knows, that a does not know that p

is consistent only if the following is consistent:

p
a does not know that p

This is consistent only if

not p

is consistent, which it is unless *p* is a tautology or self-sustaining sentence. So according to condition (A.PKK*) the KK-thesis holds, but according to (A.PK*) it does not.

So the cashing out, in terms of (A.PKK*), of *a*'s being in a *position to know* that *p*, is that *a* knows that *a* knows that *p*. There is nothing else in the S4 logic. There is certainly no use of justified true belief, for example.

But what then is *being in a position* to know that one knows that *p*? In terms of the KK-thesis, it is sufficient to know that *p*, or it is sufficient to know that one knows that one knows that *p*. This is either circular or regressive.

This just does not deal with the real epistemological issues. Assertions that someone is not in a position to know something are notoriously fallible. For example, the history of the fairly standard justified true belief account of knowledge is a minefield of claim and counter-claim, and has itself been roundly criticized.

But perhaps there is something that might reasonably follow from Hintikka's argument. It is a condition somewhat like the following, which we call the (A.PKvK*) condition:

The following set will be consistent:
"I know that p_1"
"I know that p_2"
. . .
"I know that p_k"
"It is possible, for all that I know, that *q*."
if the following *two sets* of sentences are also consistent:
(a) "p_1 is in fact the case."
"p_2 is in fact the case."
. . . .
"p_k is in fact the case."
"*q* is in fact the case."

(b) "I am in a position to know that p_1"
     "I am in a position to know that p_2"
     . . .
     "I am in a position to know that p_k"
     "q is in fact the case."

This new rule would require an additional modal operator or qualification of the epistemic operator. But what would be the logic of that operator? Above all, what kind of possible world justification could be used to explicate this new operator. There is a whole new ball game, but it is not clearly S4.

We have seen that, in any epistemic logic with both the KK-thesis and NP, it has to follow that everyone knows the KK-thesis. KKK applies to everyone.

KKK   *a knows that (if a knows that p, then a knows that a knows that p)*

Why then all the argument? Perhaps the opponents of the KK-thesis are people who know the KK-thesis to be true but don't know that they know this? If so, then they are the proof of its incorrectness.

It is important to see that the consistent sets arguments for (A.PKK*) are by no means conclusive. There may be other arguments, but to pursue them would be far beyond our remit.

If we take Hintikka's consistent sets, model sets, to be virtual possible worlds, then we can take the arguments above to be possible worlds arguments. These are in contrast to the axiomatic style arguments[29] that are often used as a basis for accepting or rejecting principles in epistemic and doxastic logic.

There has been a vast amount of debate about the KK-thesis. Our main concern has been to look at the possible worlds basis on which the S4 epistemic logic is built, and to compare that basis with the basis for weaker logics such as S0.5 and T (especially T), since T was rejected by Hintikka. It is worth noting that Lemmon explicitly rejects the KK-thesis,[30] but not for possible worlds reasons.

There are many other interesting arguments in *Knowledge and Belief*, especially those about first person knowledge and belief claims. These, and other topics, tend not to argued about in possible worlds terms. So, regretfully, we pass them by.

6.6 Knowledge, possibility and ignorance

We turn now to the possible worlds ideas of *epistemic alternativeness* and *epistemic possibility*. In applying both rules the consistency of one set, or possible world, requires the consistency of a second set, or a second world.

The second set or world is the epistemic alternative to, or what's epistemically possible given, the first set or first world. This must have some bearing on the translation of, or understanding of, statements of the form $P_a\, p$.

If we take Hintikka's original translations seriously, then $P_a\, p$ means simply, as Hintikka says, "It is compatible with everything that a knows that p".[31] We need to note that the alternatives are always "generated" by statements of the form $P_a\, p$. We have argued that the rule that best satisfies this understanding of $P_a\, p$ is most certainly the rule (A.PK*).

Hintikka suggests that the reading might be "It does not follow from what a knows that not-p."[32] Given this reading, it becomes clear that the knowledge operator in epistemic logic means somewhat more than "simple" knowledge or "just knowing". We might well take it that:

$K_a\, p$ is to be read as   *a knows that, or can work out whether, p*

This would tie knowledge, in some sense, to proof. Hintikka considers the reading:

$K_a\, p$ is to be read as   *It follows from what a knows that p*[33]

He declines to pursue this further, but seems to be quite sympathetic to it at first. Later in *Knowledge and Belief* he rejects any strong proof orientation.

It was pointed out by Austin[34] that when someone claims to know something they can be asked, "How do you know?" This contrasts with belief, where the question changes to, "Why do you believe?" The "how" question for knowledge will certainly be satisfactorily answered if a proof is produced. For example, how do we know that there is no largest prime number? We know it because we have Euclid's proof. A proof is a sufficient reason for knowing. To that extent Hintikka is certainly correct.

Another option is that S4 epistemic logic is the logic of the *commitments* of a knower. The picture given by S4 is the picture of what an epistemic agent could be said to be logically committed to by claims to know.

Earlier we remarked that there are problems about whether the "possible for" is qualified by "logically" or "epistemically" in Hintikka's reading of $P_a\, p$. In the arguments above, when we considered a denial of knowledge, a possible world was effectively generated and into it we put the negative of the proposition claimed not to be known, and the details of the agent's knowledge state.

But if someone claims to be ignorant of p, they could hardly be saying that p is true and that they are ignorant of that. They are most likely to be saying that they are ignorant about whether p is true or false. "I do not know that p" could be interpreted as opening up two possibilities, generating *two* epistemic possibilities; namely, that p is true (and I don't know that) or that p is false (and I don't know that).

This approach would rely on reading the epistemic diamond in this more literal way:

$$P_a p \quad \text{read as} \quad \textit{a is ignorant about not p}$$

So a claim not to know that p will be defensible if both its truth and falsehood are compatible with what I know. If either were incompatible, then we would have to accept its negation as possible for all we know. But that is not the same as accepting its negation as known. A logic with this approach would be very weak.[35] As Sylvan says of such weaker modal systems, "Philosophical virtue lies in weakness."[36]

6.7 Ideals and artificial intelligence

Lemmon's question, "Is there only one correct system of modal logic?", should really be "Is there only one correct system of epistemic logic?" It is clear from the debates about epistemic logic that there is concern to reflect human knowing in epistemic logic, even if there is idealization of the knower.

We can certainly see the epistemic logic enterprise in terms of the degrees of idealization of the knower provided by various epistemic logics. This perspective makes S4 into the logic for the rational, totally self-aware, totally logically aware reasoner, whose knowledge is, of course, completely logically consistent.

This perspective also makes T into the logic for the rational, totally logically aware reasoner, who may know some contingent propositions and not know that they know them. The T logic allows for incomplete self-awareness. This perspective makes S0.5 into the logic for the rational, totally logically knowledgeable reasoner, who may know some logical or contingent propositions and not know that they know them. The S0.5 logic has no automatic self-awareness.

These ideals – S4, T, S0.5 – are being suggested and discussed on the understanding that epistemic logic lives in the shadow of real agents. Such discussion has at least two interesting dimensions. One concerns the *meaning* of "knows". This is of philosophical interest. The other concerns *computational tractability*. This is of interest in artificial intelligence.

Meaning and ideal

As far as meaning goes, Hintikka's view has changed over time. He once argued that his approach was in terms of what is *meant* by the concept of knowledge. He saw his logic as providing a logical or conceptual grammar for the concept of knowledge. Soon after the publication of *Knowledge and Belief* he wrote that: "The philosophically interesting concepts which we want to study are largely embedded in our ordinary language" and "A branch of logic, say epistemic logic, is best viewed as an *explanatory model* in terms of which certain aspects of the working of our ordinary language can be understood".[37]

In the course of subsequent debate Hintikka shifted his position. Not long after the KK-thesis debate began to rage, he wrote:

> The ultimate court of appeal in deciding whether a logical principle governing some given concept is acceptable is not ordinary language, however regimented, but rather whether the principle helps the concept in question to serve the purpose or purposes it in fact is calculated to serve in our conceptual repertoire, and whether these purposes are themselves worth our effort.[38]

This indicates what Lenzen,[39] a strong supporter of Hintikka's S4 epistemic logic, might well describe as a shift from a *descriptive* to a *normative* approach to epistemic logic. The normative approach is, perforce, an idealizing approach.

The important question for the idealizing accounts is whether they are real enough or *too* ideal. Michie and Johnston point out that: "It is the task of knowledge engineering to design and construct . . . conceptual interfaces to allow people . . . and machines . . . to understand each other"[40] and "In order for any beings, human or machine, to talk to each other, they must share the same mental structures".[41] If they are anywhere near correct about this then it is important to decide whether machine knowledge and machine belief are to be more or less like human knowledge and belief. The less like, the more likely that there will be problems with interaction and understanding what is being said when a computer announces that it "knows" or "believes" something. The more like, the more descriptive. The more ideal, the more normative and unlike human agents.

Even in Lenzen's paper, cited above, he considers counter-examples to KK drawn from everyday human life, rather than asserting that the stipulated principle is more likely to serve the purposes he chooses to select for the functioning of the concept of knowledge. The concept embedded in ordinary language is difficult to escape.

Our discussion of the conceptual issues above has focused on the ways in which epistemically possible worlds might reflect conceptual issues. But it soon becomes clear that the conceptual issues are primary and the possible worlds epistemic logics are derivative.

Computational tractability

The question of computational tractability is important in artificial intelligence. There have been two movements in epistemic logic where epistemic logic is taken to include doxastic logic. These result from artificial intelligence considerations. First, there has been a move away from knowledge towards belief. Secondly, there has been a move to stronger simpler modal logics.

There are two considerations that reinforce the first move. One concerns the implementation of VP. How could one implement VP without having extensive "experiential" input to a machine so that it could decide whether its knowledge claims were correct? Consider a very simple case. Say a machine in Auckland, New Zealand, contains the sentence that it is 15°C in London, England, today. How can it check this information so that it could then move to the assertion that it *knows* that it is 15°C in London today ? The only source of information would be via its own databanks. We can envisage some time in the future when the machine might confirm a claim to know that it is 15°C in London today by consulting the input of a temperature sensor in London. But the implementation of such inputs to check epistemic claims is quite massive. However, if we focus on belief there is no immediate need to cover the implementation of VP. So it is simpler to focus on belief, where VP is of no direct concern.

The other source of pressure to move to normative doxastic logic is because belief is so subject to psychological vagaries that a descriptive logic of belief would yield practically nothing at all. Not even Con for belief would hold, because most people hold inconsistent beliefs. We will look at the problem of inconsistent belief and inconsistency tolerant belief logics in Chapter 7, but coping with inconsistency is logically and computationally complex. It is easier to argue for a stipulative or normative approach to belief than it is for knowledge. We can construct "rational" believers, or omniscient believers, or ideal reasoner-believers, or whatever we wish. We do not have to take subtle descriptive problems into account.

The second movement has been to stronger simpler modal logics. There has been a strong push towards logics as strong as S5; S4 is seen as being too weak.[42] We can add to S4 agents a fifth ability to give the S5 agent. The fifth ability has many advocates in recent knowledge representation literature.[43] It is the agent's ability, automatically, to know when they are ignorant. That is, if an agent does not know something, then they know that they do not know it. The principle is called the *negative introspection thesis* (and rather than label it with the infelicitous "NIT", I shall label it "K **not** K" for knowledge of ignorance, or knowledge of not knowing.)[44]

K **not** K   *If x does not know that p, then x knows that x does not know that p.*

It turns out that if one has K **not** K, and hence S5, then one gets the following for free:

Socrates   *If not p, then x knows that x does not know that p*

Hintikka rejected the S5 picture, which is far stronger than his S4 picture of the epistemic agent. Hintikka specifically rejects K **not** K, and hence Socrates. He writes:

> Notice, however, that you may fail – unless you happen to be as sagacious as Socrates – to know your ignorance. For [*a does not know that p*] does not imply . . . [*a knows that a does not know that p*] [45]

It does seem to be too strong for even the most ideal epistemic agent. S5 epistemic logic may even be a logic that is too strong for the knowledge of an omniscient God.

Whereas I have argued elsewhere that the normal modal logics are too strong[46] and that non-normal logics would be far better for epistemic logic,[47] this is a view that runs quite contrary to the majority view.[48] This push seems to be prompted by questions that arise out of the implementation of possible worlds semantics in machines. There has been an emphasis on technical features of finite sets of sentences, which has driven artificial intelligence epistemic logicians more and more to S5. This shift is well described by Pearce.[49]

Possible worlds technical semantics drives many epistemic logicians in application areas, and it is not altogether clear that technical matters constitute a good driver.

Appendix of principles and arguments in formal notation

VP $\qquad (K_x\, p \supset p)$

Dist $\qquad (K_x\, (p \supset q) \supset (K_x\, p \supset K_x\, q))$

Con.K $\qquad (K_x\, p \supset\, \sim K_x \sim p)$

KDist $\qquad K_x\, (K_x\, (p \supset q) \supset (K_x\, p \supset K_x\, q))$

KVP $\qquad K_x\, (K_x\, p \supset p)$

KK $\qquad (K_x\, p \supset K_x K_x\, p)$

KKK $\qquad K_x\, (K_x\, p \supset K_x K_x\, p)$

K~K $\qquad (\sim K_x\, p \supset K_x \sim K_x\, p)$

Socrates $\qquad (\sim p \supset K_x \sim K_x\, p)$

Ent $\qquad$ *If* $\vdash (p \supset q)$ *then* $(K_x\, p \supset K_x\, q)$

To deny Dist is to claim that for some agent a it is defensible to claim that the following set is consistent

$$\{K_a\,(p \supset q)\,, K_a\,p,\, \sim K_a\,q\}$$

or equivalently

$$\{K_a\,(p \supset q)\,, K_a\,p,\, P_a \sim q\}$$

If we apply the weaker rule, (A.PK*), then the set above is consistent *only if* the following (different) set is consistent:

$$\{(p \supset q),\, p,\, \sim q\}$$

This set is obviously inconsistent. So the original set is also inconsistent, and hence indefensible. So Dist is *self-satisfying*.

This can be put into the terminology of possible worlds by making the claim that the following is consistent

$$\{K_a\,(p \supset q)\,, K_a\,p,\, \sim K_a\,q\} \subseteq \textit{world } n$$

so the following is consistent by equivalence

$$\{K_a\,(p \supset q)\,, K_a\,p,\, P_a \sim q\} \subseteq \textit{world } n$$

But it is consistent *only if*

$$\{(p \supset q)\,,\, p,\, \sim q\} \subseteq \textit{world } k \textit{ (for some k)}$$

and *world k* is an epistemic alternative for *a* to *world n*.

Since the alleged contents of *world k* are inconsistent, the contents of *world n* are also inconsistent. The denial of Dist becomes inconsistent, and Dist is a logical truth.

What happens if we use the stronger rule, (A.PKK*)? The process goes:

$$\{K_a\,(p \supset q)\,, K_a\,p,\, P_a \sim q\} \subseteq \textit{world } n$$

is consistent *only if*

$$\{K_a\,(p \supset q)\,, K_a\,p,\, \sim q\} \subseteq \textit{world } k \textit{ (for some k)}$$

and *world k* is an epistemic alternative for *a* to *world n*. And this is consistent *only if* the following is, by application of VP:

$$\{K_a\,(p \supset q)\,, K_a\,p,\, \sim q,\, (p \supset q),\, p\,\} \subseteq \textit{world } k$$

Nothing is gained.

KK $\qquad$ $(K_x\, p \supset K_x K_x\, p)$

The denial of **KK** for an agent, a, gives:

$$\{K_a\, p,\ \sim K_a K_a\, p\} \subseteq world\ n$$

This is equivalent to:

$$\{K_a\, p,\ P_a \sim K_a\, p\} \subseteq world\ n$$

But it is consistent, by rule (A.PK*), *only if*

$$\{p,\ \sim K_a\, p\} \subseteq world\ k\ (for\ some\ k)$$

is consistent. And this is equivalent to

$$\{p,\ P_a \sim p\} \subseteq world\ k$$

is consistent. And this is consistent *only if*

$$\{\sim p\} \subseteq world\ m\ (for\ some\ m)$$

is consistent. And this is quite defensible. So KK is not self-sustaining when rule (A.PK*) is used.

But if we use (A.PKK*), then the denial of KK for some agent a gives:

$$\{K_a\, p,\ \sim K_a K_a\, p\} \subseteq world\ n$$

This is equivalent to:

$$\{K_a\, p,\ P_a \sim K_a\, p\} \subseteq world\ n$$

But it is consistent, by rule (A.PKK*), *only if*

$$\{K_a\, p,\ \sim K_a\, p\} \subseteq world\ k\ (for\ some\ k)$$

This is clearly indefensible, so KK is self-sustaining.

CHAPTER 7

The possible worlds of belief

7.1 Introduction

Now that we have considered Hintikka's epistemic logic in terms of its possible world basis, we shift to considering doxastic logic, beginning with Hintikka's logic and going on to consider something of the groundwork in doxastic logic that Smullyan sets out in *Forever Undecided*.[1] We will discuss Smullyan's use of doxastic logic to show what Gödel was saying in his important incompleteness theorems about the limitations of logic. Finally, we consider epistemic and doxastic predicate logic and the closely related questions of existence, quantification into epistemic and doxastic contexts, and the *de dicto–de re* distinction as it applies to these logics.

For this chapter it is especially important to be able to distinguish between modal logic and possible world semantics for modal logic. This distinction can be made in terms, for example, of the contrast between the axiomatic and deductive systems for modal logics and the possible worlds semantics for modal logics.

7.2 Doxastic symbols

If we interpret the $\Box$ as "It is believed that", then we have a *doxastic* interpretation of modal logic. Since belief, like knowledge, involves belief agents (believers), many doxastic logics use a subscript with the modal operator to indicate the agent. It is usual to replace the $\Box$ with B for belief. So we have

$B_a p$ for   *a believes that p*

and for any agent x there is the diamond equivalent of:

$$C_x\, \alpha \;=\; {}_{df} \; \textbf{not } B_x \textbf{ not } \alpha \qquad [x \text{ does not believe that not } \alpha]$$

Hintikka's doxastic logic is a multiply-modal or multi-agent D4: a non-reflexive S4.

The possible worlds of doxastic logic are often referred to as "doxastically possible worlds" or "doxastically alternate worlds". Hintikka also translates, analogously to epistemic logic:

$$C_a\, p \qquad \text{as} \qquad \textit{It is possible, for all that a believes, that p}$$

Again, in light of what was said about knowledge in Chapter 6 and the obvious analogies for belief, we use the more literal:

$$C_a\, p \qquad \text{as} \qquad \textit{a does not believe that not p}$$

Before we continue, there is a difference in principle between epistemic and doxastic logic. There is general agreement about the difference. We set it out to get it out of the way. The difference is to be seen in the contrast between the two principles. The first principle is the *veridicality principle* (VP), which we met in Chapter 6.

VP   *If x knows that P, then P*

This is in sharp contrast with belief. The form

VPB   *If x believes that P, then P*

is rejected as a principle for belief logic because a person can believe something false, and it is still belief. Believing P is compatible with the fact of P's falsehood. While false knowledge is a "contradiction in terms", false belief is a daily reality. This contrast is sometimes said to indicate a contrast between the "objectivity" of knowledge and the "subjectivity" of belief.

There is a weaker belief principle that many accept. It is a principle known as *Consistency for belief* (Con.B):

Con.B   *If x believes that P then x does not believe that not P*

If Con.B applies to believers, then their belief systems will be logically consistent. Such believers can be seen as ideal *rational* believers. This ideal runs contrary to the realities of everyday life. Many people who are not in the least irrational have contradictory beliefs. We will return to Con.B later when we discuss awareness of the consistency or inconsistency of one's own beliefs, and inconsistent possible worlds.

So, there are two features of belief that make doxastic logic quite different from epistemic logic. First, there is the failure of VPB in contrast to the uncontested sway of VP for knowledge. Secondly, most people assume that reality is consistent.[2] If this assumption is correct, then it follows from the VP principle for knowledge that knowledge will be consistent and not contradictory. A person cannot know both *P* and *not P*.

7.3 Doxastic logic

The possibilities of false belief and of contradictory belief mean that the creators of doxastic logic are more inclined to go beyond idealization to stipulation. In other words, various logics are considered from the point of view of what it would be like if agents' beliefs and believing conformed to a given doxastic logic. This is probably why there was much more philosophical interest in Hintikka's epistemic logic than in his doxastic logic.

The doxastic logic in Hintikka's work is just the same as epistemic S4, but with Con.B in place of VP. The standard name for such a logic is "D4". The principles for D4 are NP, Dist, BB and Con.B. We set these out for reference:

NP   *If L is a logical truth of this logic, then x believes that L.*

(We note that NP for belief includes the WNP for belief:

WNP   *If T is a tautology then x believes that T.*)

Dist   *If x believes that if P then Q, then if x believes that P then x believes that Q.*

BB   *If x believes that P then x believes that x believes that P.*

Con.B   *If x believes that P then x does not believe that not P.*

We note that believers who have the ability asserted by the NP for belief are said, just as for epistemic logic, to be *logically omniscient*. The combination of NP and Dist means that Hintikka's believers are also *deductively omniscient*.

If Con.B is removed, then we get the doxastic logic known as K4. This is of far greater interest to us. We simply pass D4 by and move on to other systems. We will look at these systems from a *stipulative* point of view, as logics intended to describe *ideal reasoner-believers* of a particular stipulated kind.

We now consider some of the belief logics that are stipulated in Smullyan's *Forever Undecided*. Smullyan sets out a sequence of doxastic logics. They run roughly in parallel with the S0.5, T, S4 sequence of epistemic logics. None of them has VP. The most powerful systems are K4 and G. We have shown how to set out the K4 system. We will set out G below.

Before we go on to G, we note that the sequence of doxastic logics introduced in the first half of *Forever Undecided* plays the role of gradually introducing the reader to various features given to ideal or stipulated reasoner-believers. Smullyan uses his favourite Island of Knights and Knaves as a foil for his development. It is the island where the knights always tell the truth, and the knaves always speak falsehood, and everyone is either a knight or a knave. There is no need for us to go through all the details, but it is certainly interesting to read the full account, and to work out the many details of the properties of the reasoner-believers.

Smullyan introduces five things, step by step: logical omniscience, deductive omniscience, self-awareness, correct belief and beliefs about whether one's belief system is consistent or inconsistent. We look at some of the logics in order to see how they work. They are all presented in terms of reasoners of various types, *type 1* to *type 4* and *type G*. The simplest is the *type 1* reasoner.

Reasoners of type 1

A reasoner-believer of *type 1* satisfies two conditions:

- he believes all tautologies; and
- for any propositions X and Y, if he believes X and believes $X \supset Y$, then he believes Y.[3]

This means that reasoners of *type 1* satisfy WNP and Dist for belief. Reasoners of *type 1* are non-reflexive S0.5 believers: S0.5 believers without VP.

Reasoners of type 4

In order to define a *type 4* reasoner, Smullyan first introduces *normal* reasoners: "a reasoner is *normal* if for any proposition p, if he believes p, then he believes that he believes p".[4] So BB is true of the *normal* reasoner. Normal reasoners have much more self-awareness than reasoners of *type 1*. But "A normal reasoner doesn't necessarily know that he is normal."[5] So for a *type 4* reasoner, we add the belief in normality. This gives the doxastic analogue of KKK:

BBB   *x believes that (if x believes that P, then x believes that x believes that P).*

Type 4 reasoners are K4 belief agents.

Consistency

Because Smullyan is describing just one believer-reasoner, and not a multi-agent system, he leaves out the x in B_x. So $B_x\, p$ becomes just Bp in his formulation. In what follows we translate logic symbols into our notation, so that formal logic's ~ becomes **not** and ⊃ becomes **imp**.

Smullyan introduces the mechanisms by means of which a reasoner will detect inconsistency. First, he introduces the symbol "⊥" for contradictory propositions in general. ⊥ can be thought of as equivalent to (p **and not** p). So if *a believes* ⊥, then *a* has contradictory beliefs. He says: "We say that a reasoner is *consistent* if the set of all propositions that he believes is a consistent set, and we shall say that he is *inconsistent* if his set of beliefs is inconsistent."[6] It follows that:

> the following three conditions are equivalent:
>
> (1) He is inconsistent (he believes ⊥)
> (2) He believes some proposition p and its negation (**not** p)
> (3) He believes all propositions.
>
> We shall say that a reasoner believes he is consistent if he believes **not** B⊥ (he believes that he doesn't believe ⊥.) We shall say that he believes that he is inconsistent if he believes B⊥ (he believes that he believes ⊥.) [7]

It follows from these definitions and equivalences that the following is true of reasoners of all types, including *type 1* (we call it CB):

CB   *If x believes that P and also believes that not P, then x believes the contradictory.*

Type 4 reasoners will believe CB. So, it is true of *type 4* reasoners that BCB:

BCB   *x believes that (if x believes P and also believes not P then x believes the contradictory).*[8]

  The point of the last formula is that it shows that *type 4* reasoners can formulate beliefs about themselves, particularly about their own consistency and inconsistency.[9] Furthermore, because these ideal reasoners believe all the logical and doxastic consequences of their beliefs – they are logically and deductively omniscient – we can say that they believe everything to which their beliefs commit them.

Reasoners of type G

The final doxastic system introduced by Smullyan is system G. He begins the introduction by defining a *modest* reasoner: "We shall now call a reasoner *modest* if for every proposition p, he believes Bp **imp** p only if he believes p (in other words, if he believes Bp **imp** p, then he believes p)"[10] and "a reasoner is modest with respect to a particular proposition p if it is the case that if he believes Bp **imp** p, then he also believes p".[11]

So it is true of a believer, say *a*, who is modest with respect to *p*, that MB:

MB   *If a believes that (if a believes that p then p), then a believes that p.*

Believer *a* will be modest if he is modest with respect to all propositions. Of course, a reasoner, say *a*, *believes* he is modest with respect to *p* if the following is true of him:

BMB   *a believes that (If a believes that (if a believes that p then p), then a believes that p.)*

A reasoner of *type G* is a reasoner of *type 4* who believes he is *modest* with respect to every proposition.

A *modest type 4* reasoner-believer is a *type G* reasoner-believer. They reason about themselves. Most important of all, they reason about their own consistency and inconsistency. But it turns out that there are some beliefs that they just *cannot consistently* have. It is the "cannot consistently" that is vital here. This combines with the fact that *type G* reasoner-believers have beliefs about themselves to produce some quite remarkable results, results that go back to Gödel.

We begin by noting an formal fact about negation. When we have "⊥", we have the following equivalence:

not *P*   is equivalent to   (*P* **imp** ⊥)[12]

It is relatively easy to show that reasoners of *type G* have a very interesting, and apparently paradoxical, characteristic. Suppose that a *type G* reasoner-believer believes that he is consistent. Then he believes **not** B⊥. Hence he believes the logically equivalent proposition B⊥ **imp** ⊥. Then, being modest, he must believe ⊥, which means that he is inconsistent! And so *no modest reasoner*[13] – even of *type 1* – can *consistently* believe in his own consistency.[14]

It is most important that this principle is not misunderstood. Smullyan writes:

> This, of course, doesn't mean that he necessarily *is* inconsistent; he might happen to be consistent, but if he is consistent – and a modest reasoner of type 1 – then he cannot believe he is consistent.[15]

Besides not meaning that *he is* inconsistent, it does not even mean that *we* cannot tell whether or not he is consistent from an objective and external point of view. After all, he is defined as consistent. It just means that, although he can reason his way correctly to many conclusions about himself, he cannot draw the conclusion *from within his own belief system* that he is consistent.

The use of "cannot" here is the use that tells us that, on the one hand, if believers are at first consistent, and then come to believe that they are consistent, they fall into logical contradiction, and are then not consistent any more. To remain consistent the believer must not believe anything about the consistency of their own beliefs. On the other hand, if a believer is inconsistent and comes to believe that they are consistent, then their beliefs are inconsistent anyway.

We have the principle that can be called "Gödel Two Belief" (G2B):

G2B   No *type G* reasoner-believer with consistent beliefs can *consistently* believe in their own consistency.

This limitation on the beliefs of *type G* reasoners and on the conclusions they can draw from within their belief systems is exactly the same as one of the important limits on logic set out in Gödel's second incompleteness theorem about mathematical systems and what they can prove (believe) about themselves. Gödel's second incompleteness theorem goes much further than just mathematical systems; it applies to certain kinds of self-aware rationality.

It might be of some help if we summarize what is involved in being *type 1*, *type 4* and *type G* reasoner-believers. The principles at issue are:

1. Weak necessitation   (If *T* is a tautology then *x* believes that *T*.)
2. Distribution   *If x believes that if P then Q, then if x believes that P then x believes that Q.*
3. Necessitation   (If *T* is a tautology or doxastic principle then *x believes that T*.)
4. Introspection   *If x believes that P then x believes that x believes that P.*
5. Modesty   *If a believes that (if a believes that P then P), then a believes that P.*

- *Type 1* reasoner-believers conform to 1 and 2.
- *Type 4* reasoner-believers conform to 1, 2, 3, and 4.
- *Type G* reasoner-believers conform to all five principles.

It also turns out that *type G* reasoner-believers include all the features of both *modest type 1* and *modest type 4*. We also note that there is no belief principle like VP. If there were it would be:

If **a** *believes that P, then P.*

It is the lack of this principle that distinguishes belief from knowledge.

Apart from being dazzled with the complexity of Smullyan's types of reasoner-believers, you might well ask, "What does this have to do with possible worlds?" One answer is that, particularly for *type 4* believers, we have partly dealt with this in the section about defensibility in epistemic logic in Chapter 6. But, you might ask, "What does immunity from criticism have to do with belief? After all, belief can be quite irrational and inconsistent."

The answer is that we are not dealing with an attempt to develop a logic that relates closely to human belief agency. In the case of epistemic logic, many criticisms of Hintikka's logic were based on everyday counter-examples to principles derived from indefensibility. These were met with responses about fully aware knowledge, being able to work things out, and other such points that relate to human beings. In the doxastic situation we are simply looking at the ramifications of definitions of ideal reasoner-believers. These reasoner-believers are varieties of rational believers, not believers with any old kind of belief. We are looking at the consequences of certain kinds of stipulations.

The most important outcome of these stipulations is the way in which Gödel's second incompleteness theorem applies to totally rational, modest, self-aware believer-reasoners and their systems or sets of beliefs.

It is often suggested in philosophy and in critical thinking that an enterprise worth pursuing in everyday life is making one's system of beliefs into a consistent system. It is suggested that we should consider our beliefs, find inconsistencies if they are there, sort them out, and develop a set of beliefs about which we can say, with confidence, "I have a consistent set of beliefs." In other words, we should be able to say "I do not believe contradictions." ("**not** $B_i \perp$"). It turns out that there is no *ideal* reasoner-believer who can, in the long run, come to this conclusion *from within their own belief sets or belief systems.*

This is not a matter of human failing. We are looking at ideals. This is a matter of logic, established by proof, and applying to extraordinarily rational believers. And we are talking about totally rational, self-aware believer-reasoners. So is the enterprise hopeless? Well, no. But ideal reasoner-believers will have to rely on *others* in the enterprise. They have to rely on scrutiny and assessment *from outside their belief system.* To quote the poet, they need to be able to see themselves as others see them. Others can tell if beliefs are consistent without falling into inconsistency themselves.

But these answers and animadversions don't really answer the question about possible worlds. We can come to these conclusions just by inspecting the principles of the G system. In effect, the principles of G are the axioms of G.[16] But axiom systems are not possible worlds semantic systems. So we must return to the question, "What does this have to do with possible worlds?"

7.4 Proof and possible worlds

There are some possible worlds reasons for adopting a *type 4* ideal for reasoner-believers. They are essentially Hintikka's possible worlds reasons for adopting a belief analogue of knowledge, and a disbelief analogue of ignorance. The question about possible worlds then becomes the question about why we might want to go beyond the *type 4* reasoner-believer to *type G*. This is discussed in the literature about the use of modal logics for the study of proof and unprovability, and proof systems for mathematics.

The discussion begins by taking "belief" in a G system to mean the same as "proved" or "provable", and disbelief as "unprovability". The reasoner-believer is a prover of some beliefs, and is unable to prove others. So the five principles above have to be transformed into principles about proving. For example:

- *Weak Necessitation* becomes: (If T is a tautology then *it's provable that T.*)
- *Distribution* becomes: It *it's provable that if P then Q, then if it's provable that P then it's provable that Q.*
- *Necessitation* becomes: (If T is a tautology or provability principle then *it's provable that T.*)
- *Introspection* becomes: If *it's provable that P then it's provable that it's provable that P.*

These seem to be acceptable for proof, particularly if the proof system is self-reflecting or "self-aware" in some formal sense. It is not so clear with *Modesty*. *Modesty* for proof becomes PM:

PM   *If it's provable that (if it's provable that P, then P), then it's provable that P.*

Before looking at the reasons for having Modesty, there is one more thing. It is about something missing. Where is VP? One would expect VP for proof to be there:

VPP   *If it's provable that P, then P.*

Surely if something can be proved then it will be so. But from a logical point of view it is not possible to have both Modesty for proof and VPP for proof. If both are there, then we have an inconsistent logical system. You might ask how that comes about. The explanation is quite simple. Note first that if Modesty for proof is really a principle then all sentences with that same form should be examples or instances of Modesty for proof. One of the complicated versions of Modesty for proof is where P is uniformly replaced by a contradiction such as (*q and not q*). Then we get:

PM1   *If it's provable that [if it's provable that (q and not q), then (q and not q)], then it's provable that (q and not q).*

Secondly, if we did have the VPP principle for proof then we would also have:

VPP1   *If it's provable that (q and not q), then (q and not q).*

We have also seen that, by Necessitation, we would have:

2   *It's provable that (if it's provable that (q and not q), then (q and not q)).*

PM1 and 2 together with *modus ponens* will give us the horrible conclusion that:

3   *It's provable that (q and not q).*

And 3 means inconsistency.

Rejection of VP does fit the notion of belief. So the question becomes a question about Modesty for belief. There is the intuitive problem of why, even after rejecting VP, we should have Modesty for either proof or reasoner-believers. Why not stay with an S4-style system, such as D4 or K4, for believers and believer-provers? Discussion of this question in the literature, as far as I can see, makes no use of possible worlds, as such, as the basis for making use of G, or GL, as it is called by Boolos.[17] One of the most important texts in this area is Boolos's *The Logic of Provability*. The main arguments in that text are based on making the axiomatic principles of GL match the notions of provability as expressed by Gödel in his work on mathematical systems.

The possible worlds semantics is brought in so that it can be shown, in a technical sense, that the logic of provability is a normal modal logic like S4. But this could be shown by axiomatic methods anyway. The appeal in the text is not to possible worlds, as it is in Hintikka's writing about knowledge, but to modal logic. Here we see the sharp contrast between possible worlds semantics for modal logic and modal logic itself. So if there were to be some other semantics for **GL**, such as algebraic semantics, then possible worlds could be left right out of the picture.

But there is also an indication in another place in Boolos's writings that any direct appeal to possible worlds might be very problematic. He writes:

We have written: $\Box p$ to abbreviate: $\exists x \text{Proof}(x, \lceil p \rceil)$, where $\lceil p \rceil$ is a standard representation in the language for the sentence p ... "Proof (x, y)" is a noun phrase (of our language) denoting a formula (of the theory's language) whose construction parallels any standard definition of "... is a proof of __ in the theory." Thus, for any sentence p of the language, $\Box\, p$ is another sentence of the language that may be regarded as saying that p is provable in the theory.[18]

In other words, $\Box\, p$ states that:

7.4.1.   There is a proof of p.

But the standard sense of $\Box\, p$ in possible worlds terms is that p is true in all accessible worlds. Where have all the possible worlds gone? Maybe we can give $\Box\, p$ a reading like:

7.4.2.   In every possible world there is a proof of p.

But where does that leave the diamond in $\Diamond\, p$? By reference to the definition:

$\Diamond\, p$ is defined as: *not* $\Box$ *not p*

we get, at a first approximation, that $\Diamond\, p$ for proof is

7.4.3.   In *not* every possible world is there a proof of *not p*.

and so to

7.4.4.   In at least one possible world there is *no* proof of *not p*.

On the other hand, 7.4.1 and the definition of diamond would just yield:

7.4.5.   There is *no* proof of *not p*.

Then, by the usual definitions of the interrelationship between the existential and universal quantifiers, does this give the following for $\Diamond\, p$?

7.4.6.   Every proof is of p.

That just seems very strange. Stranger still would be the result of applying the usual definitions of the interrelationship between the existential and universal quantifiers to 7.4.3 to get:

7.4.7.   In at least one world every proof is of p.

Possible worlds just get in the way. The usual readings of the box and diamond in GL are easier to cope with if we forget possible worlds and concentrate on proof. So we read $\Box\, p$ as "p is provable" and read $\Diamond\, p$ as "*not p* is *not* provable." The point is not that there is anything suspect about the modal logic of provability, but that possible worlds give nothing to the case except technical depth.

Furthermore, it is shown by Boolos that GL is not S5. It is, in some sense, weaker than S5. When the logical structure of proof is seen in terms of GL and the logical structure of logical possibility is best seen in terms of S5, then logical necessity and logical proof are not of the same logical structure. It then seems that not everything that is logically necessary will be provable. And that is the point that Gödel wanted to make.

7.5 Inconsistency and para-consistency

One major problem with belief logics based on classical logic is that they cannot cope with inconsistent belief, other than by simply rejecting it. We have seen how paradoxically problematic consistency is for reasoner-believers. These believers have belief sets that are *classical*. In Hintikka's terminology, when they do not believe that *p*, then their beliefs, if rational, have to be consistent with *not p*. Just as epistemic logic requires that knowledge has to be compatible with ignorance, in doxastic logic, on Hintikka's plan, belief has to be compatible with disbelief. But compatibility is *classical* compatibility. In that case, no one is allowed to have inconsistent beliefs. Classical logic is utterly intolerant of inconsistency, and is reduced to uncontrollable inferential idiocy in the presence of contradiction.

It is vital, therefore, that inconsistency-tolerant logics be investigated as a base on which doxastic logic can be built. Such non-classical logics are to be found in the family of *para-consistent* logics. These logics have been thoroughly investigated. Now is the time for us to acknowledge their application as a base for doxastic logic. We have no real space for a full account of para-consistent logic. We can only point out the area of investigation.

The problem that classical logic has with inconsistency can be exemplified by the classical theorems of the form:

EFQ   *If both P and not P, then Q.*

Such theorems are called *ex falso quodlibet* (whatever you wish follows from contradiction). So when a contradiction is deduced from a set of beliefs, it also follows, *ex falso*, that any proposition, including every possible contradiction, follows validly from that set of beliefs. There is no restriction of the consequences of inconsistency to related or relevant beliefs. So if we apply a classical inference engine to drawing conclusions from an inconsistent set of beliefs, a malignant inconsistency spreads across absolutely everything.

This does not, however, happen in real-life belief systems. Reasonable people isolate inconsistency, suspend judgement or follow other inconsistency handling procedures. Classical inference systems cannot deal so easily with the inconsistency of real-world belief systems. So when doxastic logics are built on a classical base they are equally unable to cope sensibly with inconsistency. One standard classical response has been to develop restricted doxastic logics by interpreting doxastic logics as logics for rational belief. But this interpretation begs a wide range of questions concerning rational and reasonable belief in favour of classical logical consistency. Not only is there no conceptual impossibility about declaring that someone has inconsistent beliefs, but it is by no means clear that everyone with logically inconsistent belief systems is irrational. There are at least three important concerns.

First, it is not clear that a necessary condition for a rational belief system is classical logical consistency. Secondly, it is not even clear that the attributions of rationality should depend on the logical structure of a system of beliefs. It can be argued that rationality should depend on the way in which an agent deals with contradictions when they are detected in a system of beliefs. Thirdly, there is a need to develop some taxonomy for inconsistency in belief systems. We might consider a taxonomy related to the *depth* of its occurrence. Some inconsistencies occur on the *surface* of belief systems. The most obvious are the *prima facie* contradictions of the form *"p and not p"*.

Because of the classical threat of global inconsistency there is a fairly standard, but not uncontroversial, expectation that a rational agent will resolve such contradictions. But in some contexts it might be better to leave such inconsistencies unresolved for the time being. In this case we need a logic that will at least quarantine the inconsistency. Para-consistent logics will do just this, since they lack *ex falso quodlibet* and its related theorems. Such logics will help us to deal with contradiction in a more rational fashion than indicated by classical logic. On the other hand, not all inconsistency is on the surface. Some inconsistencies are very deeply buried in belief systems. They often become apparent only after the malignancy has been widely spread, even to totally unrelated areas. If a logic lacks *ex falso quodlibet* it will give us an inference system that is inoculated against the spread of more deeply buried contradiction.

Much more work remains to be done on logical systems for belief. We will return to some further discussion of this question in Chapter 10.

7.6 Epistemic and doxastic predicate logic

We turn briefly to epistemic and doxastic predicate logic. There are two topics of interest: existential import and quantification into epistemic and doxastic contexts.

We have already seen that some of the problems of existential import can be avoided with free logic. It should be no surprise to discover that Hintikka's epistemic and doxastic predicate logics are free logics. In particular, consider the statement:

7.6.1.   *a believes that Holmes exists.*

This translates easily to:

7.6.2.   *a believes that* **(Some x)(x = h)**

Similarly:

7.6.3.   *Although Holmes does not exist, a believes that Holmes does exist.*

This translates easily to:

7.6.4.   **not (Some x)(x = h) and** *a believes that* **(Some x)(x = h)**

If we used standard predicate logic with existential import for quantifiers and individual constants, then the last translation would be contradictory simply because the left conjunct, **not (Some x)(x = h)**, is a contradiction. If we used standard predicate logic with existential import then 7.6.2 would attribute a trivial belief to *a* because the content of *a*'s belief would be a logical truth. Standard predicate logic with existential import is clearly quite out of court in both cases.

It is no wonder then that in Hintikka's epistemic and doxastic logics he uses free logic. In free logic, **not (Some x)(x = h)** is read as "h does not exist". It is particularly important for belief logic that at least the existential import of names be avoided; otherwise the logic prevents the representation of beliefs about nonexistent individuals and, in particular, beliefs that nonexistent individuals do exist and beliefs that existent individuals do not exist. In the context of belief it will not do to take a swipe at nonexistent individuals in the fashion of Plantinga: "How, exactly, does the question of nonexistent objects rear its ugly head?"[19] In belief logic, like it or no, there are nonexistent objects everywhere.

In an earlier discussion we resolved to do without existential import for both proper names and for quantifiers. We resolved to use existence as a "linguistic" predicate, and to leave open the status of the linguistic predicate as a real predicate in Kant's sense, or a property in McGinn's sense, or whatever. This resolve means that we can use the language and logic of predicate logic without the difficulties arising from existential import.

The translation of 7.6.1 is just:

7.6.5.   *a believes that* **Eh**

where **Ex** is for *x exists*. The translation of 7.6.3 is simply:

7.6.6. **not Eh and** *a believes that* **Eh**

We have covered these issues in Chapters 4 and 5.

We turn to the problem of quantifying into epistemic contexts. This problem is just a variation of the *de dicto–de re* problem, which we looked at in Chapter 4. The problem appears in its most acute form when we contrast the following two formulas:

7.6.7.   *a believes that* **(Some x) Fx**
7.6.8.   **(Some x)** *a believes that* **Fx**

Formula 7.6.7 is fairly easy to interpret. It is the *de dicto* formula. It simply says that:

7.6.9.   *a believes that at least one thing is* **F.**

Given that *believes that*, in doxastic logic, is an interpretation of *box*, formula 7.6.7 means that, in every doxastically accessible world for agent *a*, at least one item is **F.** Formula 7.6.7 is the doxastic analogue of:

7.6.7a. □ **(Some x)Fx**

But, what does 7.6.8. mean? It is the doxastic analogue of:

7.6.8a. **(Some x)** □ **Fx**

That was interpreted as stating that an item from the world in which 7.6.8a is true, say *world n*, is an item which is **F** in all worlds to which *world n* has access.

7.6.10. *There is at least one item of which a believes it to be* **F.**

By application of the same possible worlds interpretation, 7.6.8 states that an item from the world in which 7.6.8a is true, say *world n*, is an item which is **F** in all worlds to which *world n* has doxastic access for agent *a*.

There is an interesting *de re–de dicto* contrast in epistemic logic. Consider the following uncontroversial sentence from epistemic logic and its translation:

7.6.11. *a knows that* **(Some x) (x = h)**

In free logic this translates easily to:

7.6.11t. *a knows that* **h** *exists.*

But what is the sense of the *de re* sentence:

7.6.12. **(Some x)** *a knows that* **x = h**

If one uses a free logic where the quantifier has existential import, then, as a first move, the translation has to be something like:

7.6.12t. *At least one existing item is known by a to be* **h**.

It is easy to see that there are two things to be taken account of in 7.6.12. First, it does not follow from 7.6.12 that 7.6.11 (*a knows that* **h** *exists*). Secondly, it does follow from 7.6.12 that **h** *does exist*, even though 7.6.11 does not follow. So whatever the translation, we have to be careful not to say something that assumes that *a* knows something that is not plainly said. But what, then, does 7.6.12 say that *a* knows? Hintikka's answer is that:

7.6.13. *a knows who* **h** *is*.

This answer takes no account of the two points made above. Indeed, it as if the whole purpose of using free logic has been forgotten. My response[20] is that 7.6.11 says:

7.6.14. *At least one entity, known by a as* **h**, *exists*.

In case the words "as **h**" look too quotational for comfort, we can say:

7.6.14. *At least one entity, known by a to be* **h**, *exists*.

It seems to me that Hintikka casts his net both too wide and too narrowly with 7.6.13. Knowing who someone or something is does not require that they or it exists. One can sensibly answer the question "Who is Mr Micawber?" in the full knowledge that Mr Micawber does not exist. Further, it is not sufficient for knowing who someone is to know their name. It might help, but in most contexts one needs also to know some salient description to know who they are: "Mr Micawber is a friend of David Copperfield."

But, say we ring the changes and abandon free logic for standard quantifier logic, but with possibilist quantification over entities that could exist. What, then, are we to make of 7.6.12? Hintikka can just as well say again:

7.6.15 *a knows who* **h** *is*.

Similar points to those above can be made about knowing who. But there is one interesting thing to which Hintikka's persistent reading points: the notion of knowing a thing or knowing a person, in contrast to both knowing how and knowing that. Is there some way of integrating knowledge by acquaintance into epistemic logic?

My more literalist translation will be:

7.6.16. *At least one entity, known by a to be* h, *might exist.*

This translation could also point to the "*a* knows h" reading.

Appendix of formulas of doxastic logic

VP	$(K_x P \supset P)$
VPB	$(B_x P \supset P)$
Con.B	$(B_x P \supset \sim B_x \sim P)$
Dist	$(B_x (P \supset Q) \supset (B_x P \supset B_x Q))$
BB	$B_x P \supset B_x B_x P$
BBB	$B_x(B_x P \supset B_x B_x P)$
CB	$(B_x P \ \& \ B_x \sim P) \supset B_x \perp$
BCB	$B_x((B_x P \ \& \ B_x \sim P) \supset B_x \perp)$
MB	$B_a(B_a p \supset p) \supset B_a p$
BMB	$B_a(B_a (B_a p \supset p) \supset B_a p)$
EFQ	$((P \ \& \sim P) \supset Q)$
7.6.2.	$B_a(\exists x)(h = x)$
7.6.4.	$\sim (\exists x)(h = x) \ \& \ B_a(\exists x)(h = x)$
7.6.5.	$B_a Eh$
7.6.6.	$\sim Eh \ \& \ B_a Eh$

7.6.7.	$B_a(\exists x)Fx$	7.6.7a.	$\Box(\exists x)Fx$
7.6.8.	$(\exists x)B_a Fx$	7.6.8a.	$(\exists x)\Box Fx$

CHAPTER 8
Time and many possible worlds

8.1 Introduction

There is an interpretation of quantum physics that is known as the *many worlds interpretation*. The interpretation is not, by any means, a majority view, but it is much discussed, and is much beloved by authors of fiction, especially the authors of science fiction. In this chapter we will look at the many worlds interpretation from the perspective of possible worlds.

Our considerations will be much assisted if we begin by looking at time from a possible worlds perspective. There are logics for time that have been developed on the basis of standard modal logics with possible world semantics. These logics provide an interesting background for the discussion of the many worlds interpretation of quantum physics, as we shall see.

8.2 Possible worlds and time

States of the universe at any point in history can be seen as possible worlds. Such states are sometimes called "time-slices", but we will call them "instant states". The state of the universe at one particular instant state, say right *now*, could be seen as possible world n. World n is the possible world in which it is true that you are reading this book, the Earth is orbiting the Sun, and the Sun is in the Milky Way galaxy. The state at the next instant can be seen as possible world k, the next after that as possible world l. Earlier instant states are *before* the later instant states; later instant states are *after* the earlier ones. The accessibility connections between possible worlds can be seen as either time-lines from instant state to instant state, or causal connections, or just the temporal relations of *after* or *before*. If world *n* has *access* to world *k*, then *n* is *after k*. If *n* is *after k* and people in *n*, say us, can *see* into *k*, then in *n* we can "see back" into the past, or remember the past. So begins *modal temporal logic*.

Consider a sequence of possible worlds, as in Figure 8.1, where the possible worlds are instant states of the universe in a sequence of instants of time:

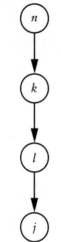

Figure 8.1

The accessibility arrows can be seen as pointing towards the future, with the flow of accessibility being the flow of time. Possible world *n* (now) might be the instant state of the universe at the present, *k* might be the instant state of the universe at the next instant of time, and so on into the future. We could extend the diagram with possible worlds before world *n*, and then we would represent instant states of the universe into the past. Of course, if *x* is after *y* then *y* is before *x*.

In modal temporal logic, the box and diamond are translated as follows:

$\lozenge p$ translates as   *At some instant in the future*: *p*

and $\square p$ translates as   *At all instants in the future*: *p*

Given *L* = *There is life on Earth*, we would translate:

1. $\lozenge$ **not** *L* as   *At some instant in the future there will be no life on Earth.*

2. $\lozenge\square$ **not** *L* as   *There will be some instant in the future such that at all instants later there will be no life on Earth.*

3.   (*L* **and** $\square$ *L*) as   *There now is and always will be life on Earth.*

There is an alternative, past tense, interpretation of the box and diamond. Then we have:

$\Diamond p$ translates as   *At some instant in the past*: *p*

and $\Box p$ translates as   *At all instants in the past*: *p*

In order to take advantage of both possibilities, it is usual to change the symbols for the future from $\Box$ to **G** and from $\Diamond$ to **F**. **G** is read as "It is always *going* to be the case that" and **F** is read as "At some instant in the *future* it will be the case that". For the past we replace the $\Box$ and $\Diamond$ with **H** and **P**. **H** is read as "It always *has* been the case that" and **P** is read as "At some instant in the *past* it has been the case that".

With these symbols the translations of 1–3 above are:

1s.   **F not** L

2s.   **FG not** L

3s.   (L **and G**L)

These symbols are not really the most important thing. They simply show us, at a very superficial level, how modal logic can be interpreted to translate some temporally qualified propositions. Given this facility, there are more important questions about the way the *logic* of time works.

There need to be, at least, some principles that allow the past, present and future to be related to each other in some logical fashion. Two principles have been suggested. They are:

4.   *If from some instant in the past it is always going to be the case that p, then p is the case now.*

5.   *If at some instant in the future it always had been the case that p, then p is the case now.*

These translate, respectively, to:

4s.   (**PG**p **imp** p)

5s.   (**FH**p **imp** p)

These principles do not give us a full logic for time. A full logic depends on how we understand the *sequence* of instant states. The immediate question for the modal logicians will be, "Which modal logic is the best for representing the sequence of instant states as sequences of possible worlds?" The answer will depend on what we think should be the structure of the sequence of time instants. The structure of the time sequence will depend on what is allowed and what is forbidden.

8.3 Lines, branches and loops

Consider the apparently simple structure where the sequence is strictly *linear*, as in Figure 8.2. The arrows point from past to future.

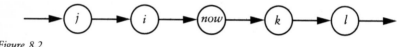

Figure 8.2

There are logics that require that the sequence be linear. One such system is CL (Cocchiarella's linear time). There is no need for us to go into the technical details of CL. CL is to be contrasted with logics for time that allow *branching time*. The branching picture is shown in Figure 8.3.

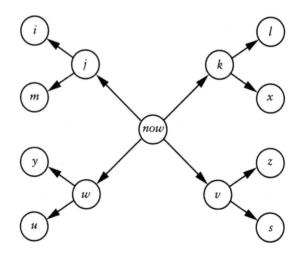

Figure 8.3

It is difficult to know just what the picture means, apart from the obvious fact the there are branchings from the *now* to both the past and future. One of the temporal modal logics that allows such branchings is known as CR (for Cocchiarella's relativistic causal time). CR *allows* for linear time, but does not *require* it, while CL does *not allow* branching but *requires* linear sequences of time instants. The technical details can be found in several places. The distinction between what is *allowed* and what is *required* by logics for time is a crucial distinction.

The CR logic allows for many things. Another intuitive picture of past, present and future, allowed by CR, is in Figure 8.4. For example, some people see the past as a fixed single line, or sequence, of instances up to the present. The future is full of possibilities. In Figure 8.4 the future is a set of branching possibilities. This is allowed by CR, but not CL.

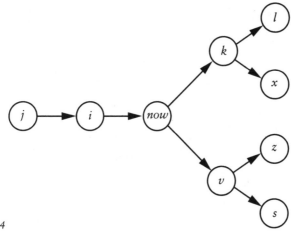

Figure 8.4

Once again, what do the branchings mean? Do they simply mean possibilities, or do they mean something stronger, whatever "stronger" might be?

There is something quite surprising that is also allowed in both CL and CR. It is looping time. The picture could be as in Figure 8.5.

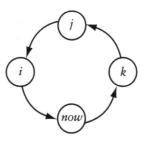

Figure 8.5

Figure 8.5 is a picture of *circular* time: *now is before k, k is before l, l is before m*, and *m is before now*. This circular time is non-ending and non-beginning. Circular time is not what we would have expected for non-ending and non-beginning time.

It is possible, within possible worlds semantics, to have semantic systems that are non-looping. Looping is just not allowed. We can have non-looping linear time with a logic known as asymmetric CL, or CLA. We can similarly have non-looping branching time with an asymmetric CR, or CRA. These systems are not held in great favour by the aficionados of formal modal logic. These *asymmetric* logics lack the formal property of completeness: they are incomplete. Some logicians think incompleteness is a fatal flaw, but that is another story that we will note, but not explore here.

Another possibility in CR is where the branches converge as in Figure 8.6. This is like Figure 8.3, but with convergence added. The arrows in some cases *converge*. The two sequences, *j, s, k,* and *j, n, k,* are convergent; as are *n, k, x* and *n, t, x*.

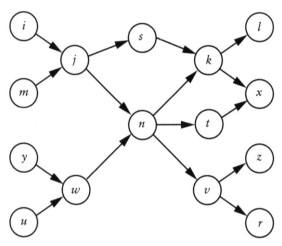

Figure 8.6

We have now set out the sorts of pictures of time painted by some relatively straightforward modal logics. There are more complex pictures required by some modal logics. We will turn to one complexity in §8.4. At this stage, we simply note two things about modal temporal logic. First, possible worlds represent states of the universe at particular instants. Secondly, the accessibility relation can be seen, in its simplest role, as representing nothing more than *before and after*. The before–after relationship involves either linear looping, linear non-looping, branching looping or branching non-looping, or a mixture of these.

8.4 The actual and the possible

We should also be careful in the use of possible worlds semantics. For example, we need to understand what a diagram like Figure 8.3 is supposed to tell us about the relationship between time and possibility. It is tempting to see the branches as "possibility" branches instead of seeing them as branches allowed by just one reading of "before and after". The diagram just tells us about a system of states that CR allows to be related by the before–after relation. The fact that CR allows such a system might be a good reason for declaring that the logic is not a suitable logic for time. We might argue that, in the world we live in, only one sequences of states correctly describes the past, and only one will describe the future. So we should accept only a logic with a linear accessibility (before–after) relation for time. Questions about what might have been the case, or what might be the case in the future, should be left to the logic of possibility. We should beware of diagrams leading us to confuse notions of temporality (instant state possibility) and logical possibility.

Some diagrams in temporal logic assign a special status to one sequence of instant states, the *actual* sequence: real history rather than possible history. For example, we might have a diagram such as Figure 8.7. The darker line of arrows in Figure 8.7 might mark out the *actual history* of the universe. T_1 is some time into the past from n, and T_2 is even further into the past. The other arrows can be taken as indicating, at least, instant states that were possible. Some philosophers might want to say that these states are also "real" states, but that the states that we remember, and of which we are and were conscious, are the ones linked by the dark arrows.

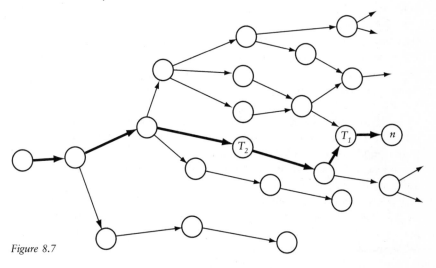

Figure 8.7

Now consider the same structure as in Figure 8.7, but with additional dark lines (Figure 8.8). Which is the "real" T_2? Should we just be able to raise questions by darkening lines in a diagram? We can, even if for purely speculative reasons. Does T_1 have several "real" pasts? These questions are quite strange. We will return to these strange questions in §8.6.

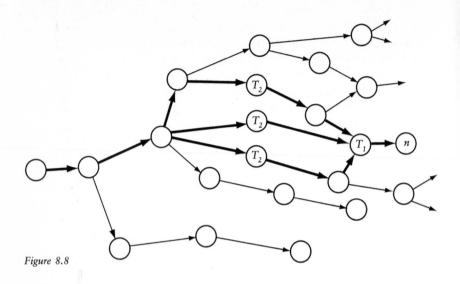

Figure 8.8

8.5 Past, present and future

Temporal modal logic has some versions that have interesting things to suggest about the relationship between any *now* and the instant states that are before and after it. The sequence of time instant states can be either *discrete* or *continuous*. One analogy for this distinction is that time can be granular like a sequence of grains of sand, or smooth as a silken cord. Granular time is discrete time. If time were granular then the universe would "skip" from instant state to instant state. The *now* would be a distinct instant state to which the universe had skipped, and from which it would skip when it moved on to the next instant state. If time were smooth as silk, continuous, then the universe would not skip from instant state to instant state. But something even more interesting is involved for continuous time.

We begin by looking at two simple facts about sequences of numbers in mathematics. First, we need to note that some mathematical sequences can have a first element or number and no last element or number. For example, the positive sequence of whole numbers starting with 1 has a first number, namely 1, but can go on for ever and never stop. No matter what number we might suggest as the last number, another number can be added by simply adding 1 to it. There is no last number. So the positive whole number sequence has a first element but no last element. Secondly, there is the converse. Some mathematical sequences can have a last element or number and no first element or number. For example, the sequence of negative whole numbers ending with −1 has a last number, namely −1, but has no negative beginning.

So some mathematical sequences have a first element but no last, and some have no first element but do have a last. We can represent these facts with the

Figure 8.9

two arrows in Figure 8.9 The first has a first and no last, the second has a last with no first. The arrow heads point in the direction of larger and larger numbers. There are other sequences as well, but we do not need to worry about them here.

From a mathematical point of view, the sequence of instant states can be seen as points on a line: a time line. Any such line can be "cut" into two sections. Such a cut can be represented by Figure 8.10. The arrow head in the centre points to the cut. The *now* can be seen as a cut that divides the past from the future.

Figure 8.10

Given the facts about mathematical sequences with or without firsts and lasts, there are four very interesting combinations of firsts and lasts at cuts:

(a) there is a first and a last at a cut[1]
(b) there is a last but no first at a cut
(c) there is no last but there is a first at a cut
(d) there is neither a last nor a first at a cut.[2]

These options can be represented diagrammatically (Fig. 8.11).

If a line is continuous, smooth as silk, then *every* cut is a (b) or (c) cut.[3] The present, the *now*, divides the past from the future. But in a continuous sequence of instant states, where, or what, is the present? It cannot be the first of the future if the cut is as in (b). If it was, then there would be no present, because there is no first of the future in (b). So, it would have to be the last of the past, if the cut is as in (b). It cannot be the last instant state of the past if the

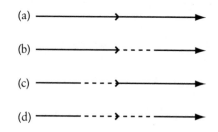

Figure 8.11

cut is as in (c). If it was, then there would be no present, because there is no last of the past in (c). So it would have to be the first of the future if the cut is as in (c).

Are the cuts as in (b) or as in (c)? Is the present the last of the past with no next instant state in the future, or is it the first of the future with no last instant state of the past? Whichever you opt for, it will apply to every now in the sequence of instant states.

If, on the one hand, we say that the future instant states of the universe are caused by the instant state of the universe right now, then there is a problem with the picture presented in (b). The "right now" is the last instant state of the past. There is no first instant state of the universe in the future for the present instant state of the universe to cause. So, given (b), the causal link between now and the future is quite mysterious.

If, on the other hand, we say that the present is caused by the immediate past instant state of the universe, then there is a problem with the picture presented by (c). The "right now" is the first instant state of the future. There is no last instant state of the past universe to cause the present instant state of the universe. So, given (b), the causal link between the past and right now is quite mysterious.

Which do you prefer to be mysterious: the causal link between now and the future or the causal link between the past and now? Or is there a deeper problem? These mysteries are a consequence of seeing the history of the universe as a continuous sequence of instant state possible worlds. We need not have this problem if we portray the history of the universe as a sequence of discrete instant state possible worlds. There is a temporal logic, known as GHli, where every cut is as in (a) above.[4] There is no mystery about causal links, except for the intuitive perception that each instant state of the universe seems to "stand alone". The question then becomes a question about how each instant state was generated by the previous instant state, and how matter and energy were transmitted to the next instant state.

It might well be suggested that we should abandon the sequence of instant states possible worlds approach to time and the universe. Perhaps it would be best to adopt the spaciotemporal worm approach, where the whole history of the universe is taken to exist in the form of the worm. There are no temporal instant states to worry about: the worm is just a "solid" entity. But it is not as easy as that. The same problems will arise when we consider the relationship between the parts of the worm.

The question above was what is the relationship between instant states of the universe in temporal sequence? With the worm we have the analogous question of what is the relationship between temporal cross-sections of the worm?

8.6 Many parallel worlds

In Squires's discussion of the many worlds interpretation of quantum physics, there is an interesting diagram.[5] The essence of that diagram is replicated in Figure 8.8 above. There is both branching and converging. But Squires points to a *realistic* interpretation of the diagram. That interpretation would claim that at T_2 there are three "real" streams of history.

The diagram indicates one way in which the many worlds interpretation of quantum physics has been taken by some writers. Although Squires's own view of the many worlds interpretation is more like "many views of one world",[6] others take up a realist interpretation. For example, in his science-fiction novel *The Time Ships: The Authorized Sequel to The Time Machine*,[7] Stephen Baxter puts the following words into the mouth of the narrator:

> At every moment, in every event (I summarized), History bifurcates. A Butterfly's shadow may fall *here* or *there*, the assassin's bullet may graze or pass on without harm, *or* lodge itself fatally in the heart of a King ... To each possible outcome of each event, there corresponds a fresh version of History. "And all of these Histories are *real*," I said, "and – if I understand it right – they lie side by side with each other, in some Fourth Dimension, like the pages of a book."[8]

No doubt there will be much demurral at this reading of the many worlds interpretation, but it has been advocated. It is highly compatible with the realist understanding of time, when time is represented by means of possible worlds for instant states as in Figure 8.8.

There are at least two things to note. The first concerns the relationships between the worlds in the many worlds interpretation. The second concerns the very representation of time in terms of lines and sequences of instants.

First, it is clear from the many worlds interpretation that each different world is actually generated from some world. The branching in Figure 8.8 shows the generation of each world, except the first on the left, from some other world or worlds. This means that the worlds are both physically possible, in terms of quantum theory, and physically interconnected. This is not the same as possible worlds that are related purely by logical possibility and logical necessity, and not by physical causation or some physical relationship describable by theoretical physics. We will see, in Chapter 10, that David Lewis requires that possible worlds have no causal or spatiotemporal relationship at all. They are utterly distinct. So, the possible worlds of David Lewis are not the many worlds of quantum theory.

The physical relationship between worlds in the many worlds interpretation is what prompts some people to believe that the worlds are all real, not just possibilities. If we look back to Figure 8.7, then we see that one could take the dark line to mark out the actual history of the world; the rest is all mere possibility, albeit physical possibility.

The second thing of interest is to indicate the way in which possible worlds semantics bears on the contrast between the presentist and tenseless accounts of time. I do not have the space to deal with this contrast in great detail but can point you in the direction of the debate. But we can look at a point made by Bigelow[9] about the way in which the line analogy has come to dominate the way in which people look at time. Bigelow claims that "Time travel stories . . . are essentially inconsistent." But the inconsistency is deeply buried by spatializing time: "Stories can be told that do *appear* to be *internally self-consistent*, provided that you set them within the context of a metaphysics that *spatializes* time, and that does this at a very deep level."[10] The general drift of Bigelow's argument is that if one pushes the idea of four-dimensional space-time to the point where one is taking the temporal dimension to be of a kind with the three spatial dimensions, then one is likely to have an account of time that is misleading, and open to the generation of inconsistencies.

In the same paper, Bigelow argues that one of the ways in which Lewis and others support their arguments is by a misreading of quantifiers. He says:

> It turns out that, when you describe the continuity of time, in exact mathematical parallel with the continuity of space, you find yourself using the existential quantifier "there are . . ." and saying that *there are* past, present, and future things which stand in a certain important relation to one another. So you are asserting the *existence* of things which are not present.[11]

Since Bigelow holds that the quantifiers have existential import, and says so quite strongly in this paper,[12] the "there are . . ." cannot be read by him in any other way.

So if one takes the tenseless account of the spatiotemporal world with strong existential import, that is the spatiotemporal worm account, then one has an account of the world that is essentially like Parmenides' account of a changeless existent world that only appears to change. Parmenides called it the "motionless continuous plenum". He also thought it to be finite, but if it is allowed to extend infinitely in either the temporal and/or spatial dimension, then we have the infinite Parmenidian worm. The world is a four-dimensional plenum, and it does not and cannot change. It *appears to change* because we can be conscious of only a succession of time slices. Change, from the perspective of the Parmenidian worm, is essentially epistemic or psychological.

8.7 Time and necessity

Temporal modal logic is of importance in considering issues to do with causality, freedom, determinism and necessity. For example, the picture in Figure 8.4 depicts the idea of the past as fixed and the future as full of possibility. Diodorus of Megara is often said to have maintained that both necessity and possibility are definable in terms of time. There is much argument about what Diodorus was actually supposed to have said, and I have no space to enter into exegetical arguments, so we will look at the following two theses as of interest in their own right:

1. All true past tensed propositions are necessarily true.
2. Propositions which are or will be true are possibly true propositions.

The first thesis picks up on the intuition that the past *cannot* be altered. Prior gives the interpretation, "Whatever has been the case cannot now not have been the case."[13] This gives us:

1′.   (P p imp $\Box$ P p)

or

1″.   (P p imp not $\Diamond$ not P p)

The second thesis "cashes in" the idea that if something is not now true and never will be, then it's not possible for it to be true.

2′.   ((not p and not F p) imp not $\Diamond$ p)

or

2″.   ($\Diamond$ p imp (p or F p))

The last of these is highly compatible with possible world semantics where the truth of $\Diamond$ p in a world entails that p is true in some world, either the same one or one to which there is access. Possible worlds semantics can assist in discussing these notions.

8.8 Time and computation

We turn for a moment to an area where possible worlds have, in some sense been used, and then bypassed. Temporal logic has been applied in areas where considerations of temporal sequences are of importance. Planning and project management are common areas of application. For example, in the building of a large inner-city tower block it is crucial that some tasks are completed before others are begun. The available storage spaces will be limited. Some materials will have to be delivered and used before others are delivered. Some materials, such as concrete, can be delivered and used immediately, so there is no need for storage space to be available. The complexities of these sequences of events in the construction schedule, and their relationship to storage and use, can be worked out by computers that reason about sequences of events over time.

Temporal logic, it might seem, is a "natural" for providing a logic for reasoning about sequences of events in project management, building schedules and all sorts of sequential arrangements. But it has turned out that modal temporal logic is not the best logic for computation in this kind of practical world. The instant-oriented logic of possible worlds is too complex.

The instant and state-of-the-universe approach is not the only way to approach temporal reasoning. An important alternative is the "time interval" approach.[14] It is probably true to say that, in the applications of temporal logic, the time interval approach has become quite dominant.

If we reflect on the processes that have to be managed in any project, then we will notice that they all occupy periods or intervals of time. The important features of interval based reasoning is that we need to know the basic relationships between intervals. It turns out that there are just 13. Before and after are just two of the relationships. There is totally before, totally after, overlapping, inclusion, starting together, finishing together, identity, abutting and so on. The basic relationships are crucial, not whether time is linear, branching or looping.

Of course, someone might well advocate the treating of intervals as "extended" possible worlds or sets of instants. But converting intervals into sets of instants is a complex and computationally wasteful process.

While a great deal of the work in temporal representation and reasoning began with modal temporal logic, the work has moved on. In this area, the possible worlds account of time has not driven artificial intelligence and software applications.

CHAPTER 9
Real possibility

9.1 Introduction

If possibilities are real, what follows? Lots of things. But, if we use possible worlds to explain the nature of possibility, does the reality of possibilities mean that possible worlds must be real?

Some argue for a "yes" answer. Famously, David Lewis was the chief of those in the twentieth century arguing for a "yes" answer.[1] Perforce, we will spend a great deal of time in this chapter considering Lewis's ideas, but not in the detail they deserve. Lewis takes the possible *worlds* account of possibility and necessity, and some other modal notions such as ought, with utmost seriousness. An analogy has been drawn between his approach to possible worlds and Gallileo's ideas about the heliocentric solar system.

At the time of Gallileo there were two astronomical pictures of the solar system: Gallileo's picture and Ptolemy's picture. Ptolemy's picture had the Earth at the centre of the solar system, and everything orbited about the Earth. The vast majority of astronomers accepted the Ptolemaic account. The Ptolemaic picture was more in accord with everyday intuition, common sense and observation. There is an excellent picture-book account of Ptolemy's account that shows how closely it follows observation.[2] It was not a "silly" account.

Gallileo's picture, by contrast, had the Sun at the centre of the solar system, and the planets, including Earth, orbited the Sun. His motto was, "The earth moves". This solar-centric account is quite contrary to everyday, and every night, common-sense observation. Gallileo based his solar-centric picture of the solar system on the fact that the picture gave the simplest and most elegant and most serviceable explanation of the movements of the planets. The mathematics of the solar-centric picture were simpler than the mathematics of the system which put the Earth at the centre of the solar system. The Ptolemaic picture was not just a little less elegant than the solar-centric from a mathematical point of view. It was very complex, very inelegant and, in some respects, quite *ad hoc* from a mathematical point of view. After Gallileo publicly supported the view that the Sun was at the centre of the solar system, and the planets orbited around the Sun, he was urged to assert that the picture was just a mathematical convenience, merely serviceable. He was urged to treat his picture as an *ersatz* system, a virtual system. The Earth did not *really* move. The Earth was really at the centre of the universe.

When Gallileo was eventually forced by the Catholic Church to recant, it is said that after he had said the words of recanting, he stamped softly on the ground and whispered, "It does move anyway."

Lewis is with Gallileo. He wants us to treat the possible worlds explanation of possibility with deadly seriousness. Although Lewis appeals to serviceability, we should not forget that the pressure on Galileo was to accept the serviceabilty of the solar-centric view without accepting its realism. So we cut to the main argument. Lewis says: "If we want the theoretical benefits that talk of possibilia brings, the most straightforward way to gain honest title to them is to accept such talk as the literal truth."[3] This is Galileo's way. This is not instrumental, not merely serviceable: it is fact. Furthermore, the idea works, and that is not a minor thing.

> Why believe in a plurality of worlds? – Because the hypothesis is serviceable, and that is a reason to think that it's true. The familiar analysis of necessity as truth at all possible worlds was only the beginning. In the last two decades, philosophers have offered a great many more analyses that make reference to possible worlds, or to possible individuals that inhabit possible worlds. I find that record most impressive. I think that it is clear that talk of *possibilia* has clarified questions in many parts of the philosophy of logic, of mind, of language, and of science – not to mention metaphysics itself.[4]

"They exist." In his work he considers several accounts that treat the possible worlds accounts as epistemic or logical or linguistic conveniences, and calls them "ersatz" accounts. So the line is drawn in the sand.[5] Where are we to stand? On Lewis's side or not? Or should we leave the beach without a firm view?

9.2 Conditionals again

One way of seeing how Lewis might have come to have his view would be to start with conditionals. I am not offering any speculations or arguments for

Lewis's having actually done this. That's a matter for those who want to write an intellectual biography of Lewis.[6] All I want to do is show how one might go along this path and finish up at a lookout point with Lewis's view across a rich landscape of possible worlds.

Conditionals have been at the centre of the development of modal logic and the possible worlds accounts of modality from the late nineteenth century. Some even argue that there are prefigurings of this in ancient philosophical logic.

Say we reject the material conditional account of conditionals and want to give some other account of conditionals. One kind of conditional that is very problematic from the point of view of the material conditional is the counterfactual or "contrary to fact" conditional. A counterfactual conditional is a conditional with a known (or believed) to be false antecedent. If the material conditional account applies to counterfactuals then, since a material conditional is true when the antecedent is false, all counterfactuals are true (or should be believed so). So on a material conditional account, it will be true that if Hitler had invaded England then his army would have reached London in five days, and it will also be true that if Hitler had invaded England then his army would not have reached London in five days. But the claim that both counterfactuals are true just does not seem to be correct.[7]

The problem with counterfactuals is a problem about what would make one true and another false. When we begin to look closely at counterfactuals we turn up modality. We see "might", "must", "would definitely" and other such phrases. Possibility is lurking in the wings. For example:

9.2.1.   *If Auckland were the capital city of New Zealand, then it might have a good suburban electric train system.*[8]

9.2.2.   *If Auckland were the capital city of New Zealand, then it would definitely have a good suburban electric train system.*

Sentence 9.2.1 makes claims about what *might* follow from Auckland's being the capital city, while 9.2.2 makes claims about what *must* follow. We can predict that a possible worlds account of 9.2.1 will involve *at least one* possible world because of the "might", and a possible worlds account of 9.2.2 will involve *all* possible worlds of some sort because of the "would definitely".

And that is how it turns out for Lewis. One way of deciding on the truth of 9.2.1 would be to consider *at least one possible world* in which Auckland is the capital city of New Zealand, and to ask whether it is also true *in that world* that Auckland has a suburban electric train system.

One might argue that, since the parliament of a nation is usually in the capital city, the politicians have to spend their time there. Politicians make sure that facilities are good where they spend their time, and they would spend money on a good suburban electric train system. So 9.2.1 is arguably true, because of what is true in some possible world in which there are nations, capital cities, parliaments and politicians just like there are in the actual world.

The falsehood of 9.2.1 would require that every possible world like ours – worlds with nations, capital cities, parliaments and politicians – would be a world in which it does not follow from Auckland's being the capital city of New Zealand that Auckland has a good suburban electric train system.

In the case of 9.2.2 one might argue that in all possible worlds like ours – worlds with nations, capital cities, parliaments and politicians like ours – it would be inevitable that politicians would spend money on a good suburban electric train system in the capital city. The falsehood of 9.2.2 might be argued for by asserting that there would be at least one possible world – like ours as far as nations, capital cities, parliaments and politicians are concerned – in which Auckland was the capital city of New Zealand, and in which there are no electric trains at all. One might point to the capital of Australia, Canberra, as a like case where the capital city does not have any suburban train system at all. In such a world the antecedent of 9.2.2 would be true, but the consequent false, and so 9.2.2 is false because it makes claims about *all possible worlds* in which Auckland is the capital city of New Zealand.

9.3 Existent possible worlds

Let us stand back from the discussion of whether either of 9.2.1 and 9.2.2 is true, and consider how the question of truth is being settled. Possible worlds, and the similarity of one world to another, are the basis for settlement.

At this point it is also important to make two additional points to keep the record straight. First, what I have sketched above is not the detail of Lewis's possible worlds semantics for counterfactuals. His possible worlds semantics for counterfactuals is more complex. Nevertheless, the key ideas are possible worlds and similarity of worlds. Second, it should be noted that the same sort of approach was set out in Robert Stalnaker's "Theory of Conditionals", which was published earlier than Lewis's *Counterfactuals*. Stalnaker's approach is less complex than Lewis's, and sets out a strikingly elegant theory. Lewis shows that Stalnaker's theory is a special case[9] or restricted form of his own. The general approach of both Lewis and Stalnaker has been referred to as "The Classic Stalnaker–Lewis Theory of Conditionals".[10] Stalnaker does not come to the same conclusion as Lewis about the ontological status of possible worlds, even though the formalities of Stalnaker's theory are a special case of Lewis's more complex theory. This bears out Lewis's point that the question of ontological status does not depend on logic, but on metaphysics.

Now, back to the main line of consideration. After Lewis presents his similar possible worlds analysis in *Counterfactuals*, he says, "It is time to face the fact that my analysis rests on suspect foundations."[11] His response to his own rhetorical assertion is this:

I believe that there are possible worlds other than the one we happen to inhabit. If an argument is wanted, it is this. I believe, and so do you, that things could have been different in countless ways. But what does this mean? Ordinary language permits the paraphrase: there are many ways things could have been besides the way they actually are. *On the face of it, this sentence is an existential quantification* [my italics]. It says that there exist many entities of a certain description, to wit "ways things could have been." I believe that things could have been different in countless ways; I believe permissible paraphrases of what I believe; taking the paraphrase at its face value, I therefore believe in the existence of entities that might be called "ways things could have been". I prefer to call them "possible worlds".[12]

The italicized sentence above and the one that immediately follows it show just how the assumption of the existential import of quantifiers is deeply ingrained in the tradition to which Lewis adheres. He simply assumes that ordinary language quantifiers have existential import. The assumed existential import carries straight over into his metaphysical assertions. He is cautious about carrying quantification across into analysis. "I do not make it an inviolable principle to take the seeming existential quantifications in ordinary language at their face value." He is determined to hold to the principle unless "(1) taking them at face value is known to lead to trouble, and (2) taking them some other way is known not to."[13] But like so many twentieth-century philosophers, he does not address the assumption of existential import. So the argument is to be that possible worlds exist because, in this case, he does accept the ordinary language quantified assertion that there are possibilities, and, since the quantifier is assumed to carry existential import, possibilities exist. If they exist they are real. So we get modal realism.

There is a subsidiary claim. "If our modal idioms are not quantifiers over possible worlds, what else are they?" This rhetorical question gets its considerable force from existential import. So "It is possible for Auckland to be the capital city of New Zealand" is to be taken as "In at least one *existing* possible world Auckland is the capital city of New Zealand." If existential import is abandoned for quantification, then the latter becomes something weaker: "In at least one possible world Auckland is the capital city of New Zealand."

What is a possible world if it is *not* an *existing possible* world? Indeed, what is a possible world if it *is* an existing possible world? Lewis addresses both questions, but he begins with the claim that only *existent* possible worlds can give a proper account of possibility.

We have already discussed existential import in Chapter 4. I have argued that the doctrine of existential import for quantifiers is deeply flawed. The flaws show up no more clearly than in modal predicate logic. If it is assumed in modal predicate logic, then we render the logic useless for just those things for which one would expect the logic to be useful. We question the content of the intuitive and common-sense basis to which Lewis appeals for modal realism.

But there is more. Lewis also appeals to quantification with both existential and *possibility* import. Not only does the existential quantifier have existential import, but it must be read so that 9.3.1 translates to 9.3.1t:

9.3.1 **(Some x) Fx**
9.3.1t. *Some possible entity is F (and it exists).*

For the purpose of the possible world semantics and "possibly *p*" we would get:

9.3.2 **(Some x) (Wx and p is true in x)**
9.3.2t. *Some existent possible entity is a world and in it p is true.*

This is to doubly beg the question of the explanatory power of utilizing quantifiers over a domain of possible and existent entities for an account of real possibility in terms of possible and existent worlds.

It could be argued that I am labouring the point about possibility import and existential import: if something exists, then it has to be possible. So if there are existent worlds, then they must be possible worlds. That is, existential import brings possibility import with it, free of charge. Not everyone will agree, especially those of a dialethic persuasion. They may well argue that existent worlds in which there is change are worlds in which some propositions are both true and false. Worlds in which there are propositions that are both true and false are impossible worlds. So on the dialethic doctrine, worlds in which objects exist and change are existent impossible worlds.

We set aside the dialethic impossible worlds for the moment, and return to them in Chapter 10. We note that Lewis utterly rejects impossible worlds.[14] For the moment we will discuss existential import and possibility import on the basis that the former entails the latter. Nonetheless, the latter does not entail the former, and Lewis is assuming not only possible worlds, but existent possible worlds.

McGinn is opposed to both these assumptions. His criticism begins with the preliminary point that possible worlds semantics and metaphysics treat the terms "possibly" and "necessarily" as logical operators on sentences. The literature is filled with the technical expressions "*Possibly p*" and "*Necessarily p*" where *p* is a proposition expressing sentence. He then makes his main point:

> We take what looks superficially like an operator and interpret it by means of an existential or universal quantifier over "worlds" – however exactly those entities are to be construed. But the objection I want to make to this is that such a translation is either circular or inadequate; specifically, we need to use the modal

notion being translated in order to get the translation to come out right.[15]

Above all, the quantifiers have possibility import.

> So let us consider some proposition of the form "possibly *p*": this is meant to go over into "there is a world in which *p*" or "for some world *w*, *p* in *w*". Now the question I want to ask is: does the notion of "world" here invoked include or exclude *impossible* worlds? Suppose it includes them. Then "possibly *p*" will be true if "*p*" holds in an impossible world.[16]

If this is so, disaster follows. Necessarily false propositions will be possibly true because they are true (as well as false) in impossible worlds. This will not do at all if we are to get the sorts of accounts of modal logic and of metaphysics given in possible worlds semantics, accounts standardly given in Lewis and all over the place. But the quantifier is being restricted to possible worlds in most accounts, and restricted further in Lewis to existent possible worlds. What, then, is the basis of the restriction? It is based on prior notions of possibility and existence.

One response that Lewis might make here is the "matter of fact" response: there just are these worlds, like it or no. And we can, indeed we must, use them to solve the problems. This response becomes dogma unless we can be given an account of how this is known. And appeal cannot be made to either the usefulness of quantifiers or the volume of philosophical writing. Even if we agree with the point that we know that things *might* have turned out differently, we are presupposing possibility.

If McGinn is anywhere near correct, then we have to reconsider the metaphysical arguments for interpreting possible world systems of logic in a modal realist way. But McGinn (and I) are pushing against a huge weight of orthodoxy.

The state of the dialectic here is that we can argue against basing the interpretation of possible worlds semantics in a realist way on the doctrine that quantifiers have existential import. If that argument succeeds, then one cannot just dismiss possible worlds logic. There are alternative interpretations. There are alternatives that are not hostile to possible worlds, but that account for possible worlds in a way that is not realist. We look at those below. If the anti-basis argument fails, we can look at some of the "internal" problems of the realist view. We do that in §9.4.

9.4 What world is that?

There are at least three major problems with Lewis's real worlds: cross-world identification, actuality and identity of worlds.

Trans-world non-identity

The first problem is a problem about the relationship between the items *in* one world and items *in* another. In particular, when we say that *Auckland* might have been the capital city of New Zealand, Lewis's story is not that the Auckland of this actual world could be different in some way, a way explicated by a possible world, but that some other city called "Auckland" in another possible world is the capital city of New Zealand. There is, in that world, a *counterpart* of Auckland. That counterpart city in that other world is just like Auckland in every respect except for those respects in virtue of which it is capital city there and not a capital city here. But it is a different city because it is not the actual city of Auckland.

There is, according to Lewis, no overlap.[17] The worlds:

> are isolated; there are no spatio-temporal relations at all between things that belong to different worlds. Nor does anything that happens at one world cause anything to happen at another. Nor do they overlap; they have no parts in common . . .[18]

This counterpart doctrine makes sense only if one accepts that there are many possible worlds, each of which exists as a fully fledged reality, independent of the others, and with its own independent contents. The contents of each world will be real, but, unlike the world in which we live, they will not be *actual* like the contents of this *actual world* in which we live. There is a sense in which the existential reality of each possible world requires the counterpart doctrine.

The distinctness of worlds raises the question of the meaning and force of the idea that people and things *in* the actual world "could have been different". A great deal rides on this issue for Kripke. Given his view that names are rigid designators, they designate exactly the same entity across all worlds, then he has a complaint about the distinctness of worlds which is that if when:

> we say "Humphrey might have won the election (if only he had done such-and-such)" we are not talking about something that might have happened to *Humphrey*, but to someone else, a "counterpart". Probably however, Humphrey could not care less whether someone *else*, no matter how much resembling him, would have been victorious in another possible world.[19]

Lewis's response is to say that although we should respect Humphrey's intuition that "it is *he himself* who would have been victorious in another [possible] world," it is nevertheless the case that "we are in equal agreement that Humphrey – he himself – is not part of these other worlds."[20] But we are not in equal agreement. It is quite important to be clear about how we understand the "he himself" before we concede agreement, and that's where the different readings get their bite.

Read writes in similar vein to Kripke:

> If we wonder what would have happened if Edmund had been brave, we are wondering what would have happened if our Edmund, the real Edmund, had been brave, not some mere counterpart of him.[21]

In Lewis's own terms, the "real Edmund" in Read is the *actual* Edmund. And most would, at first sight, agree with Read. It's the Edmund of this world who we wonder about. But Lewis would have it otherwise. Accepting that Lewis is, in Read's terms, a Platonist, then his account of what might be comes out like this:

> It is certainly a natural concomitant of Platonism, and supported by argument, to reject the idea that Edmund might inhabit different worlds. If each world has concrete reality, then Edmund cannot be in two worlds at once. When we wonder what Edmund would be like if he were brave, we are thinking about someone very like Edmund – or as much like him as anyone could be – who was brave.[22]

This is a contrast exactly like the contrast we considered in Chapter 4: the contrast between taking the modal operator in *It is possible that e is B* as operating on the whole of *e is B* or operating on *B*. We can take *e* as primary, and then work out what is true in each possible world of the *e* from the actual world, or we can take the operator as primary and see what, in each world, is true of the entity called "*e*" in that world. Lewis is opting for the latter. In Lewis's possible world system, the domain of items is utterly distinct from world to world. But that clashes with our intuitions in the case of Edmund.

Consider the counterfactual conditional:

> *If Edmund had been brave, then the Queen's scheme would have failed.*

If Edmund is actually not brave, then we are interested in what would follow in the world or worlds where it is true that Edmund is brave, contrary to fact. Read's demand is that *Edmund himself* be in both the actual world, in which he is not brave, and in the world where he is brave. The domains of both worlds have to have Edmund (and the Queen) in common. Then we see the ways in which Edmund might have been brave. There are formal systems that accept this demand. So, as Lewis points out, logic will not help. It will just do what we demand. We have to resort to metaphysical accounts of what is *in* possible worlds.

It is important to realize that, even if the existential reality of possible worlds was abandoned, the counterpart approach could still be sustained. But most of the powerful arguments for separate worlds and counterparts from world to world would have vanished.

The second problem is the problem of actuality. But one world is privileged. Lewis gives the possible world in which we live the status of being *actual*, whereas the other real (existent) possible worlds are not actual.

> Ours is the actual world; the rest are not actual. Why so? – I take it to be a trivial matter of meaning. I use the word "actual" to mean the same as "this-worldly". When I use it, it applies to my world and my worldmates; to this world we are part of, and to all parts of this world.[23]

So other possible worlds are non-actual possibles or unactualized possibles. The actual world is possible, existent and actual. What is the distinction between existent and actual? Just that *we* are *in* the actual world, that's all.

But these things are never so simple. Bricker writes:

> According to David Lewis's brand of realism about possible worlds, actuality is "indexical" and relational: the actual world is *this* world, the world we inhabit; to be actual is to be appropriately related to *us*. And that is all. *Being actual* confers no special ontological status; our world and the other possible worlds do not differ in ontological kind. The difference, so to speak, is that we are here and not there.
>
> The alternative for the realist is to hold that actuality is absolute, that there is an ontological distinction of kind between the actual and the merely possible. In my opinion, this is the only viable option for the realist. Our conceptual scheme demands that actuality be *categorical*: whatever is of the same ontological kind as something actual is itself actual. To hold then, as Lewis does, that the actual world and the merely possible worlds do not differ in kind is incoherent.[24]

Strong words, indeed. But if Bricker is correct the question of what it means to say that possible worlds exist becomes problematic. Other possible worlds exist in the sense that our world exists, but there is actual existence and existence that is not actual. This begins to look very strange. Bricker's only option for the realist is beginning to look like the beginnings of a *reductio ad absurdum*.

The third problem is the problem of world identity. How do we tell what world is what? It might seem right, at first, to say that there are existent possible worlds, but how do we distinguish one from the other and, even more importantly, decide whether the world of which you speak is the same as the one of which I speak? There are two sides to this problem: the question of distinguishing one world from another; and the question of being able to say when my assertions about one part of a world are assertions about the same world about which you are talking when your assertions are about a remote part of the (allegedly) same world. Some philosophers have raised one or other of two questions about real possible worlds: a question about the internal nature of worlds, especially the nature of their unity; and a question about the distinctness of one world from another. Lewis argues that spatiotemporal relations tell the whole story:

> things are worldmates iff they are spatiotemporally related. A world is unified, then, by the spatiotemporal interrelation of its parts. There are no spatiotemporal relations across the boundary between one world and another; no matter how we draw boundary within a world, there will be spatiotemporal relations across it.[25]

This passage, and others like it, have been like a red rag to a bull. Philosophers, as is their wont, have set about inventing counter-examples to both the internal unity and world-to-world differentiation in Lewis's realism. This question was mentioned in Chapter 1 when we discussed the worlds or universes of *Sliders*. If we say that each of the universes of *Sliders* are distinct possible worlds, then, because there can be traffic between universes, and things in or from one universe can cause things to happen in the other, there is not complete spatiotemporal and causal separation between possible worlds. This is not Lewis's view.

The first basic question is a query about what kind of spatiotemporal theories Lewis wants to use. An immediate answer must be spatiotemporality of the best science, especially physics. Even here there will be problems. Someone might then ask about the possibility of a Newtonian possible world. Someone else will ask about a possible world that conforms to the science of 10,000CE rather than that of 2002CE.[26] In fact, Lewis does spend some time discussing the possibility of Newtonian possible worlds.[27] He shifts slightly to declare that:

> What I need to say is that each world is interrelated . . . by a system of relations which, if they are not the spatiotemporal relations rightly so called, are at any rate analogous to them. Then my task is to spell out the analogy.[28]

Maybe the term "interrelated" should have been "intrarelated". Anyway, the picture is fairly clear, and Lewis does go on to spell out the conditions for viable analogy. But it does mean that possible worlds that contain entities that are not interrelated spatiotemporally are either impossible worlds or counter-examples. The standard counter-example in the literature is where a world consists of "island universes".

Bricker argues that a world might consist of the usual spatiotemporal universe together with isolated duplicates of individuals in the universe. Each duplicate and the spatiotemporal whole are islands. He argues for the principle:[29]

(PS)   *Principle of Solitude.* For any world-bound individual, possibly, a duplicate of that individual exists all by itself.

He takes the example of where God

> is not pleased with everything he sees. Perhaps only one thing pleases him – say, Leibniz. Then, according to the principle of solitude, God could choose to actualize Leibniz, and nothing else.[30]

The argument is interesting, even if the case is cruel beyond belief.

What does become clear is that Lewis, to avoid these cases, will have to restrict the quantificational account of possibility not only to existent worlds, but to physically possible worlds of some kind. Curiouser and curiouser.

The question of the distinctness of worlds is one that Lewis is explicitly and disarmingly agnostic about. There may be indiscernible worlds, or maybe not.

> The problem of indiscernible possible worlds is the harmless part. My modal realism does not say whether or not there are indiscernible worlds; and I can think of no very weighty reason in favour of one answer or the other.[31]

Bricker has much more to say about this, but it's in order to deny the indiscernibility of worlds.

9.5 An epistemic alternative

There is no lack of alternative accounts of what the *ways* are of "the ways things might have been different". Alternatives to Lewis's existent possible worlds are to be found in either epistemic, linguistic or abstract entities. And there are many others as well. Read uses the contrast between three sorts of approaches: the rejectionism of Quine, the Platonism of Lewis and actualism. For Quine, he says, "the theory of modalities becomes a questionable theory, ultimately to be dismissed by his arguments against analyticity and meaning".[32] Read rejects Platonism (Lewis's realism) and asks whether there is not some "sensible middle ground" between Lewis and Quine:

> There is, and it constitutes some form of actualism, sharply distinguishing the actual world from the range of possible worlds. There are two main forms of actualism: reductionism, itself having many variants, which seeks to construct possible worlds out of some more mundane and familiar materials; and moderate realism, in which the actual concrete world is contrasted with abstract, but none the less real, possible worlds.[33]

We will begin with one of the reductionist alternatives, the one where possible worlds are reduced to sets of beliefs or epistemic states, and their dynamics. This is highly compatible with Hintikka's view. But we turn to the work of Gärdenfors.[34]

There are many accounts of conditionals that begin with the Ramsey test.[35] This test provides an intuitively plausible starting point for theories of conditionals. The test is described by Gärdenfors:

> His test can be described as follows: In order to find out whether a conditional sentence is acceptable in a given state of belief, one first adds the antecedent of the conditional hypothetically to the given stock of beliefs. Second, if the antecedent together with the formerly accepted sentences leads to a contradiction, then one makes adjustments, which are as small as possible without modifying the hypothetical belief in the antecedent, such that consistency is maintained. Finally, one considers whether or not the consequent of the conditional is then accepted in this adjusted set of belief.[36]

Stalnaker[37] begins with the Ramsey test after rejecting both the material conditional account of conditionals, especially counterfactual conditionals, and accounts based on the idea that a true conditional should have a consequent relevant to the antecedent. He then goes on to develop an account based on possible worlds, but not the realist worlds of Lewis. Stalnaker approves of Ramsey's starting point in belief, but wants to "move on".

> Now that we have found an answer to the question, "How do we decide whether or not we believe a conditional statement?" the problem is to make the transition from belief conditions to truth conditions; that is, to find a set of truth conditions for statements

having conditional form which explains why we use the method we do use to evaluate them. The concept of a *possible world* is just what we need to make this transition, since a possible world is the analogue of a stock of hypothetical beliefs.[38]

Stalnaker uses the notation $(A > C)$ for the conditional *If A then C*, and so distinguishes his account from the material conditional represented by $(A \supset C)$.

But why move on? Why not develop the Ramsey test from within some sort of account of belief and belief change? Belief revision theory provides just such an account of both ordinary and counterfactual conditionals. And because of logical links between conditionals and possibility, an account of possibility is to be found in belief revision theory.

Peter Gärdenfors proposes a theory of conditionals in which the central ideas are those of belief sets, and their expansion, contraction and revision. A belief set is a consistent set of believed propositions represented in some first order language. There is a question about whether a belief set is essentially linguistic, a set of sentences, or a set of objects of belief, propositions. For the moment we will take the way of vacillation: "beliefs represented in a first order language". But we note in passing that the beliefs in belief revision theory are not represented in the language of doxastic logic.

A belief set is *expanded* when a belief, consistent with the beliefs in the set, is added to the belief set. A belief set is *contracted* when a belief is removed from a belief set. A belief set is *revised* when a belief, inconsistent with the belief set but not self-contradictory, is added and consistency preserved by the removal of beliefs.

Gärdenfors is one of the three people – Alchourrón, Gärdenfors and Makinson – who first developed belief revision theory in a fully formal way. The standard theory is called the "AGM" theory.[39]

- When a belief set, K, is expanded by adding a sentence expressing the new belief, say p, a belief consistent with the contents of K, then the new set is of beliefs is represented by: *K plus p*.
- The belief set that results from K by abandoning a belief, say p, is the set represented by: *K minus p*.
- The belief set that results from K by revising the set with respect to p, given that in some cases p is inconsistent with the beliefs in K, is the belief set represented by: *K revised with p*.

The revision of a belief set can be defined in terms of first *contracting* the set by removing the negative of the belief to be added, and then *expanding* the belief set with the revising belief. It has been shown in the standard theory of belief revision that:

K revised with p is the same set as (*K minus not p*) *plus p*

A belief set not only is consistent, but also represents the beliefs of a believer who is both weakly logically and deductively omniscient. All the logical consequences of the beliefs in K are included in K. Logical consequence is logical consequence based on classical first-order logic. It follows that:

(a)   Every belief set contains all the tautologies of first-order logic.
(b)   For any sentences A and B, if the set contains (A **imp** B) and A, then it will contain B.
(c)   No belief set contains any contradiction.[40]

Condition (a) is effectively weak logical omniscience, and with (b) leads to deductive omniscience.[41] Belief sets are said to be "deductively closed". Condition (c) requires that through each of the three kinds of changes the resultant belief set be consistent.

In order to avoid the immediate objections that are prompted by deductive omniscience, there is often a move to distinguish a small subset of beliefs in the belief set as the "real" or "explicit" beliefs. This small set is often called the "base set" of beliefs. The whole set less the base set is often called the set of "implicit" beliefs.

For each of the changes there is a set of logical postulates that will preserve consistency, and other reasonable features of belief sets.[42] The simplest change process is expansion. When a new belief is added to a belief set (with which it is consistent) then all the consequences of that belief are also added, by virtue of deductive omniscience or deductive closure. The new belief, without all its deductive consequences, can be added to the base set, and so we can distinguish the growing set of explicit beliefs, as distinct from the growing belief set.

The most problematic of the change processes is contraction. And because contraction is problematic, so is revision. For example, say someone believes that:

1.   *There is no milk in the fridge.*
2.   *If there is no milk in the fridge then I will have to go to the shop to buy some milk.*

and because of condition (b) (and common sense) that:

3.   *I will have to go to the shop to buy some milk.*

If they refuse to believe the last of the statements, then they will contract their belief set by abandoning that belief. But just that will not do. Condition (b) and common sense will put 3 back into the belief set at once, because it follows from 1 and 2. So they must also abandon one of the other two beliefs. If the first is unassailable, as it is likely to be, then the conditional, 2, will have to be abandoned. That would be the standard tactic for an argumentative teenager or ethics student. But, one could think of situations where the first belief is abandoned because it is based on a fraudulent report by someone who wants a lift to the shops. In that case, if the fraud is discovered, the conditional does not have to be abandoned. In the technical jargon of belief revision, it depends on which belief is most deeply "entrenched".[43]

A principle that is generally observed in AGM theory is that, whenever there is a contraction of a belief set, then there should be minimal change. The principle advocated by AGM theory:

> can be motivated by the following *conservativity principle*:
> (Cons)   When changing beliefs in response to new evidence, you
> should continue to believe as many of the old beliefs as
> possible.[44]

The AGM theory can form the basis for developing an account of conditionals along the line of the Ramsey test. Gärdenfors does just this:

> The Ramsey Test can be summarised by the following rule:
> (RT)   Accept a sentence of the form "If A, then C" in a state of
> belief K if and only if the minimal change of K needed to
> accept A also requires accepting C.

The minimal change may require expansion or revision. It will be the latter if K contains *not A*.

Gärdenfors begins with the Ramsey test and goes on to develop accounts of several kinds of conditionals. They include counterfactuals, "even if" conditionals (C, even if A), "might" conditionals (If A, then C might be) and "necessary" conditionals (If A then necessarily C.). In the course of expounding on all of this, Gärdenfors shows that one of the logical systems, from a purely formal point of view, is the same as David Lewis's system VC, a system in *Counterfactuals*. Since the logic of counterfactuals in Lewis can be used to derive an account of possibility and necessity, Gärdenfors's belief revision based logics can also be used to develop a belief revision account of possibility and necessity.

Although this is not the place to explore the technical details, it is clear that an interpretation of possibility and necessity can be given in terms of the dynamics of epistemic state change. Gärdenfors says:

> I have tried to show that various kinds of changes of belief correspond to different kinds of conditionals in a natural way. In my opinion this correspondence gives a better understanding of the meaning of conditionals, their function in arguments, and their logical properties than the semantics based on possible worlds and the similarities between possible worlds. Furthermore, the use of epistemic states as an ontological basis for the analysis does not

give rise to the ontological problems connected with possible worlds and their properties.[45]

Both Lewis and Read are critical of the reductionist approach. The belief revision account relies, in a strong sense, on sets of *sentences* (that express the beliefs). So it is a linguistic approach in an important sense. Lewis is critical of linguistic ersatzism, even though he thinks it is his strongest rival: "The best ersatzism by far is linguistic."[46]

There are two main lines of criticism. The first concerns begging the question about possibility. The second concerns the expressive power of language of any kind.

It is ironic that Lewis accuses the advocates of "linguistic" accounts of begging the question:

My first objection [to linguistic ersatzism] is that modality must be taken as primitive. First, via consistency. Not any set of sentences of the worldmaking language is an ersatz world. It has to be a consistent set . . . So in order to say which things of the right nature – which sets of sentences of the worldmaking language – are the ersatz worlds, we need to distinguish the consistent ones. That is *prima facie* a modal distinction: a set of sentences is consistent iff those sentences, as interpreted, *could* all be true together.[47]

The criticism is based on a "possibility" view of logical consistency. The possibility view of consistency is that a set of sentences is consistent if and only if it is possible for all the sentences to be true. So, consistency already assumes possibility. It is hard to escape this criticism, except to point out that Lewis falls into the same trap.

Lewis begs the same question, as we have seen, in his reliance on quantifiers with possibility import. Take your pick: do you want "virtual" worlds described by consistent sets of beliefs, or existent possible worlds? Of course, the choice is not as simple as that, because Lewis has further criticisms.

Lewis, and Read also, criticize the reductionist approach to possibility in similar ways. They say that the reductionist does not treat individuals seriously; and does not see the limits of propositional accounts of possibility. There are two major difficulties. The first concerns expressive power. This problem divides into two parts. First, there is the problem that language alone will not enable us to distinguish between worlds. Some worlds will be indiscernible from others. Secondly, there is the problem of indiscernible possible individuals.

Lewis is not overly concerned with the first indiscernibility problem, so we will set it aside. His main concern is for indiscernible individuals. This problem, he says, "is serious".[48] Before we consider his complaint, we note that he writes in introduction of these problems that:

> If ersatz possible worlds and individuals are linguistic descriptions, then we will never have two of them alike. If an ersatz possibility *is* its description, there can only be one for any given description.[49]

The "is" is in Lewis's own italics. Go no further. Here *is* the problem. Why would it be assumed that a nonexistent but real possible world or possible individual *is* its description? The only thing that I can think of is an assumption that if a description is not *of* an existing individual, then the description itself must *be* the individual. One might similarly suppose a correlated assumption that, unless there exists an individual to name, then a name of a nonexistent individual must be a name of itself. Once again, the assumption of existential import is the key. Here we have the assumption of the existential import of names. We have already pointed out that this assumption is deeply problematic, and have argued against it. In this case the assumption has the consequence that, unless the described or named individual exists, then the name or description must be of itself.

If, on the one hand, we accept these assumptions of existential import, and hold that the language of possibilities describes real possibilities, then either possible worlds exist and contain existing individuals, or the possibilities are somehow the sentences and the names and descriptions the sentences contain. If, on the other hand, we do not accept the assumptions of existential import, then we do not have to accept just the alternatives offered above. Belief sets and the names and descriptions in them are descriptions of real possibilities in which *there are* nonexistent individuals and the sentences in belief sets contain names of some existent and maybe some extra nonexistent individuals.

Lewis could not disagree more. His position about this is made crystal clear:

> For linguistic ersatzism, this is a problem about naming. If the extra individuals do not exist for us to name (or for us to declare then to be names of themselves) how can we possibly have names for them?[50]

Plantinga gives aid and comfort to this doctrine when he asks the rhetorical question already quoted in Chapter 7:

> In one regard, however, I think [the Canonical Conception of possible worlds] yields confusion rather than clarity; for it suggests that there are things that do not exist. How, exactly, does the question of nonexistent objects rear its ugly head?[51]

The question rears its ugly head only because it has been repressed rather than addressed. In this volume, we persist in the claim that one can sensibly name and talk about nonexistent individuals. Furthermore, whatever we might want to say about them, nonexistent individuals are not their own names. They *have* names like "Vulcan", "Cair Paravel" and "Excalibur", just like existent individuals *have* names like "Mars", "Windsor Castle" and "Kohinoor". By analogy with Lewis's appeal to what we all know, I declare that:

> I believe that things could have been different in countless ways; I believe permissible paraphrases of what I believe; taking the paraphrase at its face value, I therefore believe that we can talk about entities that can be called "ways things could have been". I prefer to call them "possible worlds".

Things do not have to exist for us to be able, sensibly, to talk about them and to name them. Parmenides' principle – the principle that we cannot talk about the nonexistent – is just plain wrong. That is not to say that there is no problem here. There is, but it is the problem of *how* we can and do discuss and reason about the nonexistent. The problem needs to be addressed directly. The solution will not be found by either generating existent possible worlds containing existent individuals or by sweeping the nonexistent away into the null set where Mr Pickwick is Pegasus.

Finally, I will comment about vacillation between language and propositions. We will see below that if we move to the view that belief sets are sets of (believed) propositions, then belief sets become abstract entities because sets are themselves, in a standard mathematical sense, abstract objects; and that leads to a convergence of the linguistic and abstract entity accounts of possibility. But it does depend on what account one gives of propositions, as distinct from propositions-represented-in-language (if such a distinction can be made).

9.6 An abstract entity alternative

The view advocated by Stalnaker, Read and many others is that possibilities are abstract entities, and none the less real for that. Stalnaker says that Lewis's modal realism is based on four principles. One of these is fatally flawed, but the others are reasonable. If we accept them then we have the doctrine that possible worlds exist, but they exist, not as the real world does, but in the same sense that abstract entities can be said to exist.

The starting point for Stalnaker is the *ways* things might have been, and this includes one way: the actual way that things are. Stalnaker wants to agree with Lewis's starting point as stated: "I therefore believe in the existence of entities that might be called 'ways things could have been'. I prefer to call them 'possible worlds'."[52] But Lewis's renaming of ways as "possible worlds" is not a simple innocent move. It leads to Lewis's four theses:

(1) *Possible worlds exist.*
(2) *Other possible worlds are things of the same sort as the actual world – "I and all my surroundings".*
(3) *The indexical analysis of the adjective "actual" is the correct analysis.*
(4) *Possible worlds cannot be reduced to something more basic.*[53]

Stalnaker wishes to reject thesis 2 but hold to the rest. His conclusion is that possible worlds are existent abstract entities, and so the possible worlds analysis of possibility is the analysis of "real" possibility.

The major point against 2 is that the shift from ways to worlds is a shift of kinds. The *ways the world might have been* are the same in kind as the *way the world is*. As Stalnaker writes:

> *The way the world is* is a property or a state of the world, not the world itself. The statement that the world is the way it is is true in a sense, but not when read as an identity statement. (Compare: "the way the world is is the world"). This is important, since if properties can exist uninstantiated, then the way the world is could exist even if a world that is that way did not.

This leads to the conclusion that:

> One could accept thesis one – that there really are many ways that things could have been – while denying that there exists anything else that is like the actual world.[54]

So *ways* the world is or might be are not worlds of spatiotemporal objects and energies, but are property-like possibilities. They are real but not concrete. And because they are real they exist. So, Stalnaker rejects thesis 2.

Stalnaker accepts thesis 3, which is the indexical view of actuality. This is the thesis that, of the existent worlds, the world in which *we* live and move and have our being is the actual world. The other worlds (ways) are unactualized, but existent, possibilities. This thesis has led to a literature in modal logic and philosophy about the actual. An early modal logic paper in this area is Davies and Humberstone's "Two Notions of Necessity".[55] If the reader is interested, there could be no better place to start. We pursue this no further.

Stalnaker then asks whether thesis 4 is to be accepted. He poses the question about 4 by asking whether *ways things might have been* are respectable entities in their own right. If not, are they reducible to something more fundamental? And if so, what would that be?

Stalnaker considers the view that *ways the world can be* can be reduced to *world-stories* in the manner of Adams.[56] He effectively looks at propositional ersatzism. Adams writes:

Let us say that a *world-story* is a maximal consistent set of propositions. That is, it is a set which has as its members one member of
every pair of mutually contradictory propositions, and which is
such that it is possible that all of its members be true together. The
notion of a possible world can be given a contextual analysis in
terms of world-stories.[57]

This account of possible worlds is beginning to look like the propositional
version of the belief set account we looked at above. It is not the same, but it is
very similar. The difference lies in the fact that, although belief sets are deductively closed, and the ideal believer is logically and deductively omniscient, the
believer is not *factually* omniscient.[58] As Gärdenfors points out:

An important feature of belief sets is that they need not be *maximal*
in the sense that for every sentence A either A belongs to the belief
set or [*not*] A belongs to it. The epistemic interpretation of this is
that an individual is normally not *omniscient*.[59]

It is clear that Gärdenfors's *omniscience simpliciter* is, in my terms, *factual
omniscience*.

Stalnaker says many things about Adams's account, but we consider just
two. First he writes that the notion of possibility in Adams's world-stories
account:

is a property of *sets* of propositions. Intuitively, a set of propositions is possible if all its members can be true together. This notion
cannot, of course, be defined in terms of possible worlds, or world-
stories, without circularity, but it should be a consequence of the
theory that a set of propositions is possible if and only if its
members are simultaneously true in some possible world (are all
members of some world-story).[60]

So *ways the world might be* are world-stories. World-stories are maximal
consistent sets of propositions. There seems to be slide here from *ways the
worlds might be* to sets, rather than to what is described by the propositions in
the sets. The slide might be driven by the desire to pin down possibility to
something that can be claimed to exist, and sets exist in the abstract. But what
is described by the propositions in a set, or by a world-story, may well not
exist, unless it is the way the actual world *is*.

I hate to say it, but it looks as if we are back to the aversion to the nonexistent. But the reader is asked to look at both the Adams and the Stalnaker
accounts. They have enormous amounts of detail not discussed here.

The second thing that Stalnaker discusses is a methodological issue of great
importance to this whole area of debate: "It will be useful to compare this

reduction of possible worlds to propositions with the competing reduction of propositions to possible worlds." Stalnaker is referring to the widely held view that a proposition is, in fact, the set of worlds in which it is true. It is a view that holds that, once we have worlds and truth, propositions can be eliminated. To continue:

> What is at stake in choosing which of these two notions to define in terms of the other? . . . Part of what distinguishes them is the elusive question of conceptual priority, but there are also more substantive differences . . .[61]

This raises the whole question of what is going on in the explication of possible worlds. There are at least two possibilities. On the one hand, it could be that possible worlds are being used as a useful tool for exploring the interrelationship of concepts in a network of modal concepts. This would accord with Hintikka's idea that epistemic and modal logics are explorations of the conceptual "grammar" of these notions.

> A branch of logic, say epistemic logic, is best viewed as an *explanatory model* in terms of which certain aspects of the workings of our ordinary language can be understood . . . Other more general aspects of the idea of logic as an explanatory model can also be registered. This idea is related to Wittgenstein's idea of a language game.[62]

As I pointed out elsewhere:

> Hintikka sets out in some detail what he conceives to be the relation between the explanatory model and ordinary language. They are related in much the same way as any theory is related to the data which is explained . . . The theory of meaning set out in the explanatory model is to be seen as an explanation of the *basic meaning* of the words and expressions.[63]

Conceptual priority is not at issue. The network of concepts and their interrelation is what the semantics is all about. Possible worlds provide the setting for the model.

On the other hand, it could be that possible worlds are being used for the reduction of the notions of possibility and necessity to other more basic concepts; namely, existent worlds themselves. This is the aim of Lewis's project, and also of Stalnaker's; but the outcomes are very different, as we have seen.

9.7 Mathematics again

In Chapter 4 we raised the question of the status, in possible worlds semantics, of mathematical truth. In what sense can we say that the truths of mathematics are necessarily true because they are true in all possible worlds, rather than they are true in all possible worlds because they are necessarily true? If the latter is correct, then possible worlds are of little use in accounting for mathematical necessity.

Throughout Lewis's writings about the existence of possible worlds there is the insistence that logic and mathematics are constant from world to world. Each world contains the same mathematical entities and truths about them. And one would have to assume that, for Lewis, these entities exist in each existent possible world. So long as these entities are on a par with properties and relations then there will only be the problems of how properties and relations are the same across worlds. But if it should turn out that mathematical objects are based on "raw numbers" or some such thing, then they will be individuals, and that means that if 1 exists in the actual world, it will be the counterparts of 1 that exist in other worlds.

On any such "raw numbers" account, the truths of mathematics will be necessarily true because of truth in all possible worlds. But if mathematical objects are on a par with properties and relations, then mathematical truth will be truth in all possible worlds because such truths are necessary.

Appendix: belief revision formalities

K plus A: $\quad K^+_A$

K minus A: $\quad K^-_A$

K revised with A: $\quad K^*_A$

K is the absurd belief set, $K_\perp$

Belief revision postulates for expansion, revision and contraction

The AGM (Alchourrón, Gärdenfors and Makinson) belief revision postulates are as follows. (Note that $K_\perp$ stands for the "absurd" or contradictory belief set.)

Expansion
The expansion of K by A is K^+_A

(K^+1) $\quad K^+_A$ is a belief set

(K^+2) $\quad A \in K^+_A$

(K^+3) $\quad K \subseteq K^+_A$

(K^+4) If $A \in K$, then $K^+_A = K$

(K^+5) If $K \subseteq H$, then $K^+_A \subseteq H^+_A$

(K^+6) For all belief sets K and all sentences A, K^+_A is the smallest belief set that satisfies $(K^+1) - (K^+5)$.

Revision
The revision of K by A is: K^*_A

(K^*1) K^*_A is a belief set

(K^*2) $A \in K^*_A$

(K^*3) $K^*_A \subseteq K^+_A$

(K^*4) If $\sim A \notin K$, then $K^+_A \subseteq K^*_A$

(K^*5) $K^*_A = K_\perp$ iff $\vdash \sim A$

(K^*6) If $\vdash (A \equiv B)$, then $K^*_A = K^*_B$

(K^*7) $K^*_{(A \& B)} \subseteq (K^*_A)^+_B$

(K^*8) If $\sim B \notin K^*_A$, then $(K^*_A)^+_B \subseteq K^*_{(A \& B)}$

The following *monotonicity principle* is rejected:

(K^*M) If $K \subseteq H$, then $K^*_A \subseteq H^*_A$

The following strengthening of (K^*6) is rejected:

  If $\vdash (A \supset B)$, then $K^*B \subseteq K^*A$

Contraction
The contraction of K by A is: K^-_A

(K^-1) K^-_A is a belief set

(K^-2) $K^-_A \subseteq K$

(K^-3) If $A \notin K$, then $K^-_A = K$

(K^-4) If *not* $\vdash A$, then $A \notin K^-_A$

(K^-5) If $A \in K$, then $K \subseteq (K^-_A)^+_A$

(K^-6) If $\vdash (A \equiv B)$, then $K^-_A = K^-_{B^-}$

(K^-7) $K^-_A \cap K^-_B \subseteq K^-_{(A \& B)}$

(K^-8) If $A \notin K^-_{(A \& B)}$ then $K^-_{(A \& B)} \subseteq K^-_A$

Ramsey test

(RT) $A > C \in K$ iff $C \in K^*_A$

CHAPTER 10
Impossible possible worlds

10.1 Introduction

One quite surprising development in modal logic has been the development of systems in which there are possible worlds in which some sentences are both true and false. This development has been greeted with incredulous stares of such intensity that the stares directed at Lewis's claims become shy glances. This development has been extended to the actual world, and there is a group of logicians who claim that there are some contradictions that are true, as well, of course, as being false. Note that they are not claiming that *all* contradictions are true, only that *some* are. These logicians are the *dialethic* logicians.

In this chapter we will consider some of these impossible worlds claims, and see what sense can be made of them. Impossible worlds appeared when doxastic logic was being discussed. There is also a group of logicians, the *relevant* logicians, who focused their attention on conditionals. On some relevant accounts of conditionals there are worlds in which sentences are both true and false. Conditionals have been the inspiration for many unusual things in logic, and have led to many strange uses of possible worlds. We begin with epistemic logic, move on to relevant logics, and then turn to dialethic systems of contradiction tolerant logics.

10.2 Omniscience

One of the sources of controversy in epistemic S4 is that the system describes a knower who is both logically[1] and deductively[2] omniscient. We have seen that Hintikka's original response to this was to argue that if it is true of *a* that:

> *a knows that p*
> *a knows that if p then q*

then, even though *a* might not be immediately aware of knowing that *q*, if they are reasonable and rational, they will soon agree to *q* and so come to know that *q*.

> *a knows that q*

Any denial of knowing that *q* is indefensible (in the long run, anyway).

But, for whatever reason, Hintikka seems to have had a change of heart between 1962, when *Knowledge and Belief* was published, and 1975, when "Impossible Possible Worlds Vindicated"[3] was published. In the latter he argues that epistemically possible worlds do not have to be logically possible.

His argument begins by first setting out the analysis principle:

(1) A sentence of the form "*a* knows that *p*" is true in a world W iff *p* is true in all the epistemic *a*-alternatives to W, i.e. in all the epistemically possible worlds which are compatible with everything *a* knows in W.

Then, the problem with omniscience is set out:

(2) There are *a*, *p*, and *q* such that *a* knows that *p*, *p* logically implies *q* (i.e. (*p* **imp** *q*) is logically true), but *a* does not know that *q*.

Note further that logical truth has implications for knowledge.

(3) A sentence is logically true iff it is true in every logically possible world.

Remember, from Chapter 6, that all the knowers described by Hintikka's epistemic logic know all the self-sustaining sentences. Self-sustaining sentences are the sentences whose denial is indefensible in worlds governed by certain consistency conditions. The consistency conditions set out by Hintikka are essentially those conditions that will make all the tautologies of first-order logic and all the theorems of epistemic S4 self-sustaining. So self-sustaining sentences are the logical truths of his systems. Thus when *if p then q* is logically true, all knowers should know that *if p then q*.

Now consider 2 again in terms of epistemically possible worlds. If *a* knows that *p* is true in world W, *p* logically implies *q* is true in world W, but *a* does not know that *q* is true in world W, then, if U is an epistemic alternative to W, *p*, *if p then q* and *not q* will all be true in U. So U is inconsistent, 2 is highly problematic when all knowers are logically omniscient.

The weaker omniscience, deductive omniscience, creates a similar problem. We don't have to have that *if p then q* is a logical truth. It can be just a contingent but known to be true implication. Then we might have:

(2D)   There are *a*, *p*, and *q* such that *a* knows that *p*, *a* knows that *if p then q*, but *a* does not know that *q*.

Given the "automatic" or Cartesian knowledge of all logical truths, 2D is entailed by 2, and generates the same inconsistency in world U. In the case of 2D it is easier to avoid the inconsistency, because one can simply draw to *a*'s attention the fact that they have simply forgotten for the moment something that they already know: "But you know that *p*, and if you just think for a moment you will realize that you already know that *if p then q*. So how can you say that you do not know that *q*?" The difficulty with 2 is that the agent might not have yet worked out that *if p then q*. We saw earlier that Lemmon realized that Cartesian knowledge of complex conditionals may be problematic, but urged that we not worry about it. The important omniscience problem is not that 1, 2D and 3 are inconsistent, but that 1, 2 and 3 are inconsistent.

Hintikka then says that 1–3 are not sufficient to create a contradiction unless we add principle 4:

(4)   Every epistemically possible world is logically possible. (That is, every epistemic alternative to a given world *W* is logically possible.)

It is usually assumed that any qualified possibility entails logical possibility. In other words, physical possibility, moral possibility, economic possibility and epistemic possibility all entail logical possibility. If something is not logically possible then it cannot be physically, morally, economically or epistemically possible. That assumption is now called into question. And Hintikka's original epistemic logic is called into question too.

The standard methodology, set out in Chapter 6, for considering whether a problem is created by 2 is as follows: The *ignorance claim* in world W, *a* does not know that *q*, "generates" an epistemically alternate world for agent *a*, say U, in which *not q* is true, and all that *a* knows in W is also true in U. The standard approach to knowing in epistemic logic includes an approach to not knowing. Epistemic logic is a logic for both knowledge and ignorance. A claim not to know may turn out to be indefensible. Ignorance gives epistemic logic its real leverage as a logic.

To test the defensibility of the ignorance claim in 2 we consider U. In U we get at least:

p
not q
if p then q

It must be noted that the last sentence is in U either because a knows that *if p then q* in W or because all logically true conditionals are in every world. If it is there then U is prima facie indefensible. U is logically inconsistent, and if we assume either 4 or Hintikka's original consistency conditions, then it is not epistemically possible.

The response of several logicians, including Hintikka,[4] Levesque[5] and Konolige,[6] is to place some sort of limit on the amount of reasoning that is required of an epistemic agent in order for them to become aware that sentences are true. In terms of the example above, an agent might not be able to work out that *if p then q*. If the agent is of limited reasoning capacity, then 2 fails to entail 2D because although *if p then q* is a logical truth, it is beyond the ability of any agent modelled by this system to work it out. There will be cases where 2 is correct but 2D is not. So with this limit, world U might contain just p and *not q*. At the same time, these responses are made from within the context of classical logic. There is an assumption that the logical constants, negation and conjunction and inclusive disjunction, are to have their usual classical truth-functional definitions. Non-classical logics are not seen as being part of the solution. Hintikka says:

> Attempts have in fact been made to construct a model theory of impossible worlds by adopting some sort of nonstandard interpretation of logical constants. However, this course is very dubious.[7]

Even if we grant this limitation of reasoning ability, if world U contains p and *not q*, and, as a matter of classical logical fact, *if p then q* is a logical truth, then world U is logically inconsistent. So, there has to be some sort of qualification of 4, at least for world U. There are two kinds of qualifications of 4 in the discussions. One is the limit on reasonable proof. The other is the limitation on semantic models.

It is also quite standard to distinguish between inconsistency and contradiction. Konolige writes of Ralph (the robot?):

> Ralph is noncontradictory if he does not believe ϕ and $\neg\phi$ for any proposition ϕ. Note that Ralph may be noncontradictory, while at the same time being *logically* inconsistent: he may believe ϕ and believe ψ, where ϕ *entails* the negation of ψ, without believing $\neg\psi$.[8]

Some authors distinguish between *explicit* or prima facie contradiction such as *p and not p*, and *implicit* or *deep* contradiction. Deep contradiction is logical inconsistency. The logical problem is how one can have deep contradiction without explicit contradiction in a classical logic context. We begin with the way in which limits are imposed, first with limits on proof.

Limits on proof

Konolige's arguments focus on belief, rather than on knowledge, but nevertheless there are strong analogies when we consider logical and deductive omniscience. His basic idea is that an agent will come to believe the logical truth that *if p then q* when they find a proof of *q* from *p*. Some proofs will be very long and complex. Any inspection of most typical introductory logic texts will show that quite standard deduction systems require very long proofs to establish entailments. Even if one simplifies these systems into more sensible systems,[9] the proofs can still be very long.

Some logicians, such as Konolige, place a limit on the length or complexity of a proof of *q* from *p*, and require that if proof is limited, then we cannot expect the agent to believe that *if p then q*. Nonetheless, if there is a proof, within limits, of *q* from *p*, then *if p then q* will hold at *U*. So let it be done. This is the approach of proof prevention or proof limitation. So if *if p then q* is never allowed to appear in *U*, then there is no contradiction.

Konolige describes a logic governed by limitations of various kinds. In a situation where coming to believe ϕ would be contradictory:

> Note that there several reasons why Ralph may not believe a sentence ϕ, even if it is a logical consequence of his base set [of beliefs]. He may have insufficient inference rules, so that no matter how hard he tries, he cannot derive it . . . Or, even if his inference rules are adequate, Ralph may have insufficient time to figure out that ϕ follows from the base set. In either case, Ralph, as a limited agent, cannot be said to believe all the logical consequences of his beliefs, so that the belief set is incomplete from a logical standpoint.[10]

Konolige indicates that he has in mind a partial system, or an incomplete system that is theoretically tolerant of logical inconsistency. His preferred belief model is a deduction model. The set of inference rules available is not a set that makes logical inconsistency the same as contradictoriness: "If the deduction rules are logically incomplete, then not all logically possible consequences of the base set [of beliefs] will be derived."[11]

The sorts of deduction limits that Konolige want to impose on the logic of belief are limits that reflect the limited ability of human and human-like agents. But, he argues, such limits are not possible in possible worlds semantics:

> We have distinguished contradiction, that is, believing ϕ and $\neg\phi$ for some proposition ϕ, from the case where Ralph's beliefs are logically inconsistent, but Ralph has not derived the contradiction. In the possible-worlds model, these two cases cannot be distinguished: if Ralph is logically inconsistent, he must be contradictory.[12]

Konolige's whole argument for a deduction model for belief is based on the point that the alternative semantic model, the possible worlds model, is defective and counter-intuitive.[13] The defects and counter-intuitiveness are nowhere so clear as in the problem of omniscience of whatever kind.

Konolige also considers the response, on behalf of possible worlds models, that some kind of non-standard logic might solve the problem:

> One answer is to admit *nonclassical worlds* into the possible-world model. These are worlds in which inconsistent sentences can be simultaneously true, or where classically valid sentences are not true . . . there seems to be no motivation other than a technical one for admitting nonclassical worlds. What does it mean, after all, to have an inconsistent world as one of the ways an agent thinks the world cam be?[14]

Although we return to this below, it is worth noting that Konolige rejects this proposal altogether. We will look more closely at the reasons for rejecting the proposal.

Limits on semantic models

The second approach is semantic. If the truth of a conditional that leads to an inconsistency is *deeply buried*, then it might never come to the surface. And if it never comes to the surface, then there will be no contradiction. In other words, this is a challenge to Konolige's assertion that a distinction between inconsistency and contradiction cannot be sustained in possible worlds semantics.

Hintikka advocates a system for showing that inconsistency, when it does infect a set of sentences, might be found only at a certain *depth* of semantic analysis. There is no need for us to go into the technical details of this depth analysis. There is an emphasis on "semantic reasoning" rather than on deductive proof.

In both Konolige's and Hintikka's cases there is an allowance for unbelief or ignorance, respectively, in an interesting way. An agent's unbelief or ignorance is defensible, to use Hintikka's terminology, when their unbelief or ignorance cannot be overturned without the agent's having to engage in logical proof beyond some fixed degree of complexity, or having to engage in semantical analysis to an unreasonable depth or degree. From the semantic point of view, impossible epistemically possible worlds are to be tolerated so long as inconsistency is deeply enough buried or difficult enough to detect.

There is an interesting consequence of this approach in the logic for knowledge. You will recall from Chapter 9 that when considering a's claim to know some things and not to know others, epistemic systems with possible worlds require that we place all the knowings of the form "a knows that p" in some world, say W, and all the ignorance of the form "a does not know that q" in the same world W, and discover whether the content of W is defensible.

First, given the veridicality principle, the complete content of a's knowledge will be true in W. In other words, for every sentence of the form "a knows that p", p is true in W. This content of knowing will have to be logically consistent, unless Hintikka and the other classical logicians want to be paraconsistent, or even dialethic about positive knowledge. Hintikka certainly does not want to be paraconsistent, so he will hardly want to be dialethic. Some classical logicians want only to hiss at paraconsistent logic,[15] so they will hardly want to depart from the necessary condition of classical consistency. Hintikka's comment that "Unlike its rivals as a candidate for the role of a logically nonstandard world (semantical basis of so-called 'paraconsistent' logics), this generalization is completely realistic",[16] must indicate that he thinks that paraconsistent solutions are unrealistic.

Secondly, given any ignorance sentence of the form "a does not know that q", there will have to be an epistemically alternate possible world. The alternate world is not necessarily logically possible. Inconsistency is allowed at some (maybe hidden) depth. So there will be two kinds of possible worlds in revised epistemic logic. Different conditions will govern the allowable contents of these different kinds of worlds. But tests of the defensibility of any agent's body of ignorance and knowledge will be based in the logically possible worlds, with the impossible possible worlds being dependent on, or generated by, or epistemically alternate to the logically possible worlds.

Logics that allow for different kinds of worlds are known as "non-normal" logics. These are well understood. The second kind of world, such as in Hintikka's suggested system, is usually known as a "non-normal world". In fact, Lemmon's S0.5, which we met in Chapter 6, is a non-normal logic when set out in technical detail. But the non-normal worlds of S0.5 do not allow, in any obvious way, for logical inconsistency. Not all non-normal logics allow for impossible possible worlds, but some do.

What can we say about Hintikka's approach to impossible possible worlds? First, we can certainly say that these impossible possible worlds are not the sorts of worlds that Lewis would say are real. The fact that inconsistency is allowed to dwell in the hidden depths of such worlds does not alter the fact that such worlds *are* inconsistent.

Secondly, we can say that epistemically possible worlds, being in some sense "unreal", might nevertheless be part of a reasonable explanation of ignorance, if we allow for there being impossible possible worlds. Thirdly, the notion of inconsistency being hidden at some depth in a world raises again the whole question of the logic of inconsistency. In Chapter 7 we saw that the classical account of inconsistency would require that if there is any inconsistency in a world, and the logical constants such as negation, conjunction and inclusive disjunction have classical definitions, then every sentence is true in that world. Arguments that follow the standard and classically valid *ex falso quodlibet* rule will make the world totally and utterly inconsistent. This means that no inconsistency can be hidden, because it will make for surface inconsistency – contradiction – at every turn.

If Hintikka's deep inconsistencies are to remain hidden, some sort of curb has to restrain the *ex falso quodlibet* rule. And despite Hintikka's rejection of paraconsistent solutions, his offering is paraconsistent in terms of the standard definition of a paraconsistent logic. The standard definition is that a logic, S, is paraconsistent if the *ex falso quodlibet* rule is not valid in S. It is certainly the case that the *ex falso quodlibet* rule is not valid in the non-normal worlds of Hintikka's offering.

10.3 Semi-relevant logic

There is a group of logics, mainly aimed at providing a better account of conditionals than the material conditional account, in which use is made of the set of values *just true, just false, both true and false* and *null*.[17] The first of these logics was discussed by Belnap in "How a Computer Should Think."[18]

Some of these logics have been called "contradiction tolerant logics" because, in some of them, arguments following the *ex falso quodlibet* form are not valid. That means that some of them are also paraconsistent logics.

In Belnap's four-valued logic there are what he calls "told" values. Given any proposition *p*, an agent could be *told it is true, told it is false, told both that it is true and false* (by different people or at different times) and *told nothing*. The logic that he sets out on the basis of these values is not a possible worlds logic, but the ideas embodied in Belnap's four values have been applied to possible worlds conditional logics and to belief revision systems with interesting outcomes.

One of the best known of the conditional logics is called "RM". In RM only three of the four told values are used.[19] They are *just true, just false* and *both true and false*. There are parallel but disconnected semantic conditions for truth and for falsehood. The main idea is that a conditional will be *true* if it is a necessarily true conditional, but *false* if it has a *true* antecedent and a *false* consequent. The semantics for falsehood are the semantics of a material conditional. If either the antecedent is *non-true* or the consequent is *non-false* then it is *non-false*.

A variation on RM is RM-all, which is the same as RM, but all four of Belnap's values are used. In both RM and RM-all, arguments following the *ex falso quodlibet* rule are invalid.

The most interesting thing about these logics from the point of view of possible worlds and impossible worlds is that an interesting form of logical consistency is to be found in their semantics. It follows from the disconnection of the semantics of *false* from the semantics for *true*. These semantics allow for sentences to be both *true* and *false*, but they do not allow for sentences to be both *true* and *non-true, false* and *non-false*. So it is not strictly correct to say that the worlds in this logic are logically inconsistent.

That is the case only if we affirm that truth and falsehood are the simple negatives of each other.

Lewis, and many others, argue that this is all nonsense. Lewis dismisses this in a footnote in *On the Plurality of Worlds*. He is responding to the McGinn-like complaint that his quantificational account of possibility and necessity is using quantificational modifiers that restrict quantification to worlds in which there are no true contradictions. He effectively says that without possibility import there is no world. He writes:

> This discussion of restricting modifiers enables me to say why I have no use for impossible worlds, on a par with the possible worlds. For comparison, suppose travellers told of a place in this world – a marvellous mountain, far away in the bush – where contradictions are true.

Of the report of this supposed mountain he goes on to say:

> to tell the alleged truth about the marvellously contradictory things that happen on the mountain is no different from contradicting yourself. But there is no subject matter, however marvellous, about which you can tell the truth by contradicting yourself. Therefore there is no mountain where contradictions are true. An impossible world where contradictions are true would be no better . . . If worlds were like stories or story-tellers, there would indeed be room for worlds according to which contradictions are true . . . But worlds, as I understand them, are not like stories or story-tellers. They are like this world; and this world is no story, not even a true story. Nor should worlds be replaced by their stories . . .[20]

There is more in this footnote for the keen reader. But it is clear that Lewis considers worlds not to be places where contradictions could be true under any circumstances whatsoever.

There is, however, a concession of sorts. He does not say that stories containing contradictions describe worlds, but he does allow contradictory stories. Now we are faced with nonexistence again. No worlds are described by contradictory stories. Some of the things that do not exist are worlds described by contradictory stories. If there were such worlds, then they would not exist.

How do we deal with the counterfactual? Is it trivially true? And is it also trivially true that if there were such worlds, then they would exist?

10.4 Meta-consistency

This raises the question of meta-consistency and meta-possibility. It does not look as if the relevant and paraconsistent logicians abandon consistency in their metalanguages. One of the oldest ambitions of such logicians is to use paraconsistent logic as its own metalanguage. The metalanguage of classical first-order logic is a classical "first-order" language with extensions to the domain of quantification so that there may be assertions about all properties and all possibilities. But the same kind of logical consistency as for first-order logic is used.

The sorts of impossible worlds that are often produced by the supporters of impossible worlds are not quite what they seem at first. There may be "funny" values and restricted accounts of proof but, in the end, classical consistency holds the high ground. This has led some of the paraconsistency advocates to concede that there are "moderate" accounts and interpretations of para-consistency: accounts that hold it to be epistemic rather than alethic.

CHAPTER 11
Unfinished story

11.1 A budget of heresy

I have declared or argued for several quite heretical things. First, I declared in favour of the status of first-order modal logic as an artificial language. I then gave examples that show that the language of classical logic is unreliable for the evaluation of many arguments couched in ordinary language. It was urged that more attention should be paid to the logic–language relationship. Modal logic is more reliable for some argument evaluation than non-modal logic. But we saw that there is much beyond the scope of present modal logic – the present logic of boxes and diamonds.

I argued for a renewed look at the whole question of existential import for both quantifiers and names. An appeal was made to ordinary intuitions and sensible talk of the properties of nonexistent entities. McGinn effectively denies Parmenides' law as he writes:

> It may now be asked how we can ascribe *any* properties to purely intentional objects, including the property of non-existence. Here we need to heed carefully the way we actually talk and not impose misleading models on our concepts. For we simply *do* ascribe properties to non-existent objects – we make remarks about them. Thus we say that Pegasus is a horse not a pig, the Zeus is the senior god, that Sherlock Holmes is a brilliant detective. These statement are all true and they contain predicative expressions; so, yes, we can predicate properties of non-existent entities.[1]

And just in case someone wants to claim that this is all unscientific, let me turn to Vulcan: the planet between the Sun and Mercury, not the home of the

Vulcans in *Star Trek*. I love Vulcan, because it is not only nonexistent, but scientists *named* it. Again, in McGinn's words:

> Imagine someone overhearing a conversation you are having about Vulcan and wondering what you are talking about. "What is this Vulcan thing anyway?" they ask, and you reply, "Oh, Vulcan is a planet that some astronomers mistakenly thought to exist." "So it's not a cactus you're referring to with the name 'Vulcan'?" "Definitely not, Vulcan is a planet not a cactus – and moreover it doesn't exist."[2]

His case, and mine, is that logicians can often impose misleading models on the conceptual data, and then refuse to face up to the counter-examples. But counter-examples are the stuff of philosophy, and are the means of keeping us honest.

There has been considerable emphasis on epistemic logic and the discussions surrounding it. This area of modal logic is one of the few areas where possible worlds, as such, have been used to argue for analysis and explanatory models. Hintikka's case for S4 epistemic logic is centrally semantic. At the same time, he did not use existent possible worlds but the virtual possible worlds of model sets.

The use of modal logic in the discussion of provability and ideal reasoner-believers is a discussion in which the possible worlds semantics has just not been used in any clearly significant way to establish theses. This is no reflection on what has been done. It just turns out that the logics used, logics mainly understood in terms of their axiomatizations, have possible worlds semantics. So the possible worlds semantics can be used to satisfy the search for what Hunter calls the "Holy Grail" of logic,[3] the proof of completeness.

The use of possible worlds semantics in the study of time leads very soon to the problem that interesting systems are incomplete. There are no axiomatic systems to give a deductive version of reasonable accounts of how the worlds of time should be interrelated. But then, this might not be a problem, except for those in the search of the Holy Grail.

Modal realism is the most philosophically fashionable and contestable area of possible worlds semantics at the turn of the millenium. Here, as with epistemic logic, the focus is on the worlds. We have tried to bring the two areas of discussion a little closer together. The most interesting thing about this area of argument is that it has brought to the fore a range of questions that, half a century earlier, were considered by many influential philosophers to be beyond rational discussion. Possible worlds have provided a framework, however defective and partial, by means of which possibility, necessity, existence, counterfactual conditionals and many other important questions can be sensibly discussed.

The phrase "*possible* worlds", by its very redolence, raises the question of impossible worlds. It is no coincidence that dialethic and paraconsistent logicians have made the idea of impossible worlds into something not to be simplistically dismissed. Gärdenfors says that impossible belief sets are "epistemic hell".[4] The notion might give metaphysicians deep cause to shudder, but it has struck a chord in the applications area of artificial intelligence, where inconsistent data are everywhere to be found in ever increasing data stores.

11.2 The neverending story

The story of possible worlds is a sub-plot of the neverending story of philosophy and logic. It raises again all the key issues in metaphysics. Sadly, possible worlds do not solve the problems, but they do make some of the problems more accessible.

It does, however, look as if possible worlds are not as helpful as we might have thought for a range of issues. Those include: what we mean when we say that something is *essentially* φ; what we mean by existence; how we refer to and talk about nonexistent entities; and what is going on in fiction. Some would say that, despite the work with possible worlds in ethics and the production of deontic[5] logic as a result, this is nowhere as productive as was first thought. As I write, vast research, debating and creative effort is being put into working on solutions in modal logic.

Notes

Chapter 1: Introduction

1. D. K. Lewis, *On the Plurality of Worlds* (Oxford: Blackwell, 1986), 70.
2. *Ibid.*, 80.
3. F. K. Kroon, "Parts and Pretense", *Philosophy and Phenomenological Research* **61** (2001), 543–60.
4. Especially S. A. Kripke, "Semantic Analysis of Modal Logic I, Normal Propositional Calculi", *Zeitschrift für mathematische Logik und Grundlagen der Mathematik* **9** (1963), 67–96.
5. Classical formal logic is also known as first-order logic, and is derived from the work of Frege, Whitehead and Russell.
6. Especially J. K. K. Hintikka, *Models for Modalities* (Dordrecht: Reidel, 1968).
7. For example R. A. Girle, *Modal Logics and Philosophy* (Chesham: Acumen, 2000).
8. For example W. V. O. Quine, "Aims and Claims of Regimentation" from *Word and Object*, reprinted in *Logic and Philosophy*, G. Iseminger (ed.) (New York: Appleton Century Crofts, 1968), 240–44.
9. For example A. R. Anderson and N. Belnap, "Entailment", in *Logic and Philosophy*, G. Iseminger (ed.) (New York: Appleton Century Crofts, 1968), 76–110.
10. For example R. C. Stalnaker, "A Theory of Conditionals", in *Ifs: Conditionals, Belief, Decision, Chance, and Time*, W. L. Harper, R. Stalnaker and G. Pearce (eds) (Dordrecht: Reidel, 1981), 50.
11. I abstain from the use of the mathematical terminology of "formula" and "formulae".
12. These are not the only truth-values available, but they are the most common.
13. Unless one wants to take it that mathematical objects are everyday entities in the real world.
14. There are other forms of argument such as interactive argument. Although there are dialogue logics for the analysis of interactive argument, we will focus on premise–conclusion argument.

15. For a contrasting view see D. Levi, *In Defence of Informal Logic* (Dordrecht: Kluwer, 2000).

16. R. A. Girle, "'And/or' or 'Or but not both' or Both", *History and Philosophy of Logic* **10** (1988), 39–45.

17. The conditional "If you want some biscuits there are some in the tin" seems to express a conjunction of a question, "Do you want some biscuits?" and a proposition, "There are some biscuits in the tin." But even this is not clear.

18. The *standard form* for an argument is simply a list of the premises and the conclusion, with the conclusion as the last item in the list. The conclusion is usually also marked with "So" or "Therefore".

19. In fact, negation with just any one of the other three is all that is needed for a full formal classical propositional logic.

20. M. Hunt, *The Universe Within* (New York: Simon and Schuster, 1982).

21. *Ibid.*, 134.

22. F. Jackson, *Conditionals* (Oxford: Basil Blackwell, 1987).

23. For example, T. A. Halpin & R. A. Girle, *Deductive Logic*, 2nd edn (Brisbane LogiqPress, 1978), Ch. 7, 181–206.

24. The notion of reliability which follows is set out in detail in P. Staines, "Some Formal Aspects of the Argument-Symbolization Relation", *Australian Logic Teachers' Journal* **5**(3) (1981), 1–15; P. Staines and R. A. Girle, "The Reliability of Formal Systems", in *Proceedings of the Fifth Australian Joint Artificial Intelligence Conference*, A. Adams & L. Sterling (eds), 272–7 (Hobart: World Scientific, 1992); and Girle, *Modal Logics and Philosophy*. There is a teachable version of Staines's work in R. A. Girle, *Introduction to Logic* (Auckland: Prentice Hall, 2002), Ch. 7.

25. Entailment is necessitated implication. If the antecedent is true then the consequent is true, of necessity.

26. Constructivist logicians dispute the equivalence of negation in both ordinary language and mathematical language to the negation of classical propositional logic.

27. Some logicians argue that inclusive disjunction is intentional, and not equivalent to the classical inclusive disjunction.

28. Just such translations are recommended in the vast majority of logic texts.

29. Believe me. Those who can use truth-tables can quickly satisfy themselves as to this evaluation.

30. This is another "believe me" situation. If you want to be able to show this yourself, then you will have to learn modal logic in some technical detail.

31. D. K. Lewis, *Counterfactuals* (Oxford: Blackwell, 1973), §1.8, 31–6 in the reissued edition.

32. Stalnaker, "A Theory of Conditionals", 41–55.

33. Lewis, *On the Plurality of Worlds*, 17.

34. D. K. Lewis, "Counterpart Theory and Quantified Modal Logic", *Journal of Philosophy* **65** (1968), 113–26.

Chapter 2: Possible worlds

1. Frege published his formal logic in 1879. The work was largely ignored until it was popularized by A. Whitehead and B. Russell in *Principia Mathematica* (London: Cambridge University Press, 1899).
2. Even those who disagree with features of first-order logic will begin their discussions with it.
3. Many modal logicians use "M" for possibility and "L" for necessity.
4. R. A. Girle, *Introduction to Logic* (Auckland: Prentice Hall, 2002). The extended list is on p. 130, but Chapter 7 covers reliability.
5. A good starting place is S. Read, *Thinking about Logic* (Oxford: Oxford University Press, 1995), Ch. 2.
6. H. McColl, "Symbolic Reasoning", *Mind* 5 (1880), 45–60.
7. C. I. Lewis, *A Survey of Symbolic Logic* (Berkley, CA: University of California, 1918).
8. C. I. Lewis, *A Survey of Symbolic Logic*, 2nd edn (New York: Dover Publications, 1960), vii.
9. These were published in C. I. Lewis & C. H. Langford, *Symbolic Logic* (New York: Dover Publications, 1932).
10. *Ibid.*, 497ff.
11. At the end of Chapter 1 we saw that a standard logic symbol for material implication is the hook or horseshoe, "⊃"; and the symbol Lewis used for strict implication was the fish-hook, "⇱ ".
12. Lewis & Langford, *Symbolic Logic*, 217.
13. *Ibid.*, 500–501.
14. A. Chagrov & M. Zakharyaschev, *Modal Logic* (Oxford: Clarendon Press, 1997), 115.
15. W. Kneale & M. Kneale, *The Development of Logic* (Oxford: Clarendon Press, 1962), 548–68.
16. These were usually multi-valued matrices. They were used primarily to show that apparently different logical systems were in fact different, and to show what axioms were not needed.
17. Fitting suggests two others concerning Lewis's explanations in M. Fitting & R. L. Mendelsohn, *First-order Modal Logic* (Dordrecht: Kluwer, 1998), 41–2.
18. See especially E. J. Lemmon, "Algebraic Semantics for Modal Logics I", *Journal of Symbolic Logic* 31 (1966), 46–65 and "Algebraic Semantics for Modal Logics II", *Journal of Symbolic Logic* 31 (1966), 191–218.
19. In fact, Carnap had constructed a semantics for S5 that is the same as Kripke's, but, for some unknown reason, it was not widely recognized or taken up. For details of developments see Chagrov & Zakharyaschev, *Modal Logic*, 106.
20. I will use "set-up" instead of "system" so that the latter term will only refer to *systems of logic*.
21. The technical terms, S5-*frame* and S4-*frame*, do not mean exactly the same as S5-*framework* and S4-*framework*. For a detailed technical account of *frames* see Fitting & Mendelsohn, *First-order Modal Logic*.
22. This axiom is formally redundant. This was shown by J. C. C. McKinsey, "A Reduction in the Number of Postulates for C. I. Lewis's System of Strict Implication", *Bulletin of the American Mathematical Society* 40 (1934), 425–7.

23. We dare not say it is accepted by all, but very few reject it. See E. P. Martin, "The P-W Problem" (PhD thesis, Australian National University, 1978).
24. G. E. Hughes & M. J. Cresswell, *An Introduction to Modal Logic* (London: Methuen, 1968), 218.
25. Lewis & Langford, *Symbolic Logic*, 493.
26. *Ibid.*, 497.
27. In a strictly formal sense, where negation is also counted, there are six modalities in S5 and 14 in S4.
28. They are set out (as 14) in Hughes & Cresswell, *Introduction to Modal Logic*, 48.
29. Some have argued that his preference was for S3.

Chapter 3: Possible worlds and quantifiers

1. Fitting & Mendelsohn provide an excellent technical approach to these matters in their *First-order Modal Logic*. I hope to cover similar topics with a minimum of technical apparatus. Those who wish to explore this topic from a technical point of view should look at their text.
2. He did *not* portray the structures of 3.2.3 and 3.2.4 in the form set out in 3.2.5. For a more detailed account, see Luckasiewicz, *Aristotle's Syllogistic*, (2nd edn) (Oxford: Oxford University Press, 1957), esp. 4, 7–10, and elsewhere; and for a contrasting view see P. T. Geach, *A History of the Corruptions of Logic* (Leeds: Leeds University Press, 1968).
3. To learn the predicate logic in detail see Girle, *Introduction to Logic*, or any of an almost uncountable number of introductory logic texts.
4. This explanation is not strictly correct and does not tell the whole story, but it will do for our purposes. More details can be found in Girle, *Introduction to Logic*, esp. Ch. 9, 292–302.
5. There is an excellent discussion of the standard view in Fitting & Mendelsohn, *First-order Modal Logic*, 168ff.
6. C. McGinn, *Logical Properties* (Oxford: Clarendon Press, 2000), esp. Ch. 2.
7. *Ibid.*, 35.
8. *Ibid.*, 35–6.
9. Fitting & Mendelsohn, *First-order Modal Logic*, 106.
10. Lewis, "Counterpart Theory".
11. In this methodology we depart markedly from Fitting & Mendelsohn. They make extensive use of open formulas.
12. Hughes & Cresswell, *Introduction to Modal Logic*, 183.
13. *Ibid.*, 184.
14. *Ibid.*, 183, n.131.
15. *Ibid.*, 194.
16. M. K. Rennie, *Some Uses of Type Theory in the Analysis of Language* (Canberra: Australian National University, 1974).
17. W. V. O. Quine, "Three Grades of Modal Involvement", in *The Ways of Paradox and Other Essays*, 156–74 (New York: Random House, 1953).
18. A. R. White, *Modal Thinking* (Oxford: Blackwell, 1975).
19. *Ibid.*, 165.

20. *Ibid.*
21. *Ibid.*, 166ff.

Chapter 4: Possible worlds, individuals and identity

1. The details of how this can be done will be found in many logic texts, including my *Introduction to Logic.*
2. B. Russell, "On Denoting", *Mind* **14** (1905), 479–93.
3. Fitting & Mendelsohn, *First-order Modal Logic*, 172.
4. R. Routley, "Some Things Do Not Exist", *Notre Dame Journal of Formal Logic* **7** (1966), 251–76.
5. See H. Leblanc & R. H. Thomason, "Completeness Theorems for Some Presuppositon-free Logics", *Fundamenta Mathematicae* **62** (1968), 126ff. and R. A. Girle, "Possibility Pre-supposition Free Logics", *Notre Dame Journal of Formal Logic* **15**(1) (1974), 45–62.
6. These are addressed in both technical and philosophical detail in Fitting & Mendelsohn, *First-order Modal Logic*, esp. 102.
7. This view is spelled out in detail in the famous paper by S. Kripke, "Naming and Necessity", in *Semantics of Natural Language*, D. Davidson & G. Harman (eds) (Dordrecht: Reidel, 1972).
8. The *alethic* modalities are the modalities of necessity and possibility, as distinct from temporal, epistemic or deontic modalities.
9. Fitting & Mendelsohn, *First-order Modal Logic*, 218–19.
10. Read, *Thinking About Logic,* 107.
11. The extension of a predicate is the set of items which have the property the predicate denotes.
12. Kripke, "Naming and Necessity".
13. *Ibid.*, 190.
14. For an excellent discussion of something like this see M. Davies & L. Humberstone, "Two notions of Necessity", *Philosophical Studies* **38** (1980), 1–30.

Chapter 5: Possibility talk

1. One of the most careful and comprehensive analyses of such usage is set out by White in *Modal Thinking.*
2. When we consider the things that are possible for us to know and believe then we are considering *epistemic possibility.*
3. What I am calling "qualified" or "qualifiable" possibility is called "existential" possibility by White in *Modal Thinking*, 6.
4. Lewis, "Counterpart Theory", 37.
5. This kind of possibility is called "problematic" possibility in White, *Modal Thinking*, 6.
6. *Ibid.*, 5–6.
7. *Ibid.*, 11.

8. *Ibid.*, 13.
9. *Ibid.*, 13.
10. Lewis, *On the Plurality of Worlds*, 11.
11. *Ibid.*, 11.
12. *Ibid.*, 11.
13. *Ibid.*, 12.
14. See Levi, *In Defense of Informal Logic*.

Chapter 6: The possible worlds of knowledge

1. Some of the epistemic logic material in this chapter is based on Chapter 10 of R. A. Girle, *Modal Logics and Philosophy* (Chesham: Acumen, 2000).
2. E. J. Lemmon, "Is There Only One Correct System of Modal Logic?", *Aristotelian Society Supplementary Volume* 33 (1959), 23–40.
3. J. Hintikka, *Knowledge and Belief: An Introduction to the Logic of the two Notions* (Ithaca, NY: Cornell University Press, 1962).
4. *Ibid.*, 23
5. *Ibid.*, 40.
6. J. Hintikka & M. Hintikka, *The Logic of Epistemology and the Epistemology of Logic: Selected Essays* (Dordrecht: Kluwer, 1989), 50.
7. Hintikka, *Knowledge and Belief*, 5.
8. Lemmon, "Is There Only One Correct System?", 39.
9. *Ibid.*, 40.
10. Girle, *Modal Logics and Philosophy*.
11. Hintikka, *Knowledge and Belief*, 31.
12. *Ibid.*, 31.
13. I use the word "tautology" to include *all logical truths* of first-order logic.
14. Semi-logical in the sense that "If *p* and *q* then *r*" is not a sentence of plain English, but a display of logical form.
15. Hintikka, *Knowledge and Belief*, 37.
16. Translations of these principles in the formal notation are in the appendix to this chapter.
17. Maybe this is too rash, and someone somewhere does reject it. Sceptics sometimes say that the strength of this principle is the very thing that means that there can be no knowledge. For them, this principle is correct, but there is no knowledge.
18. Epistemology is the philosophical study of the concepts of knowledge and belief.
19. Hintikka, *Knowledge and Belief*, 31.
20. Where the knowledge agent automatically knows *all* logical consequences of known propositions, the agent is *deductively omniscient*. A more detailed account of epistemic omniscience is set out in R. A. Girle, "Delusions of Omniscience", in *Proceedings of the Eleventh International Florida Artificial Intelligence Research Symposium Conference*, 18–20 May, D. J. Cook (ed.), 147–51 (Menlo Park: AAAI Press, 1998).
21. The dialethic view is that some contradictions are true. See G. Priest, *In Contradiction* (Dordrecht: Kluwer, 1987) and *Beyond the Limits of Thought* (Cambridge: Cambridge University Press, 1995).

22. Where the knowledge agent depicted by some epistemic logic automatically knows all the self-sustaining sentences (logical truths) defined by that logic, the agent is *logically omniscient*.

23. Hintikka, *Knowledge and Belief*, 17.

24. *Ibid.*, 17.

25. (A.PKK*) If a set λ of sentences is consistent and if "$Ka\, p_1$" $\in \lambda$, "$Ka\, p_2$" $\in \lambda$, ..., "$Ka\, p_k$" $\in \lambda$, "$Pa\, q$" $\in \lambda$, then the set: {"$Ka\, p_1$", "$Ka\, p_2$", ..., "$Ka\, p_k$", q} is also consistent.

26. Obtained by replacing the set {"$Ka\, p_1$", "$Ka\, p_2$", ..., "$Ka\, p_k$", q} in (A.PKK*) by $\{p_1, p_2, ..., p_k, q\}$.

27. Hintikka, *Knowledge and Belief*, 18.

28. In the knowledge representation literature KK is called the "positive introspection principle".

29. See R. A. Girle, "Knowledge, Belief and Computation", in *Proceedings of Pacific Rim International Conference on Artificial Intelligence '90*, T. Fukumura, S. Ohsuga, H. Tanaka (eds), 748–53 (Nagoya: Japanese Society for Artificial Intelligence, 1990) and "Delusions of Omniscience".

30. Lemmon, "Is There Only One Correct System?", 39.

31. Hintikka, *Knowledge and Belief*, 5.

32. *Ibid.*, 5.

33. *Ibid.*, 38.

34. J. L. Austin, "Other Minds", in *Philosophical Papers* (Oxford: Clarendon Press, 1961), 44–84.

35. R. A. Girle, "Epistemic Logic, Language and Concepts", *Logique et Analyse* **63–4** (1973), 359–73.

36. R. Sylvan, "Relational Semantics for all Lewis, Lemmon and Feys' Modal Logics, Most Notably for Systems between S0.3° and S1", paper presented to the 1986 Australasian Association for Logic Conference, Auckland, Aotearoa, 3.

37. J. Hintikka, "Epistemic Logic and the Methods of Philosophical Analysis", *Australasian Journal of Philosophy* **46**(1) (1968), 37–51.

38. J. Hintikka, "'Knowing That One Knows' Reviewed", *Synthese* **21**(2) (1970), 141–62.

39. W. Lenzen, W. "On the Semantics and Pragmatics of Epistemic Attitudes", in *Knowledge and Belief in Philosophy and Artificial Intelligence*, A. Laux & H. Wansing (eds) (Berlin: Akademie Verlag, 1995), 184.

40. D. Michie & R. Johnston, *The Creative Computer* (Harmondsworth: Penguin, 1985), 65.

41. *Ibid.*, 72.

42. Lenzen argues in his 1995 paper for consideration of logics between S4 and S5, logics such as S4.2.

43. For example, several papers in Laux & Wansing, *Knowledge and Belief in Philosophy*.

44. See J. Y. Halpern (ed.) *Theoretical Aspects of Reasoning about Knowledge: Proceedings of the 1986 Conference* (Los Altos, CA: Morgan Kaufmann, 1986).

45. Hintikka, *Knowledge and Belief*, 106.

46. Girle, *Modal Logics and Philosophy*.

47. Fitting calls these "sub-normal".

48. Fitting is one of a group of logicians who are interested in the sub-normal logics

for epistemic purposes. See especially M. C. Fitting, V. W. Marek, M. Truszczynski, "The Pure Logic of Necessitation", *Journal of Logic and Computation* 2(3) (1992), 349–73.
49. D. Pearce, "Epistemic Operators and Knowledge-Based Reasoning", in Laux & Wansing, *Knowledge and Belief in Philosophy and Artificial Intelligence*.

Chapter 7: The possible worlds of belief

1. R. Smullyan, *Forever Undecided* (Oxford: Oxford University Press, 1987).
2. Not everyone holds this view. Some *dialethic* philosophers hold that reality is contradictory.
3. Smullyan, *Forever Undecided*, 69.
4. *Ibid.*, 90.
5. *Ibid.*, 90.
6. *Ibid.*, 93.
7. *Ibid.*, 93.
8. *Ibid.*, 93–4.
9. The chapter in which this material occurs is called "Logicians Who Reason About Themselves".
10. Smullyan, *Forever Undecided*, 153.
11. *Ibid.*, 154.
12. Proof of this equivalence is in *Forever Undecided*.
13. My emphasis.
14. Smullyan, *Forever Undecided*, 153.
15. *Ibid.*, 154; and I am forced here to use "he" in the following comments.
16. This is not strictly correct, but if we add *modus ponens* and all the tautologies of propositional logic, then we will have axiomatic G.
17. G. Boolos, *The Logic of Provability* (Cambridge: Cambridge University Press, 1993). GL is named after Gödel and Löb.
18. G. Boolos, "Gödel's Second Incompleteness Theorem Explained in Words of One Syllable", in *Logic, Logic, and Logic*, R. Jeffrey (ed.) (Cambridge, MA: Harvard University Press, 1998), 412.
19. Plantinga, A. "Actualism and Possible Worlds", in *The Possible and the Actual*, M. J. Loux (ed.) (Ithaca, NY: Cornell University Press, 1979), 256.
20. R. A. Girle, "Quantification into Epistemic Contexts", *Logique et Analyse* 17 (1974), 127–42.

Chapter 8: Time and many possible worlds

1. This cut is known as a *jump*.
2. This cut is known as a *gap*.
3. Cuts in the continuous line are neither jumps nor gaps.
4. Every cut is a jump.
5. E. Squires, *Conscious Mind in the Physical World* (Bristol: Adam Hilger, 1990), 212.

6. Squires, *Conscious Mind in the Physical World*, 198.
7. S. Baxter, *The Time Ships: The Authorized Sequel to The Time Machine* (London: HarperCollins, 1995).
8. Baxter, *The Time Ships*, p. 500.
9. J. Bigelow, "Time Travel Fiction", in *Reality and Humean Supervenience*, G. Preyer & F. Siebelt (eds) (Lanham, MD: Rowman & Littlefield, 2001), 57–91.
10. *Ibid.*, 57.
11. *Ibid.*, 76.
12. *Ibid.*, 76.
13. A. N. Prior, *Past Present and Future* (Oxford: Oxford University Press, 1967), 32.
14. A comparison of the two approaches is to be found in J. van Benthem, *The Logic of Time* (Dordrecht: Reidel, 1983).

Chapter 9: Real possibility

1. An excellent basic account is in Lewis, *Counterfactuals*, esp. Ch. 4. Citations are to the reissued edition of 2001. More detail is in Lewis, *On the Plurality of Worlds*.
2. T. Osman, *The Discovery of the Universe* (London: Usborne, 1975), 14–15.
3. Lewis, *On the Plurality of Worlds*, 4.
4. *Ibid.*, 3.
5. Lewis would not, I am sure, have drawn "battle lines", to mention the other metaphor, over any philosophical controversy.
6. But it is certainly true that an almost complete, but briefer account of Lewis's views are to be found in *Counterfactuals*. This precedes *On the Plurality of Worlds* by 13 years.
7. Stalnaker, "A Theory of Conditionals".
8. Wellington is the capital of New Zealand (and has a good suburban electric train system).
9. Lewis, *Counterfactuals*, 78.
10. W. L. Harper, R. Stalnaker, G. Pearce (eds) *Ifs: Conditionals, Belief, Decision, Chance, and Time* (Dordrecht: Reidel, 1981).
11. Lewis, *Counterfactuals*, 84: the first sentence of Chapter 4, "Foundations".
12. *Ibid.*, 84.
13. *Ibid.*, 84.
14. *Ibid.*, 7 n.3.
15. McGinn, *Logical Properties*, 70.
16. *Ibid.*, 70.
17. This is discussed in P. Teller, "Against Against Overlap and Endurance", in *Reality and Humean Supervenience*, G. Preyer & F Siebelt (eds) (Lanham, MD: Rowman & Littlefield, 2001), 105–21.
18. Lewis, *On the Plurality of Worlds*, 2.
19. Kripke, "Naming and Necessity", 344 n.14.
20. Lewis, *On the Plurality of Worlds*, 196.
21. Read, *Thinking about Logic*, 99.
22. *Ibid.*, 99.
23. Lewis, *On the Plurality of Worlds*, 92.

24. P. Bricker, "Island Universes and the Analysis of Modality", in *Reality and Humean Supervenience*, G. Preyer & F Siebelt (eds) (Lanham, MD: Rowman & Littlefield, 2001), 29.
25. Lewis, *On the Plurality of Worlds*, 71.
26. For anno domini, or for CE (common era) or whatever you like.
27. Lewis, *On the Plurality of Worlds*, 74–6.
28. *Ibid.*, 75.
29. Bricker, "Island Universes", 36.
30. *Ibid.*, 36.
31. Lewis, *On the Plurality of Worlds*, 157.
32. Read, *Thinking about Logic*, 105.
33. *Ibid.*, 106.
34. P. Gärdenfors, *Knowledge in Flux* (Cambridge, MA: MIT Press, 1988), esp. Ch. 7.
35. F. P. Ramsey, "General Propositions and Causality", in *The Foundations of Mathematics and other Logical Essays*, R. B. Braithwaite (ed.) (London: Routledge and Kegan Paul, 1931), 237–55.
36. Gärdenfors, *Knowledge in Flux*, 147. It must be remarked that this is both a condensation of a general theme in Ramsey's paper, and a considerable expansion of what is in a footnote in Ramsey, "General Propositions and Causality", 247.
37. Stalnaker, "A Theory of Conditionals", 42–3.
38. *Ibid.*, 45.
39. C. E. Alchourrón, P. Gärdenfors, D. Makinson, "On the Logic of Theory Change: Partial Meet Functions for Contraction and Revision", *Journal of Symbolic Logic* 50: 510–30.
40. See Gärdenfors, *Knowledge in Flux*, 24.
41. Girle, "Delusions of Omniscience".
42. The formal postulates for expansion, contraction and revision are in the appendix to this chapter.
43. There is a vast literature about contraction and entrenchment. The easiest place to start is in Gärdenfors, *Knowledge in Flux*.
44. Gärdenfors, *Knowledge in Flux*, 67.
45. *Ibid.*, 156.
46. Lewis, *On the Plurality of Worlds*, 165.
47. *Ibid.*, 150–51.
48. *Ibid.*, 157.
49. *Ibid.*, 157.
50. *Ibid.*, 158.
51. Plantinga, "Actualism and Possible Worlds", 256.
52. Stalnaker, "A Theory of Conditionals", 84.
53. Lewis, *On the Plurality of Worlds*, 227 *passim*.
54. Stalnaker, "A Theory of Conditionals", 228.
55. M. Davies & L. Humberstone, "Two Notions of Necessity", *Philosophical Studies*, 38 (1980): 1–30.
56. R. M. Adams, "Theories of Actuality", in *The Possible and the Actual*, M. J. Loux (ed.) (Ithaca, NY: Cornell University Press, 1979), 190–209.
57. *Ibid.*, 204.
58. An agent is factually omniscient if and only if for every proposition the agent knows whether it is true or false.

59. Gärdenfors, *Knowledge in Flux*, 25.
60. Stalnaker, "A Theory of Conditionals", 231.
61. *Ibid.*, 231.
62. Hintikka, "Epistemic Logic", 40–41.
63. Girle, "Epistemic Logic, Language and Concepts", 361.

Chapter 10: Impossible possible worlds

1. Where the knowledge agent depicted by some epistemic logic automatically knows all the self-sustaining sentences (logical truths) defined by that logic, the agent is *logically omniscient*.
2. Where the knowledge agent automatically knows *all* logical consequences of known propositions, the agent is *deductively omniscient*.
3. J. Hintikka, "Impossible Possible Worlds Vindicated", in *The Logic of Epistemology and the Epistemology of Logic,* J. Hintikka & M. Hintikka (eds) (Dordrecht: Kluwer, 1989), 63–72.
4. Hintikka, "Impossible Possible Worlds Vindicated".
5. H. J. Levesque, "A Logic of Knowledge and Active Belief", in *Proceedings of the National Conference on Artificial Intelligence* (Austin, TX: University of Texas at Austin, 1984).
6. K. Konolige, *A Deduction Model of Belief* (Los Altos, CA: Morgan Kaufmann, 1986).
7. Hintikka, "Impossible Possible Worlds Vindicated", 65.
8. Konolige, *A Deduction Model of Belief*, 88. The symbol ~ means **not**.
9. For example, one might eliminate the tedious and nit-picking use of commutation, association and idempotence and allow short-cuts or more general rules of inference. For example, one might have a more explicitly metalinguistic rule of simplification such as: From any conjunction infer either conjunct.
10. Konolige, *A Deduction Model of Belief*, 20.
11. *Ibid.*, 23.
12. *Ibid.*, 91.
13. *Ibid.*, 91–2.
14. *Ibid.*, 108–9.
15. See the caption in J. P. Burgess, "Common Sense and 'Relevance'", *Notre Dame Journal of Formal Logic* 24 (1983), 41.
16. J. Hintikka, "Reasoning about Knowledge in Philosophy", in *The Logic of Epistemology and the Epistemology of Logic,* J. Hintikka & M. Hintikka (eds) (Dordrecht: Kluwer, 1989), 24.
17. The four values are the members of the power set of the set of values: {true, false}.
18. N. D. Belnap, "How a Computer Should Think", in *Contemporary Aspects of Philosophy*, G. Ryle (ed.) (Stocksfield: Oriel Press, 1976), 30–56.
19. J. M. Dunn, "A Kripke-Style Semantics for R-Mingle Using a Binary Accessibility Relation", *Studia Logica* 35 (1976): 163–72.
20. Lewis, *On the Plurality of Worlds*, 7 n.3.

Chapter 11: Unfinished story

1. McGinn, *Logical Properties*, 41.
2. McGinn, *Logical Properties*, 42.
3. G. B. B. Hunter, *Metalogic* (London: Macmillan, 1971), 93.
4. Gärdenfors, *Knowledge in Flux*, 51.
5. Deontic logic is the modal logic of obligation, where $\Box p$ is read as "*p* is obligatory".

Bibliography

There are several volumes below which have excellent bibliographies. One of the best is Fitting and Mendelsohn (1998). Read (1995) also has excellent guides to further reading.

Adams, R. M. 1979. "Theories of Actuality". In *The Possible and the Actual*, M. J. Loux (ed.), 190–209. Ithaca, NY: Cornell University Press.

Alchourrón, C. E., P. Gärdenfors & D. Makinson 1985. "On the Logic of Theory Change: Partial Meet Functions for Contraction and Revision", *Journal of Symbolic Logic* 50: 510–30.

Anderson, A. R. & N. Belnap 1968. "Entailment". In *Logic and Philosophy*, G. Iseminger (ed.), 76–110. New York: Appleton Century Crofts.

Austin, J. L. 1961. "Other Minds". In *Philosophical Papers*, 44–84. Oxford: Clarendon Press.

Baxter, S. 1995. *The Time Ships: The Authorized Sequel to The Time Machine*. London: HarperCollins.

Belnap, N. D. 1976. "How a Computer Should Think". In *Contemporary Aspects of Philosophy*, G. Ryle (ed.), 30–56. Stocksfield: Oriel Press.

Bigelow, J. 2001. "Time Travel Fiction". In *Reality and Humean Supervenience*, G. Preyer & F. Siebelt (eds), 57–91. Lanham, MD: Rowman & Littlefield.

Boolos, G. 1993. *The Logic of Provability*. Cambridge: Cambridge University Press.

Boolos, G. 1998. "Gödel's Second Incompleteness Theorem Explained in Words of One Syllable". In *Logic, Logic, and Logic*, R. Jeffrey (ed.), 1998. Cambridge, MA: Harvard University Press.

Bricker, P. 2001. "Island Universes and the Analysis of Modality". In *Reality and Humean Supervenience*, G. Preyer & F Siebelt (eds), 27–55. Lanham, MD: Rowman & Littlefield.

Burgess, J. P. 1983. "Common Sense and 'Relevance'", *Notre Dame Journal of Formal Logic* 24: 41–53.

Chagrov, A. & M. Zakharyaschev 1997. *Modal Logic*. Oxford: Clarendon Press.

Davies, M. & L. Humberstone 1980. "Two Notions of Necessity", *Philosophical Studies* 38: 1–30.

Dunn, J. M. 1976. "A Kripke-Style Semantics for **R-Mingle** Using a Binary Accessibility Relation", *Studia Logica* 35: 163–72.

Fitting, M. C., V. W. Marek & M. Truszczynski 1992. "The Pure Logic of Necessitation", *Journal of Logic and Computation* 2(3): 349–73.

Fitting, M. & R. L. Mendelsohn 1998. *First-order Modal Logic*. Dordrecht: Kluwer Academic Publishers. [This is the best available text for modal predicate logic, and the philosophical problems embedded in and underlying the logic. This book has an excellent bibliography.]

Gärdenfors, P. 1988. *Knowledge in Flux*. Cambridge, MA: MIT Press.

Geach, P. T. 1968. *A History of the Corruptions of Logic*. Leeds: Leeds University Press.

Girle, R. A. 1973. "Epistemic Logic, Language and Concepts", *Logique et Analyse* 63–4: 359–73.

Girle, R. A. 1974a. "Quantification into Epistemic Contexts", *Logique et Analyse* 17: 127–42.

Girle, R. A. 1974b. "Possibility Pre-supposition Free Logics", *Notre Dame Journal of Formal Logic* 15(1): 45–62.

Girle, R. A. 1988. "'And/or' or 'Or but not both' or Both", *History and Philosophy of Logic* 10: 39–45.

Girle, R. A. 1990. "Knowledge, Belief and Computation". In *Proceedings of Pacific Rim International Conference on Artificial Intelligence '90*, T. Fukumura, S. Ohsuga & H. Tanaka (eds), 748–53. Nagoya: Japanese Society for Artificial Intelligence.

Girle, R. A. 1998. "Logical Fiction". In *PRICAI'98: Topics in Artificial Intelligence*, Hing-Yan Lee & Hiroshi Motoda (eds), 542–52. Singapore: Springer.

Girle, R. A. 1998. "Delusions of Omniscience". In *Proceedings of the Eleventh International Florida Artificial Intelligence Research Symposium Conference*, D. J. Cook (ed.), 147–51. Menlo Park: AAAI Press.

Girle, R. A. 2000. *Modal Logics and Philosophy*. Chesham: Acumen.

Girle, R. A. 2002. *Introduction to Logic*. Auckland: Prentice Hall.

Halpern, J. Y. (ed.) 1986. *Theoretical Aspects of Reasoning about Knowledge: Proceedings of the 1986 Conference*. Los Altos, CA: Morgan Kaufmann.

Halpin T. A. & R. A. Girle 1978. *Deductive Logic*, 2nd edn. Brisbane: LogiqPress.

Harper, W. L., R. Stalnaker, G. Pearce (eds) 1981. *Ifs: Conditionals, Belief, Decision, Chance, and Time*. Dordrecht: Reidel.

Hintikka, J. 1962. *Knowledge and Belief: An Introduction to the Logic of the Two Notions*. Ithaca, NY: Cornell University Press. [This is the first extended treatment of epistemic logic with heavy emphasis on semantics.]

Hintikka, J. 1968. *Models for Modalities*. Dordrecht: Reidel.

Hintikka, J. 1968. "Epistemic Logic and the Methods of Philosophical Analysis", *Australasian Journal of Philosophy* 46(1): 37–51.

Hintikka, J. 1970. "'Knowing that One Knows' Reviewed", *Synthese* 21(2): 141–62.

Hintikka, J. 1989. "Impossible Possible Worlds Vindicated". In *The Logic of Epistemology and the Epistemology of Logic: Selected Essays*, J. Hintikka & M. Hintikka (eds), 63–72. Dordrecht: Kluwer.

Hintikka, J. 1989. "Reasoning about Knowledge in Philosophy" . In *The Logic of Epistemology and the Epistemology of Logic: Selected Essays*, J. Hintikka & M. Hintikka (eds), 17–35. Dordrecht: Kluwer.

Hintikka, J. & M. Hintikka (eds) 1989. *The Logic of Epistemology and the Epistemology of Logic: Selected Essays*. Dordrecht: Kluwer.

Hughes, G. E. & M. J. Cresswell 1968. *An Introduction to Modal Logic*. London: Methuen.

Hunt, M. 1982. *The Universe Within*. New York: Simon and Schuster.

Hunter, G. B. B. 1971. *Metalogic*. London: Macmillan.

Jackson, F. 1987. *Conditionals*. Oxford: Basil Blackwell.

Kneale, W. & M. Kneale 1962. *The Development of Logic*. Oxford: Clarendon Press.

Konolige, K. 1986. *A Deduction Model of Belief*. Los Altos, CA: Morgan Kaufmann.

Kripke, S. A. 1963. "Semantic Analysis of Modal Logic I, Normal Propositional Calculi" *Zeitschrift für mathematische Logik und Grundlagen der Mathematik* **9**: 67–96. [This was the "breakthrough" paper in the formal semantics of possible worlds.]

Kripke, S. 1972. "Naming and Necessity". In *Semantics of Natural Language*, D. Davidson & G. Harmon (eds), 253–355. Dordrecht: Reidel. [This is the paper that triggered enormous twentieth-century debate about the philosophical implications of possible worlds semantics.]

Kroon, F. K. 2001. "Parts and Pretense", *Philosophy and Phenomenological Research* **61**: 543–60.

Laux, A. & H. Wansing (eds) 1995. *Knowledge and Belief in Philosophy and Artificial Intelligence*. Berlin: Akademie Verlag.

Leblanc, H. & R. H. Thomason 1968. "Completeness Theorems for some Presuppositon-free Logics," *Fundamenta Mathematicae* **62**: 126ff.

Lemmon, E. J. 1959. "Is There Only One Correct System of Modal Logic?" *Aristotelian Society Supplementary Volume* **33**: 23–40. [This was one of the first papers about the epistemic application of modal logic.]

Lemmon, E. J. 1966. "Algebraic Semantics for Modal Logics I" *Journal of Symbolic Logic* **31**: 46–65.

Lemmon, E. J. 1966. "Algebraic Semantics for Modal Logics II" *Journal of Symbolic Logic* **31**: 191–218.

Lenzen, W. 1995. "On the Semantics and Pragmatics of Epistemic Attitudes". In *Knowledge and Belief in Philosophy and Artificial Intelligence*, A. Laux & H. Wansing (eds), 181–97. Berlin: Akademie Verlag.

Levesque, H. J. 1984. "A Logic of Knowledge and Active Belief". In *Proceedings of the National Conference on Artificial Intelligence*. Austin, TX: University of Texas at Austin.

Levi, D. 2000. *In Defence of Informal Logic*. Dordrecht: Kluwer. [This is an important attack on the standard rhetoric about the use of formal logic for argument analysis.]

Lewis, C. I. 1918. *A Survey of Symbolic Logic*. Berkley, CA: University of California. [This was the first attempt to give an extended systematic account of the varieties of modern formal modal logics.]

Lewis, C. I. 1960. *A Survey of Symbolic Logic*, 2nd edn. New York: Dover Publications.

Lewis, C. I. & C. H. Langford 1932. *Symbolic Logic*. New York: Dover Publications.

Lewis, D. K. 1968. "Counterpart Theory and Quantified Modal Logic", *Journal of Philosophy* **65**: 113–26.

Lewis, D. K. 1973. *Counterfactuals*. Oxford: Blackwell. [Just as C. I. Lewis was one of the most important modal logicians in the early twentieth century, and S. Kripke in the mid-twentieth century, D. K. Lewis was one of the most important in the late twentieth century. This book, in my view, is the really groundbreaking work of David Lewis.]

Lewis, D. K. 1986. *On the Plurality of Worlds*. Oxford: Blackwell. [Many philosophers and logicians see this work as Lewis's most important work.]

Auckasiewicz, 1957. *Aristotle's Syllogistic*, 2nd edn. Oxford: Oxford University Press.

McColl, H. 1880. "Symbolic Reasoning", *Mind* 5: 45–60.

McGinn, C. 2000. *Logical Properties*. Oxford: Clarendon Press. [This is a notable work of many heresies.]

McKinsey, J. C. C. 1934. "A Reduction in the Number of Postulates for C. I. Lewis's System of Strict Implication", *Bulletin of the American Mathematical Society* **40**: 425–7.

Michie, D. & R. Johnston 1985. *The Creative Computer*. Harmondsworth: Penguin.

Osman, T. 1975. *The Discovery of the Universe*. London: Usborne.

Pearce, D. 1995. "Epistemic Operators and Knowledge-Based Reasoning". In *Knowledge and Belief in Philosophy and Artificial Intelligence*, A. Laux & H. Wansing (eds), 1–27. Berlin: Akademia Verlag.

Plantinga, A. 1979. "Actualism and Possible Worlds". In *The Possible and the Actual*, M. J. Loux (ed.), 146–65. Ithaca, NY: Cornell University Press.

Priest, G. 1987. *In Contradiction*. Dordrecht: Kluwer.

Priest, G. 1995. *Beyond the Limits of Thought*. Cambridge: Cambridge University Press.

Prior, A. N. 1967. *Past Present and Future*. Oxford: Oxford University Press. [This is one of Prior's groundbreaking texts in the logic of time.]

Quine, W. V. O. 1953. "Three Grades of Modal Involvement". In *The Ways of Paradox and Other Essays*, 156–74. New York: Random House.

Quine, W. V. O. 1968. "Aims and Claims of Regimentation" from *Word and Object*. Reprinted in *Logic and Philosophy*, G. Iseminger (ed.), 240–44. New York: Appleton Century Crofts.

Ramsey, F. P. 1931. "General Propositions and Causality". In *The Foundations of Mathematics and other Logical Essays*, R. B. Braithwaite (ed.), 237–55. London: Routledge and Kegan Paul.

Read, S. 1995. *Thinking about Logic*. Oxford: Oxford University Press.

Rennie, M. K. 1974. *Some Uses of Type Theory in the Analysis of Language*. Canberra: Australian National University.

Routley, R. 1966. "Some Things Do Not Exist", *Notre Dame Journal of Formal Logic* **7**: 251–76.

Russell, B. 1905. "On Denoting", *Mind* **14**: 479–93.

Smullyan, R. 1987. *Forever Undecided*. Oxford: Oxford University Press.

Squires, E. 1990. *Conscious Mind in the Physical World*. Bristol: Adam Hilger.

Stalnaker, R. 1968. "A Theory of Conditionals", *Studies in Logical Theory, American Philosophical Quarterly*. Oxford: Blackwell. Republished in 1981 in *Ifs: Conditionals, Belief, Decision, Chance, and Time*, W. L. Harper, R. Stalnaker & G. Pearce (eds), 41–55. Dordrecht: Reidel. [This account of conditionals is one of the key accounts in contrast to David Lewis's account.]

Staines, P. 1981. "Some Formal Aspects of the Argument-Symbolization Relation", *Australian Logic Teachers' Journal* **5**(3), August: 1–15.

Staines, P. & R. A. Girle 1992. "The Reliability of Formal Systems", *Proceedings of the Fifth Australian Joint Artificial Intelligence Conference*, A. Adams & L. Sterling (eds), 272–7. Hobart: World Scientific.

Sylvan, R. 1986. "Relational Semantics for all Lewis, Lemmon and Feys' Modal Logics, most Notably for Systems between S0.3° and S1". Paper presented to the 1986 *Australasian Association for Logic Conference,* Auckland, Aotearoa. [Sylvan can properly be said to be "Sylvan (née Routley)".]

Teller, P. 2001. "Against Against Overlap and Endurance". In *Reality and Humean Supervenience*, G. Preyer & F. Siebelt (eds), 105–21. Lanham, MD: Rowman & Littlefield.

van Benthem, J. 1983. *The Logic of Time*. Dordrecht: Reidel.

White, A. R. 1975. *Modal Thinking*. Blackwell: Oxford.

Whitehead, A. & B. Russell 1910. *Principia Mathematica*. London: Cambridge University Press.

Index